Getting Away with Murder

Also by Lynda La Plante

Jane Tennison series
Tennison
Hidden Killers
Good Friday
Murder Mile
The Dirty Dozen
Blunt Force
Unholy Murder
Dark Rooms
Taste of Blood
Whole Life Sentence

DC Jack Warr series
Buried
Judas Horse
Vanished
Pure Evil

Widows series
Widows
Widows' Revenge
She's Out

For a completed list of Lynda's works, please visit:
www.lyndalaplante.com/books

Lynda La Plante was born in Liverpool. She trained for the stage at RADA and worked with the National Theatre and RSC before becoming a television actress. She then turned to writing and made her breakthrough with the phenomenally successful TV series *Widows*. She has written over thirty international novels, all of which have been bestsellers, and is the creator of the Anna Travis, Lorraine Page and *Trial and Retribution* series. Her original script for the much-acclaimed *Prime Suspect* won awards from BAFTA, Emmy, British Broadcasting and Royal Television Society, as well as the 1993 Edgar Allan Poe Award.

Lynda is one of only three screenwriters to have been made an honorary fellow of the British Film Institute and was awarded the BAFTA Dennis Potter Best Writer Award in 2000. In 2008, she was awarded a CBE in the Queen's Birthday Honours List for services to Literature, Drama and Charity.

✉ Join the Lynda La Plante Readers' Club at
www.bit.ly/LyndaLaPlanteClub
www.lyndalaplante.com
❚ Facebook @LyndaLaPlanteCBE
🐦 Twitter @LaPlanteLynda

Lynda La Plante

Getting Away with Murder

A Memoir

ZAFFRE

First published in the UK in 2024 by
ZAFFRE
An imprint of Zaffre Publishing Group
A Bonnier Books UK company
4th Floor, Victoria House, Bloomsbury Square, London, WC1B 4DA
Owned by Bonnier Books
Sveavägen 56, Stockholm, Sweden

Copyright © La Plante Global Ltd, 2024

All rights reserved.
No part of this publication may be reproduced,
stored or transmitted in any form by any means, electronic,
mechanical, photocopying or otherwise, without the
prior written permission of the publisher.

The right of Lynda La Plante to be identified as Author of this
work has been asserted by her in accordance with the
Copyright, Designs and Patents Act, 1988.

A CIP catalogue record for this book is
available from the British Library.

Hardback ISBN: 978-1-80418-385-4
Trade Paperback ISBN: 978-1-80418-386-1

Also available as an ebook and an audiobook

1 3 5 7 9 10 8 6 4 2

Typeset by IDSUK (Data Connection) Ltd
Printed and bound in Great Britain by Clays Ltd, Elcograf S.p.A.

Every reasonable effort has been made to trace copyright holders of material
reproduced in this book, but if any have been inadvertently overlooked the
publishers would be glad to hear from them.

Zaffre is an imprint of Zaffre Publishing Group
A Bonnier Books UK company
www.bonnierbooks.co.uk

My sister Gilly – my harshest critic, my constant encouragement and most beloved friend – still laughing together after all these years.

Contents

Preface	xi
Chapter 1: The Little One	1
Chapter 2: Learning by Heart	15
Chapter 3: RADA	26
Chapter 4: *Calamity Jane*	43
Chapter 5: *Performance*	62
Chapter 6: *Widows*	82
Chapter 7: *Widows' Revenge*	106
Chapter 8: *The Legacy*	118
Chapter 9: *Civvies*	134
Chapter 10: Meeting the Mafia	143
Chapter 11: The Costa del Crime	158
Chapter 12: *Prime Suspect*	166
Chapter 13: *Entwined*	187
Chapter 14: *Civvies* – The Return	204
Chapter 15: Bars, Brothels and Broads	223
Chapter 16: *The Governor*	241
Chapter 17: *Trial and Retribution*	260
Chapter 18: Star Turns	276
Chapter 19: Lorcan	289
Chapter 20: Catching a Killer	300
Chapter 21: A New Chapter	312
Chapter 22: *Tennison*	324
Chapter 23: In My Prime	345

Preface

Ask me about any of the characters in my books, the twists and turns of a plot line or the reason a scene got filmed the way it did, and I remember everything. Ask me about my own life, and I haven't the faintest clue. I suppose I've spent much of it looking outwards, plucking anecdotes and jokes, mannerisms and dialogue from everyone I've ever met.

But 'The Memoir' got commissioned and 'The Memoir' has loomed large in my mind for the past year or so. Why on earth did I agree to do it? I've never been great at peering in. I've had to bring out my files, notebooks and photographs to piece much of the past together. Some days I've howled with laughter. Other days it's felt like tiptoeing barefoot over broken glass – memories that shatter the emotions. Sleepless nights, I've had a few. *Why* did I do that? *How* did I do that? Lynda, what the *hell* were you thinking? And some days I've forgotten absolutely everything. What year did I get married? Turns out I was ten years out!

Age creeps up on you. Unbelievable that I turned eighty-one this year. Eighty-one? If any of my friends reach this age I think, *Christ Almighty! They're getting on a bit!* I simply don't see myself as old. And I don't feel it, either.

'May I say, you're looking remarkable for your age,' a receptionist told me only a couple of years ago. I'd arrived at hospital for a procedure and filled out one of those laborious medical forms.

'Why, thank you!' I was seventy-nine at the time, feeling rather anxious about hitting the big 8-0.

'Well, whatever you're doing it's working!'

'So kind.' I smiled.

I've never had Botox. Or a face lift. Or any other kind of lift. All my body parts remain my own. I still work every day, averaging two novels a year alongside several TV projects. *Must keep me young*, I thought.

The doctor looked somewhat surprised too.

'Lynda, my God! I had no idea you were ninety-seven!'

Ah. Did I mention I'm dyslexic and I'd forgotten to put my glasses on?

Admittedly, there is the odd occasion when I've felt every bit my age. My eightieth birthday was spent in a swanky London restaurant with my son, Lorcan, and his girlfriend. They chose the restaurant; I paid the bill – it was eye-watering.

'Madam, would you like the meat matured in Somerset sun and simmered with the bark of a tree for twenty-four hours?' the waiter asked.

No, thank you.

'No, really, Ms La Plante, the chef has bathed it in rhubarb and sprinkled it in beetroot dust!'

I'm the sort of person who's repelled even by sushi. If I have to poke a dead fish, I'm off. Give me good old-fashioned meat and two veg any day. As for the portions served in restaurants these days? I've got eyeballs that are larger. And don't young people dress for dinner anymore? I turned up in a sequinned jacket looking like a Russian whore; my son came dressed like he'd climbed out of a tent at Glastonbury. It's no wonder we were politely moved from the open dining hall to behind a pillar.

At home I feel as though I'm turning into my mother: every day circling in red pen what I want to watch in the TV guide, then yelling at the screen if I have to sit through one more bloody commercial. Juggling which remote is for what device has become a circus act.

So much has changed since I began my career aged fifteen in 1958. Far too young, when I think about it now. I've been an actor, screenwriter, producer and author. I've seen a lot, and been through a lot in a tough industry. I've met the great, the good and the bloody awful. And I hope I've gained some wisdom along the way that I can share.

In other respects, so little has changed. Storytelling has been my life, all of my life. I wrote my first TV series on a prehistoric typewriter and now I'm making podcasts. I've yet to master TikTok, and I'm hoping I can dodge that medium. But exactly the same fascination with the world drives me. I love exploring the light and the dark that everyone has within them. As you'll discover, I have all that and more in me too! So strap in for the ride. It's going to be one helluva journey.

Chapter 1

The Little One

Why was I tied to a wooden wave-breaker looking out across the Irish Sea? A good question, and one I was asking myself. I'd been there for two hours. My brother Michael had left me and run off to play with his friends.

'Do you want to come to the beach?' he'd asked. That kind of invite didn't happen very often. Michael was four years older than me and I was more of an irritant than a friend.

'You can be a Native American squaw!' he promised, bringing out a thick rope from his pocket and tying my hands behind my back and then to the breaker. 'Or a hostage!'

How incredibly exciting, I thought. I was desperate to play with Michael. I fell for that trick every time and now here I was, knee-deep in the sand dunes with a brisk north-west wind buffeting my hair.

The beach at Blundellsands stretched for miles. At low tide you could see the mudflats glisten as they swept out to sea. To the south, the industrial skyline of the Wirral Peninsula sat nose-to-tail with the city of Liverpool. For much of my childhood, it and the surrounding area of Crosby was my universe.

We didn't have a TV back then – not for some time, in fact. And when we did get one we rarely watched it. In March 1943, when I was born, the first domino in Hitler's armies had toppled and would continue to fall. The Second World War loomed large in the nation's consciousness, but not in my memories. I was Enid Blyton on roller-skates. Never indoors, always at the beach or astride my bike racing through Sniggery Woods, a narrow tangle of thicket near my parents' house. Our imagination took us places, which is probably one reason I was tied to a post gazing out to the Irish Sea.

Yet for all the constancy and flatness of the surrounding countryside, nothing I know about my childhood is as steadfast. My recollections are jagged. I know that my parents started off in a dark, rambling house where they were living when I was born. When they moved to a larger, perfect square-of-a-house on Moor Lane in Crosby, my father drove us there.

'This is the house,' he announced.

I must have been around five years old. Old enough to remember its crowning glory.

'Look . . .' he stood proudly and pointed upwards to the roof.

'Look at what?' my mother asked.

'No drainpipes.'

I'm not even sure my mother was privy to my father buying that house, but whoever visited was made to stand outside and gaze up, as we had done.

'Not a drainpipe in sight!' my father would say.

'Well, where are they?' the visitor would ask, as predicted.

'All hidden on the inside,' he would nod self-satisfyingly. In his eyes, this aspect of the house's drainage system meant our family – the Titchmarshes – had made it.

Like the pipes, much about our household was hidden on the inside. To this day, I've never joined it all together. Never had much interest in doing so, if truth be told. The past is the past. I'm defined by my non-memories – so many missing pieces rather than one complete picture. I still don't know what job my father, Bill, did. A salesman of some sort, I believe. He travelled a lot. My mother Florence – Flossie to her family – was a stay-at-home wife and exceedingly beautiful. Tailor-made suits bought from department stores in Liverpool. Perfect nails. Perfect pitch-black hair, which she tinted to cover the grey. My mother turned grey rather early.

Her maiden name was Harrison, I think. Apparently, many of her antecedents, the Southwoods, are buried in the little churchyard in St James's Church just off Piccadilly Circus in London. But even that fact is porous. I've never looked. I only ever met one grandmother, my maternal grandmother Gertrude, and only because she lived with us. For all the ten brothers and sisters she was rumoured to have had I didn't know a single one.

One day, when I was very young, my mother answered the door to find Gertrude had a visitor.

'There's an Arthur Southwood here to see you,' she called out.

My grandmother's face remained completely blank.

'Who?'

'An Arthur Southwood. Says he wants to talk to you.'

'Oh yes ...' Gertrude replied flatly. 'He's my brother. You'd better show him in.'

As I recall, Arthur was a dapper man with the same hawk nose as Gertrude. He must have stayed less than five minutes before I watched him trot back across the front yard. Weeks later he turned up with a large Persian kitten. It was the last I ever saw of Arthur. The kitten was beautiful – soft white fur and piercing jade eyes – but it pissed everywhere and upset my father.

My father's side of the family was just as invisible. A nephew recently sent me part of our family tree. My father had three siblings. Incredible news to me! I'd heard of his brother, David, but his two sisters had never been mentioned.

My nephew sent a Bible as well, which apparently belonged to my father. Tucked inside was a piece of paper with a list of Christian names, but no surnames. The only reference to my father's name is on a letter from a man also called Titchmarsh who had arrived from Australia. He'd wanted to track down his family in the UK and believed they were related. In his handwritten scrawl across the top, my father had written 'Don't bother'.

And then there was my older sister, Dail: ever present in our house, though never present in my lifetime. A painting of her hung in the hallway. Dail was striking. Coal-black hair and china-blue eyes. She was the only child of my parents' to have my mother's colouring. Michael, like myself and our sister Gill, who was two years my junior, inherited my father's flame-red hair.

'I have four children,' my mother used to say. 'My first was Dail. The most beautiful one.' For her, Dail remained forever a child. She never grew old. From the day she died at the age of six, she was the underlying, unspoken void that filled the expanse of our house. Up until that point, my parents had been religious. High up in the Anglican Church, I believe. But not after Dail's death. 'There can be no God who would take a child like that,' my mother would say.

It was just before Christmas in 1942 when my mother was called to discover Dail on the roadside near the convent school she attended. A Catholic school was not my parents' religion, but it was the nearest school to our home and thereby considered the safest. But an older girl had led Dail from the school gates and across the busy main road to admire a Christmas tree hung with baubles and lights. Dail was hit, caught between the rolling double wheels of an articulated lorry, and dragged for some distance. She lived, but no more than a couple of weeks, and with horrific injuries to her brain and little body.

No one in my family talked about it. Not my parents. Not my brother, who'd been two years younger and who I suspect never accepted me as a replacement sibling. It was only Gertrude who talked about her at all, telling me once that she thought it disgusting that the doctors had let my mother sit by Dail's hospital bed every day and scream like she did. My mother was thirty-three years old and six months' pregnant with me at the time.

Instead, underneath all the noise and activity of our home there were silent cross-currents. Gertrude and my father never spoke to one another. Ever. They drifted past each other in rooms and hallways like malevolent spirits. I never knew the reason why, only that it had something to do with my sister's death.

At dinner we sat around a large table in the dining room. Suddenly, I'd become aware of my father's hand hovering past my nose.

'Lynda, tell your grandmother to pass the salt,' he would say.

Gertrude would lean over and hand it to me without ever glancing at Bill. 'Tell your father, here it is.'

Each other's existence was erased. To us, it was normal behaviour.

At times, my mother became unreachable for other reasons. The effect of unimaginable trauma, I now assume. But as children, we were unaware. Her hearing began to fade not long after Dail's death. Mid-sentence she would stop dead, without any warning. Her eyes would stare out, vacant, as if she'd been hit by a sledgehammer. Sometimes she pulled herself out of it, but on other occasions my father would magically appear.

'Come on, Flossie, let's go for a walk,' he'd say, gently guiding her up from her chair and leading her out of the room.

I heard the odd story, too. Apparently, I'd still been in my high chair when I'd leaned over and tapped the crust of an apple pie my mother had made. My mother was no great cook, but she prided herself on her apple pies.

'Hard! Hard! Hard!' I'd shouted as my spoon bounced off the pastry.

Gertrude told me years later that my mother simply got up and disappeared. The last words Dail had spoken on the day she died were: 'Hard as nails!' She'd tapped her spoon on my mother's apple pie in precisely the same way.

Photographs of me from that age are virtually non-existent. Of the few that exist, I was dressed almost identically as Dail. A plain dress and a white brocade bib. The same outfit she wore in the painting.

'Is that me or Dail?' I used to ask my mother.

I could never be Dail, nor do I think I was ever explicitly expected to be so. Though perhaps I always felt that I was never good enough. I was shown her school notebooks once. Unbelievably neat handwriting, in the most perfect lines. Dail was beautiful but also exceptionally clever.

I'm also certain that my mother was periodically taken away, although I never knew where. 'Your mother's gone for a rest,' I was told. Another cryptogram, the lines of which I needed to read between. The only other time that I became aware of my mother's grief was in the run-up to Christmas. Then, it noticeably broke the surface and she became anxious and irritable.

Seared into my mind is one occasion, years after I'd left home, when we visited my brother who had moved to Yorkshire with his wife and young family. As we walked under the arch and through the courtyard leading to his house, my mother froze.

'Take it down! Take it down!' she began yelling.

Her cries were sharp and shrill, like a terrier barking.

A Christmas wreath hung on my brother's front door. It was identical to that which had been placed on Dail's grave so many years before.

'What's she talking about?' my brother frowned at me.

'It's the wreath. Just take it down,' I told him through gritted teeth.

When my mother died in 2005 the only items that she wanted buried with her were Dail's school tie, hat, ribbon and her little teddy bear.

In the years since, I've spoken to many victims of crime and parents of dead children. I've learned that it's impossible to cut out pain like that. It's always there, never leaves you. But if you'd ever visited the Titchmarsh home, it was rarely a mawkish place – surprisingly the opposite, in fact. Today in the downstairs of my home, I have a hanging plaque. It reads: a good laugh is sunshine in a home. It's the motto I've lived by all of my life and it was my parents' dictum too. Even now, whenever my sister Gill and I meet up we spend most of our time in hysterics. The slightest thing can set us off. Up front, our lives in Moor Lane were also filled with uproarious laughter.

One might conclude that losing a child in such tragic circumstances prompted my parents to withdraw somewhat from parenting, which may be true. Or perhaps they simply wanted us to live each day fearlessly, like there was no tomorrow. Whatever the reason, our childhoods were blissfully free. Never mind that I got lost in Sniggery Woods picking blackberries that hung thick throughout the late summer, or got tied to a post for hours on Blundellsands Beach. No one worried. No one checked up on us and no one warned us of any danger. It was idyllic beyond belief.

We were taught to swim from an early age. After all, we lived by the sea. But my mother also took us regularly to the lido at Southport Beach, where so many from the North-West flocked in the summer sun. Freshly washed beach towels were our constant companions and we splashed around in the water while my mother lay on a sun lounger bordering the oval Victorian pool. She looked like Katharine Hepburn in sunglasses, with all the manners of Hyacinth Bucket.

I never knew how my parents met, or when or where they were married. I knew nothing about their lives. They were, and remain, a complete enigma. But together they were rock solid. A powerful, centrifugal force around which everybody gravitated – everybody except their own extended family. Parties at our house were unbelievable! My brother Michael was the first in the neighbourhood to have a birthday bash with bangers and chips and baked beans. My father devised incredible games with wonderful prizes. Parents fought to get their children an invite.

Their friends Sybil and Eric were a mainstay of my parents' whirlwind social circle, always turning up well dressed for drinks and nibbles.

'Sybil will be arriving shortly,' my mother would announce. 'We have to get the cocktails ready.'

Time would be spent in the kitchen mixing punches and fashioning cucumber sandwiches. My parents' lives revolved around the golf club, the rugby club, charity balls and formal functions. My father was a rather loud, lean, and sporting man. My mother was as energetic – as a young girl she'd been a mascot for Liverpool Football Club and followed The Reds avidly. But she was also stinging in her sarcasm and a stickler for good manners and pronunciation. God forbid we'd ever turn out talking Scouse!

Once I accompanied her to pick up my little sister, who'd gone to the home of the local butcher for a children's birthday party. Although only two years separated us, Gill and I were never close as children and only became so in later life. She had her friends and I had mine.

'I've come to pick up Gill,' my mother announced on the doorstep.

The butcher lived in an incredibly fancy house, and his wife was polite and hospitable. When she looked down and saw me she said, 'Goodness, Florence, if we'd known Gill had a sister she should have came too.'

'Oh really?' My mother looked as if she was sucking on a lemon. 'She should have came too, should she?' she said mockingly.

And then there was Gertrude – Christ Almighty! Gertrude. Get on the wrong side of her and you'd live to regret it. She'd been the matriarch of her family. Freakishly tall at six foot, she had an angular face and a very nasty temper. Gertrude wasn't a nurse by profession, but as the eldest daughter in her family she'd delivered babies, sewed fingers back on, tended to the sick. Walking alongside her was terrifying. She wore large dress hats and clutched an umbrella with an iron grip. Moving traffic? No obstacle whatsoever! She strode out in front of cars waving her brolly.

'They will stop for us,' she declared confidently.

I must have been around seven years old when she took me to the Adelphi Hotel in Liverpool. Perhaps I had been going to the dentist in Rodney Street, as Liverpool was never a regular destination, yet I can still picture skipping up the Adelphi's front steps and entering its giant marble foyer. To have lunch there was a real treat, but when it got served I didn't feel so lucky.

Gertrude clicked her fingers in the air. 'Waiter! Come here!'

'Can I help you, madam?'

'Young man, this is not chicken. It's rabbit,' she said, waving her hand dismissively at her plate. 'I ordered chicken.'

'I'm very sorry, madam, but that is chicken.'

'Now listen here, young man. Are you telling me I don't know the difference between a chicken and a rabbit?'

When I looked around the room all the other guests' eyes were fixed on our table.

Gertrude's face was tight with anger. 'This has four legs!' she screamed as I sank further into my seat.

For a woman who claimed not to have had a drink before the age of fifty, Gertrude certainly made up for it. With gusto! She had crates of beer delivered to the house, which she stacked up outside.

If my brother ever had friends over you would inevitably hear her cry, 'Which one of you has drunk my beer?' Gertrude would stand waving a stick at Michael's friends in the back yard. 'These are empties in this crate! Not consumed by me, I might add. Come on, who was it?'

'Sorry, Mrs Southwood.'

Gertrude was a demon whist player to boot. She was always at the Conservative Club in Crosby playing cards or attending one function or another. Aintree Racecourse was also a place she liked to be seen. She'd befriended its owner and was a regular at the Grand National festival or afternoon racing. Gertrude didn't just have a flutter, she knew every horse running, every jockey and every trainer. She studied the form and placed bets. Heavy-duty bets, too. My mother always knew when she'd been on the phone to the bookies because she replaced the receiver back-to-front.

Lunacy. Utter lunacy. It's the only way that I can describe our house.

My father would leap-frog from bright idea to bright idea.

'I've bought a goat. It will be arriving at four o'clock to cut the grass. The pony that's tethered to the hedge – I want it removed before it gets here.'

Later that day I found my father hammering a post into the ground and tying the poor goat to it. By the next morning it had chewed through the rope, the flowers, the hedge. Everything but the grass.

'Unbelievable!' My father looked on in horror.

Michael was known as 'The Bird Man'. One summer he built an aviary in the back garden with wire and pipes and mesh from the local hardware store. After saving up his pocket money he'd also ordered a hawk from London Zoo and I'd find him in a fencing mask teaching it how to spread its wings and circle in the air before landing back on his glove to peck at a tidbit of meat.

Herbert, the seagull, was also a firm fixture.

'Herbert, where's your bin?' If you called out, he'd hop onto an upturned dustbin lid and toddle around it, tap, tap, tapping his beak on the metal edge.

A crow with its wing in a splint was also often glued to Michael's shoulder.

'I will not eat with that crow on your shoulder!' my father bellowed if it ever accompanied Michael to the dining table.

'A bird-watcher!' my father would cry. 'Whatever did I do to get a bird-watcher?'

Puppies; cats; horses; rabbits; birds. My father's feet were always being chewed by some creature. We were the Durrells minus the Greek sunshine.

Holidays were equally insane. My father refused to pre-book anywhere. He wanted a full inspection of the hotel before he parted with any money. We would turn up en masse to destinations like Colwyn Bay or Anglesey, Bournemouth or Brighton at the peak of the summer season in a huge grey Vanguard car that looked like a whale. Inevitably, we'd end up staying in lop-sided hotel rooms that no one wanted. My little mouse Whitey always accompanied me and lived in my pocket. We'd only been allowed one mouse but when we bought her we picked out the fattest who was, of course, pregnant. Of the ten babies born I was allowed to keep Whitey.

'Would you like to see my mouse?' I remember saying to one woman parked in a wheelchair in the conservatory of a hotel in Colwyn Bay.

'Yes, young lady, I would.'

She was rather elderly, and a complete stranger. I kissed my teeth and Whitey popped out, at which point the woman slumped over in her chair and I was removed rather promptly.

Then there were the kitchen scissors of which I seemed terribly fond. Years later when my mother was interviewed for Melvyn Bragg's *The South Bank Show* he asked her, 'What do you think made Lynda create this world of crime?'

'Well, she was lethal with a pair of scissors!' my mother replied. My parents took no interest whatsoever in my entire career, but that was one fact my mother had been right about.

One time, the play *Camelot* was being staged by the local amateur dramatics society. My friend Jane Maxwell-Brown's mother was in charge of costumes and kept a large wicker basket filled with them. One day, I cycled to Jane's – I'd written a little play and Jane and I had planned to take the costumes back to my house and act it out in the garage. We gathered them up, took them home and disappeared for hours.

All of a sudden, we could hear Jane's mother's voice.

'Is Jane with Lynda?'

'I think they're in the garage,' my mother boomed back.

'It's just it's the first night of *Camelot* tomorrow and I've been to the costume basket. There isn't a costume in sight.'

'Well, I don't think they would have taken the costumes for the production.'

When my mother eased up the garage door Jane and I looked like munchkin Cinderellas. We'd cut down the full-sized dresses and pointy hats to fit us. We'd trimmed every single sleeve. The veils were in shreds. Jane Maxwell-Brown's mother was incandescent and stayed up half the night sewing the costumes back together.

I was also caught trimming the hair of the girl next door. Kathleen had tumbling curly locks, in my eyes begging to be cut. And when I eventually persuaded her, I leant a ladder against the wall in our back yard, climbed it and disappeared over to give her a crew cut. I wasn't allowed to play with her after that. Of course, nothing was ever my fault. Gertrude was forever calling me into her room and holding up an evening gown to the window as beams of bright sunlight shone through the gaping holes.

'Can you please tell me about these, Lynda?'

'Moths, I think.'

'These would have to be very large moths.'

'Well, it's definitely moths.'

'And your doll, Lynda. Do you recognise this black lace on its head now masquerading as a hat?'

'Ah. Got me there . . .'

You'd think that surrounded by all of that, my parents may have steered me towards a career filled with make-believe, but nothing could have been further from the truth. Neither of them had any interest in the theatre or writing or in the arts whatsoever. When I was a child, my father carried around a little play I'd written in his top pocket. It was so misspelled that it bordered on farce. A story about a 'norty girl who stoal a bicycle and fel off it'. Perhaps those early scribbles were the start of my need to tell stories and write them down. Affectionately, my father humoured me but he never would have considered it likely to become the trajectory of my life. Instead, he rolled his eyes: 'This is my daughter. The writer.'

The closest my mother ever got to having any kind of expectation was taking me to ballet classes, which I did from around the age of three. I was good, too. But one day, aged around ten, I swung up and over the swing in the play-park and crashed down onto my knees. Gertrude covered each leg in poultices of scalding-hot white bread and sugar to bring the swellings down, but after that I was never the same. I'd been such a skinny child, but the minute I stopped my rigorous ballet training, I put on weight. That exposed another problem that hadn't been visible before. My wrists were completely twisted – as if they'd been sewn on backwards. When my mother took me to The White Lodge in London aged around twelve to audition for a place to train with the Royal Ballet, but at the very moment I stepped forward and into first position I heard one of the tutors say, 'Oh, she's deformed. Thank you very much, dear. The audition is now over.'

'Well, she didn't get it from my side of the family,' my mother barked.

I had been refused immediately. To say that my mother was heartbroken would be a gross exaggeration. There was little aspiration for me or my sister other than to marry a respectable husband and become perfect housewives and hostesses; a life in ballet was the exception to that. Michael, on the other hand, was given all the private tutoring he needed in the hope that he would one day go on to become a doctor. It's exactly what he did. My education was really very simple: speak properly, dress immaculately and know how to fillet a fish. That's all Lynda Titchmarsh was destined to do in life.

Chapter 2

Learning by Heart

Streatham House School was around fifteen minutes' walk from our house on Moor Lane and the nearest to a real-life St Trinian's as one could get. Violet and Maude Harvey, the sisters who ran it, seemed to have no clue what was going on under the roof of the most unruly private girls' school in Crosby. Both overweight and with shelf-like bosoms, they were the epitome of wonderful old aunties. Vowels tumbled around in their mouths.

'Euuuw dooo come in,' you would hear if you ever knocked on the door of the front sitting room where they resided and sipped tea, dressed in their neat blouses tied with bows and their hair in perfect buns.

I attended Streatham House from primary age and stayed there for all of my education. The classrooms sat above the polished staircase with its wide banister. There was no central heating. Instead, we continually swapped places around the large fireplaces that decorated every room.

'Everybody change!' At that, those freezing by the sash windows would alternate with those broiling by the coal fire.

The main hallway was always ice-cold. And in the drill hall, a more modern building next to the main Victorian building, there was a hole in the wall big enough to climb through. In the ten or so years I attended it never got fixed and gradually grew larger. If we were ever late we'd sneak through it and around the corridor to the assembly hall or into class. Anyone found entering via the hole would be severely reprimanded.

At some point during my school career Violet Harvey died, though exactly when I'm not sure. I have a vision of myself outside the school gates clutching a neat posy of pussy willows that I'd picked myself.

One teacher, Miss Asprey, stood making the announcement.

'Very sadly, Miss Violet has passed on,' she said.

'Well, when she comes back, could you give her these?' I said, stretching out my hand to pass her the flowers.

Lessons were minimal. Home Economics was abandoned after someone accidentally blew up an oven in the kitchen, but not before I was taught how to use a proper fish board and filleting knife. Filleting a fish is still one of my finest achievements and a skill that has remained with me. Curtseying for royalty? That, too, was an unforgettable lesson. As if royalty would come to Crosby! If anyone had visited they'd more likely see us sliding down the banisters in our white dresses, red ties and Panama hats.

Sports were another source of hysteria. Tennis was played out in the garden. If the net fell down Miss Roper refused to fix it. 'Leave the net as it is!' she shouted. It was barely off the ground – no match at all. And lacrosse was banned because Streatham House had inflicted far too many injuries on the nearby Merchant Taylors' School girls' team. Hockey was an open invitation to escape sports lessons. The fields where we played were covered in cow shit.

'Any girl with dung on their feet, stop playing and make their way to the changing rooms immediately.' Naturally, we trod in it deliberately.

Wednesday walks were also a highlight. We'd march in a line up and down the high street, but teachers never noticed if girls peeled off and sneaked into WHSmith. Back then, everyone collected plaster-of-Paris moulds and regularly stole them from the shelves. One girl, Sylvia, was even dealing in them. She'd often sidle up next to me and say, 'I've got a Snoopy for sale, but I'll part-exchange it for a hedgehog.' I always resisted the urge to steal, but one day I tagged alongside the others. I was so slow, all the moulds got swiped before I could pocket one and all I was left with was a roll of Sellotape, which I shoved into my blazer pocket.

Around two days later Miss Harvey called a special assembly. Standing alongside her was a uniformed policeman.

'Girls, I have something to say. This is a terrible time for Streatham House School. There has been theft from Smiths, and Constable Harris – do step forward, Mr Harris – is here to find the culprits. If you've stolen anything, honesty is the best policy. Please raise your hand.'

After a short silence, my hand shot up.

'What did you take, Lynda?'

'A roll of Sellotape, Miss.'

I was the only one to confess. Yet if the Constable had opened up every wooden desk he would have found each one groaning with fairies and Snow Whites and gnomes.

Often I found myself on the 'silly table', which was tantamount to the dunce's corner. Can you imagine it being called that now? These days I also would have been labelled as dyslexic. I've never been diagnosed with the condition but from a young age I suffered a form of word blindness. The alphabet was a complete blur to me. Bs became Ds and Hs were Ms. Mostly it wasn't a problem, except for when it came to English Literature. Miss Ash noticed something very peculiar when I read aloud. The book got passed from pupil to pupil and we'd each have to read a paragraph.

'Lynda, how could you read the story with the book upside down?' She pulled me aside after class one day having spotted that I wasn't reading at all.

'I make it up,' I confessed.

'So, you can't see what's on the page?'

'I can't see anything!'

'Is there something wrong with your eyesight?'

There wasn't anything wrong. It was simply that everything looked like one continuous word. I couldn't hear the sounds of letters, either – to me, there was no difference between the 'A' sound of an apple or the 'A' sound of an ape.

Far from letting me suffer in silence, Miss Ash was wonderful. She created a phonetic alphabet and took me for extra lessons. From there a whole world opened up – poetry, especially. I became an obsessive poetry lover. I read anything I could get my hands on, probably over-compensating for my difficulties. In the end, I became better read than most.

Away from school, I had another source of education, although not one my mother ever approved of. Uncle Stanley, the only other blood relative I knew, lived in a large house with an unkempt garden a mile down the coast overlooking the beach at Waterloo. Who exactly Stanley was to me I still have no idea – possibly a nephew of Gertrude's. On the day he came to our house, I'd never seen anything like him: thick black hair and a tanned, weatherbeaten face, wearing a navy pin-striped suit jacket over a white T-shirt. Who dressed like that? No one that I knew. And he flaunted so many tattoos! He took an interest in me because I was so mesmerised by him. Stanley Hugill was a conjurer of faraway worlds.

Secretly after school I'd pedal on my bike to his house. It was filled with rarities gathered from around the globe, much of which is now housed within the Museum of Liverpool. Stanley had run away to sea when he was thirteen years old. He collected sea shanties like he collected curios and when he died in 1992, aged eighty-five, he was known as 'The last of the Shantymen'. I can still remember the smell of the rich caramel tobacco burning from his pipe and the heavy incense around the house. Its walls were covered in Indian headdresses and oil paintings, idols and ceremonial swords. He had no qualms about showing me death masks and weaponry.

One story was that in 1929 he'd led the singing of the pump shanty 'Fire Down Below' aboard a square-rigged merchant ship called the *Garthpool* days before the vessel was wrecked off the Cape Verde Islands. It was the last sailing ship to ever trade under the British flag, which Stanley also salvaged and kept in Waterloo. I adored Stanley's stories, but they were never fairytales. They were dark and menacing. In my mother's eyes, Stanley was dangerous. Surprising to me, though, he did once show me a picture of her dressed head-to-toe in full traditional Japanese regalia.

Nelly, Stanley's mother, also lived at the house in Waterloo but I only recall meeting her once or twice. Rumour had it that she was a gypsy. Her inky black pigtails and tawny skin made me believe so. She read palms, too. But if I ever asked my mother about Nelly, she curtly said, 'I don't know anything.'

The top floor of the house was where Stanley's brother, Harold, mainly lived. It had been converted into a Buddhist temple. I understood that Harold was once destined to be a concert pianist but that a Doodlebug had landed in the back garden during the war and deafened him. The grand piano in the sitting room was erected on stilts so that he could feel the vibrations in the floor when he played. As for the circumstances surrounding his conversion to Buddhist monk, they remain a complete mystery.

Harold's death was also shrouded in secrecy. I only knew because I overheard my mother talking on the phone.

'No, I can't do that. Absolutely not. I won't be going,' she said.

Apparently, Harold had gone up to the temple, starved himself to death and been found in his saffron robes. The coroner had wanted my mother to identify his body. She point-blank refused.

The last time I saw Stanley was when he turned up at the stage door when I was performing in repertory theatre at the Liverpool Playhouse in the 1960s, when I was in my twenties.

'You don't remember me, do you?' he said.

By now Stanley had long grey hair in pigtails and looked how the country singer Willie Nelson does now.

'Of course I do. You're Uncle Stanley!'

In the intervening years he'd moved to Wales, married and had children, although rumour had it that he had already been betrothed to a Polynesian girl.

That evening he was performing at the Liverpool Empire with the English folk foursome the Spinners and invited me along. It was unbelievable! When Stanley was brought out on stage it was to a standing ovation. The crowd hushed and he tapped his foot.

'This is a song for when we beat the oars,' he said, before launching into one of the most haunting renditions of the traditional folk song 'Maggie May' I'd ever heard. After that, Stanley and I exchanged letters for the remainder of his life. His were beautiful – the work of a man filled with a childlike sense of adventure, not someone in their sixties, seventies, or eighties. He spoke eleven languages. Some letters were sent from America where he'd been living with a Navaho tribe. He'd taken magic mushrooms, he told me.

But returning to my school days, having absorbed so many of Uncle Stanley's stories I became somewhat of an oddity back at Streatham House School. I could often be found at the back of class demonstrating to the other girls how Japanese warriors committed suicide, cross-legged and on a mat. Stanley had shown me on his own authentic mat, blood-soaked from warriors past. I'd plunge my ruler into my abdomen to show how the knife cut from left to right and then up to the heart.

'Did you know that if they die before the stomach is cut open all their sins are absolved?' I told my classmates eagerly.

'Lynda, what exactly are you doing?'

'Hara-kiri, Miss.'

'Harry who?'

'Hara-kiri. It's how the Samurais kill themselves.'

My mother was called in on several occasions.

'Mrs Titchmarsh, Lynda has been showing the girls Hara-kiri!'

The macabre was always fascinating to me. If we had a babysitter, I would stay up to watch *The Little Red Monkey,* a murder mystery spy thriller set in the Cold War. I loved it, but it did give me nightmares.

On another occasion, my friend Victoria and I sneaked inside the local cinema. I was probably around eleven years old.

'Shall we go to the matinee?' she'd asked.

'I'm not allowed to go to the cinema on my own.'

'It's OK. I know a way in. There's a back door we can get through.'

Off we pedalled to The Regent. Sure enough the exit door was open, and when we crawled through to the seats there was a special afternoon showing of a film on the Holocaust. We watched open-mouthed as skeletons were shovelled into mass graves.

'I think they're dolls,' Victoria tugged at my sleeve and whispered.

'Yes, dolls . . . they must be dolls,' we concluded.

If only that *had* been true. We were removed not long after and my mother came to fetch me.

I failed my eleven-plus exam. It caused some disquiet at home, but it was soon forgiven.

The funny thing was I'd been very confident. I'd sailed through it.

'How did it go?' my father had asked me.

'Piece of cake.'

'Why so, Lynda?'

'Well, they asked the stupidest questions. What's the heaviest: a pound of feathers or a pound of coal? Not going to fool me! It's a pound of coal.'

'Ah. I can see I'm going to be paying for you the rest of my life,' he said. As far as a vocation was concerned, I had absolutely no direction. It is still preposterous to me that I followed the career path that I did, given the lack of encouragement I was given or exposure to the arts. Other than school plays, my parents hadn't taken me to a single performance.

Instead, it was by pure chance that when I reached secondary school one teacher changed my life. Miss McCormack opened up worlds to me that felt hidden and mainly forbidden. I'm not sure exactly when she arrived, where she came from or why she ended up at a girls' school in the North-West but she shone like a gemstone in silt. She'd been an actor and took us for drama, poetry and reading classes. I'd never seen such a woman: tall and slender but busty with pretty A-line skirts cinched in with a tight belt. Her little stilettos had pointy toes. Whenever she crossed her legs I'd marvel at how svelte her ankles were and how her skirt fell sophisticatedly to one side.

Miss McCormack also had a snipe nose and slightly bucked teeth, but beautiful eyes. She was exceedingly critical. If you got a 'That was good' from her it *really* meant something. She'd move around the class skipping past any pupil whose recitations didn't pass muster.

'Give me a few sentences on why you like Byron and then a few lines of your most favourite poem . . .'

'She walks in beauty, like the night . . .'

'Oh no. Very boring. That really was sleep-making, dear. Next . . .'

She taught me a technique that I still use over and over in lectures. If anyone was caught chattering, she'd lean in and say, 'I'm sorry. If I'm boring you, perhaps you'd like to tell everyone what you were talking about . . .' She'd hold the pause for so long that the sound of girls squirming in their seats became excruciating.

Yet Miss McCormack was the only teacher whose lessons I worked hard for. By now, thankfully I'd improved so whenever I read aloud, I ached for the day when she would say, 'A little more lift on the end of the line please, Lynda, but getting better.'

And it was never just poems that we recited parrot-fashion in Miss McCormack's class. She talked to us about who the poets were, their lives, the scandals surrounding them. We imagined them as people and I became transfixed. She asked lunatic questions. Questions that blindsided everyone, such as, 'And Byron. Do we think it's plausible he was having a sexual relationship with his half-sister?'

When the whole class started tittering, she would say, 'Do you find that funny? Why do you find that amusing? Was he indeed simply proving his attractiveness to the opposite sex because he had a club foot?'

One by one we'd have to stand up and explain what we found so hilarious, but also explain our thoughts. Dreadful for some, I'm sure, but it only made me want to read more Byron. More Percy Bysshe Shelley. More of all the great poets.

Then she'd turn her attention to the female authors like Mary Shelley, parts of whose life she would act out in front of the class. Mary, for instance, had such a terror of her father that she'd taught herself how to sit in front of him and not move a muscle.

'Now watch me,' Miss McCormack would say and she'd remain like a statue for minutes, as if she were perfecting stillness as an art form. *What?* Nobody in Crosby taught girls like that! And it was Miss McCormack who changed the trajectory of my entire life.

'Would you like to be an actor, Lynda?' she asked me one day.

It sounded better than marrying or filleting fish, even though I didn't know what being an actor actually entailed.

'Yes, all right!' I agreed.

'Right-o, Lynda. We'll have to work on your elocution and your posture.'

From there, Miss McCormack took me through the series of exams set by the London Academy of Music and Dramatic Art, known as LAMBDA. I could recite whole chunks of *The Faerie Queene* by Edmund Spenser, a wonderful poem that reworked the Arthurian legends, but phenomenally difficult with its complex Old English dialect. I memorised each and every line.

As I practised my recital, Miss McCormack would warn me, 'You keep moving, Lynda. You mustn't move your hands.' Ballet had been second nature to me, but she taught me to stop fidgeting and read confidently. I got through my bronze, silver and gold levels.

'Do you know of a school called RADA?' she asked when I was around fourteen years old.

'No. Never heard of it.'

'Would you like to try to go?'

'Yes please.'

'Right. Well, we might have to lie about your age. I'm not sure they take girls as young as you.'

'OK.'

Acting? RADA? It all felt so remote to me, like a great adventure, so I went along with it. From Miss McCormack I was sent to a Mrs Atkins, who lived in the centre of Liverpool in a house with a large front room filled with books and a piano. She would help me train for the audition. Mrs Atkins was getting on a bit, probably in her eighties by then, but she sat on her stool peering at me through her thick round glasses. She wore open-toed sandals and had thick tree-trunk legs, the kind that old ladies have.

'Dear, the voice is good but if you're going to act, you're going to have to throw yourself around a bit,' she said. Acting, it seemed, required far more physical expression than reciting poetry did.

She often sang at the top of her voice and tapped her knee up and down underneath her bright pleated skirt to keep time.

I would be expected to copy her.

'That's it, dear. Doing well but a bit more movement,' she would shout encouragingly.

After a few months, Mrs Atkins announced, 'Right, dear. I think you are ready . . .'

Chapter 3
RADA

I was fifteen years old when I took the early morning train from Liverpool Lime Street to London's Euston Station, armed with every lesson I'd learned from Miss McCormack and Mrs Atkins and a taxi fare provided by my parents to deliver me safely to the Royal Academy of Dramatic Arts in Gower Street.

If I was nervous, I don't recall it. To me, going to an audition felt like a game, more so because I wasn't exactly overburdened with expectation. Not only did I have little understanding of what RADA was, but when I first told my father I wanted to go he hadn't a clue either. 'RADA? That's lovely, Lynda. Is it a pub?' he asked in all seriousness.

The ambitious monologue I'd rehearsed was from *The Lark*, a 1952 play by the French playwright Jean Anouilh dramatising the trial and execution of Joan of Arc. Somehow after I'd stepped through RADA's heavy wooden doors and into the studio theatre, the white high-heeled shoes I'd worn, plus the stiff petticoat ballooning out from under my dress, felt cheap and trivial compared to the gravitas of the institution. If Mrs Atkins had wanted me to 'throw myself around a bit', then my dress and high heels constrained me.

'Excuse me. Do you mind if I take my shoes off?' I called over to the tutors sat in the half-light of the auditorium.

'No,' a voice called out flatly, giving me licence to go one step further.

'And my underskirt? Do you mind if I take that off too?' I asked, bending down to yank off the crinoline net.

'So long as you're not taking off anything else, Miss Titchmarsh. Now please, just get on with it,' the voice uttered witheringly.

Now liberated, I breathed from my diaphragm, filling up my lungs like a tank, and I began to project my voice commandingly and precisely. Mrs Atkins' voice rang in my ears: 'Don't stay static, dear. Move! Move!' And after a few minutes of flinging myself around, I finished to a prolonged silence . . .

'Thank you very much, you may go. Next!'

A couple of weeks later a very courteous letter popped through the letterbox. It turned out the idiot girl who'd entered the room that day had some potential after all. A partial scholarship was duly offered to me to be topped up by my father's income.

Where I would stay when I got to RADA ended up being taken care of by my grandmother Gertrude. An acquaintance of hers from the Conservative Club in Crosby had a connection to a Lady Russell in London – none other than the daughter of Sir William Howard Russell whose dispatches from the Crimean War in the mid-nineteenth century had marked him out as one of the first modern war correspondents.

Lady Russell had no children of her own but rented rooms to young girls like me in Albert Hall Mansions, an elegant ribbon of Victorian redbrick apartments directly behind the Royal Albert Hall. Given that the arrangement had been made through Gertrude's distinguished circle, I felt duty-bound to play by Lady Russell's rules. Yet compared to home, there seemed so many.

Rule number one was that I was never allowed to cook. The flat was in the basement, and if I was at home I was expected to confine myself to my poky bedroom off a long, dark corridor. Rule number two concerned the communal lift by the faded marble staircase. It was strictly out of bounds. Apparently, the renowned conductor Sir Malcolm Sargent lived on an upper floor and woe betide if he ever had to share a lift with one of Lady Russell's adolescent lodgers, thereby exposing her set-up that I suspect wasn't altogether above board. Apparently, one other girl was living alongside me, but I never heard or saw her once. The only trace of her was a floater left one day in the shared loo, over which Lady Russell Howard subjected me to a rigorous interrogation.

A third rule I learned the hard way. Any interior decoration of my room sent Lady Russell into near apoplexy. As well as at times working for the BBC, she had been an accomplished equestrian who had ridden horses through flaming hoops. From floor to ceiling my bedroom walls were covered with paper cut-outs of various jumping events alongside prize-winning horses. I found them creepy and on my first night peeled them off.

Ordinarily I have a photographic memory for faces but, other than two protruding front teeth, hers remains vague in my mind. All I can picture is Lady Russell calling me into her quarters and ordering me to iron every single cut-out before reattaching them to the wall. As she seethed she scratched at the lattice of burn scars covering her wrists, sustained while jumping through the red-hot rings of fire. She did that often, and I can still hear the sound of her fingernails scraping against her dry skin.

At RADA, any acting potential that the tutors may have seen during my audition turned out to be sadly lacking once term began. Lessons were so boring! Preposterously so, in my view. Movements like a curtsey that I'd been perfecting in ballet since the age of three gobbled up hours of time. In Restoration Comedy tutorials I watched as my contemporaries agonised over how to coquettishly flutter a fan. Again, ballet had taught me everything I needed to know. What did set me alight, though, was the study of the plays themselves: Strindberg; Chekhov; Molière – marvellous writers who took my understanding of character, drama and literature to another level. Aside from that, I looked to the periphery for a richer seam of education than I could ever have found on the course itself. Quite honestly, I laughed my way through RADA.

Other than Miss McCormack and Uncle Stanley back home, I'd never met a pick-and-mix of people so bizarre than at RADA. They were entirely removed from my realm of experience. In my year, there was a forty-something cab driver with no apparent acting ability whatsoever. Another student, Elsa from Sweden, was aged around thirty with a sing-song voice and sweetly refused to do anything outside of her comfort zone. 'This exercise is not for me, thank you. It's so difficult.'

By contrast, Nidal Ashka, a smoky-eyed enchantress with a deep rasp to her voice, was prone to breathtaking melodrama.

'I am Nidal Ashka from the Lebanon and I refuse to work with this man.'

'But he's your tutor!'

She sucked her teeth and gave a gallic shrug. 'Do I care?'

Then there was a girl who went on to marry a prominent Lord. She made it her mission to sleep with every man on the course, including several tutors. She carried with her a calendar on which she crossed off her conquests, and even managed to bed the assistant of the Exercise and Movement teacher. Clearly a girl of myriad talents, she was also a prolific shoplifter who brazenly lifted the finest silk scarves from Harrods. 'You can take anything!' she announced.

The small group I gravitated towards consisted of the actor Donald Pleasance's daughter Angela and also Gemma Jones, both of whom went on to become accomplished actors. Carol Cleveland, who later found fame in the *Monty Python* films, became a very firm friend and remains so to this day. She found RADA equally as hilarious. Carol had grown up in the US and had been crowned

Miss Pasadena before arriving in the UK. To me she seemed wondrously glamorous: tall, curvaceous and sophisticated with luscious red hair and a soft American accent. In height, I reached her elbow at best, making us the most peculiar double act.

Through Carol I met the actor Ian McShane, who she'd started dating, and his friend John Hurt was also part of our inner circle. Like me, Ian came from the North, so we felt an immediate bond, although his hometown had been Manchester. He was also uninterested in lessons, even though he went on to become a big Hollywood star, and in that first year he and I became partners in crime, resulting on one occasion in me being the only student to be kept back a term for misbehaviour.

Every morning we were required to place our names on a board kept in reception to show that we'd arrived but Ian, always with a devilish sparkle in his eye, spotted an opportunity. 'I know where they stash that board once classes begin. I'll show you,' he whispered to me.

Ian noticed that every morning after enrolment the board got relocated to a cupboard fronted by a locked half-door. So long as I could reach it, we could add our names. This meant we could turn up at any time we wanted. All Ian needed to do was give me a leg-up so I could stretch over.

For weeks afterwards he and I would casually stroll up Gower Street, stopping for a chat and a cappuccino when we should have been in class. But one time, just as I was hanging over the cupboard door, backside in the air, a righteous voice punctured the silence. 'What on earth do you think you are doing?'

When I hoisted myself up and looked around, Ian was nowhere in sight. Instead, John Fernald, RADA's then principal, was staring at me. He had grey slicked-back hair and a look that could cut glass.

'I was . . . I was getting my name,' I blurted out meekly.

'To do what?'

'To put it against . . . "arrived" . . .'

'And why were you doing that, Miss Titchmarsh?'

It all smacked of being ten years old and back at school, and I carried a deep shame about being kept back a term, especially when I had to confess it to my parents. What's more, the first term had been so tedious!

In many respects, I was still so incredibly naive. It was the late 1950s and if London was ever starting to swing, it certainly wasn't for me. To start with, I had no money. I was also underage so I couldn't get into bars or nightclubs. And my understanding of sex hadn't even reached elementary level. My mother had taught me precisely nothing about the facts of life.

'Lynda, do you do Biology with rabbits and things at school?'

'Yes.'

'Oh jolly good.'

That was the sum total of my sex education. I did have a boyfriend, though: a broad-shouldered, chisel-jawed, dependable and one hundred per cent platonic boyfriend called Richard Greenwood who I'd first met because he played in my brother's rugby team in Blundellsands. Richard went on to study at Cambridge before joining the England rugby union team. His son, Will Greenwood, eventually followed in his footsteps and also represented England. I adored Richard and he felt the same. Throughout my entire two years at RADA he and I would meet during the holidays – the most innocent of relationships kept together by a longing to see each other and his beautifully handwritten letters. Some were penned on that waxy Bronco brand toilet paper that was commonplace back then. I still have those letters somewhere.

I've since wondered what my life would have been like if Richard and I had ever married but as my acting career took off I moved beyond his calm and steadfastness. Part of me knew the relationship wouldn't work long-term and when a girl he was at Cambridge with came to see me in London to tell me she was in love with Richard and to ask whether I intended on marrying him, I confirmed that while I was his girlfriend I didn't plan on doing so. Evidently, Richard found my blessing of this relationship hard as he sent me the most heartfelt letters asking why I hadn't wanted us to remain an item. I had no real answer, other than my gut feeling. I wasn't yet twenty. I had no notion of what I wanted to do with my life and little interest in settling down.

At RADA my clique were always trying, in every way possible, to get me to go out with John Hurt. Because he was friends with Ian McShane, John tagged along like a puppy whenever Ian was taking Carol out. While John was entertaining, he was also pale-faced and skinny with a shock of reddish hair. Not attractive to me whatsoever. He was also a rather nervous young man who painted as a hobby and would turn up scruffily dressed in an unwashed T-shirt and jeans covered in brush marks and oil stains. One time he did make a strange attempt at impressing me.

'I want to tell you something very personal,' he said.
'Oh yes, and what is that?'
'I have no hair on my body . . .'
'Oh really?'

I found John's oddness confusing. Even when he made an effort and raided RADA's prop department, turning up in an awful brown suit one evening to take me out, I wasn't persuaded. Yet Ian McShane was always in the background, putting in a good word.

'Are you two ever going to get together?'
'No, I really don't think so.'

But I didn't just 'think'. I knew I did not want to go on a date with John Hurt. Not ever. Besides, I hadn't much of a clue what to do on a date and I doubt John did either. We were so wet behind the ears.

I recall during one break a girl called Morag approached me. I'd been in awe of Morag from afar with her cropped hair and tight jeans, and her suede-lined leather handbag with its clicky fastener that I coveted. A stylish plume of smoke always drifted up from her Gitanes cigarettes.

'Lynda, have you been fixed up with a gyno?' she asked.

'No, have you?'

'Well, of course I have! Since the age of twelve. But I'm not sure he's any good. I was wondering if you had one . . .'

I longed to be as sophisticated as Morag, so I couldn't admit that I was oblivious to what a gyno was, let alone had one. Later on in the canteen I asked Ian, John and the actor Terry Taplin if they knew.

'What's a gyno?'

Ian had no idea. Neither did John.

'Well, why's Morag got one?'

Terry, a student with an extraordinarily pointy nose and dreadful Tourette's, seemed to have the answer.

'I know what they are! They're the guys who map out the flags on Ordnance Survey maps.'

'Well, why would Morag ask if I had one of those?'

'I don't know. It's very strange!'

As for homosexuality, that was unfathomable to me. I had no idea gay men or lesbians existed.

'What's gay?' I recall quizzing Ian McShane.

'Your classmate Bernie. He's one.'

'Is he? But *what* is he?'

'Lynda. They're men that go with men. And lesbians are women that go with women,' Ian said, rather exasperated.

'What? But *how*? Surely not!'

I became a little more streetwise after I moved out of Lady Russell's apartment, but not by much. That came about because a few months into my first year it became clear that I was living under the roof of a complete lunatic. As well as working at the BBC, Lady Russell also claimed to have been a private secretary to Laurence Olivier, the whole truth of which I do not know. One of her favourite outrages was about how she and Olivier had been so close but how his second wife Vivien Leigh, whom he was divorcing, had been a troubled nightmare. Lady Russell was writing an exposé of her time with Olivier, including revelations that Leigh was a sex maniac whose rapacious appetite led her to pick up a different man every night.

One evening she announced that a very special visitor – Olivier himself – was coming to see her and I was under strict instructions to remain in my room. At the time I had no real appreciation of Laurence Olivier's acting talent, but I did know he was revered and Lady Russell behaved as if royalty were arriving. Looking back, I suspect she was madly in love with Olivier and felt her memoir would right all the wrongs she believed had been meted out to him by that harlot Vivien Leigh. That evening she sprayed the hallway with heavy scent and arrived at my door in a neatly tailored dress covering her matronly figure.

'Lynda, you must remember. Do not come out of your room. Do not even go to the toilet. Laurence Olivier will be arriving shortly to discuss my memoir. It is the meeting of my life.'

From my end of the corridor I pressed my ear against the door. Soon after the bell sounded I heard a low, plummy voice greet Lady Russell. The drawing-room door shut and I strained to make out the muffled conversation. After a while I got desperate for a pee and silently edged my door open, creeping out to the bathroom where I sat, legs dangling on the old Victorian toilet for what seemed like an eternity. The exchange didn't sound agreeable at all. Voices became more and more animated. Olivier's reached a crescendo and he exploded in a hot rage, 'You print one word of this and I'll have you up in front of every court in England. I'll sue you, you two-faced hag!'

I didn't dare come out from the bathroom. I listened on as Olivier roared abuse. Then there was the crash-bang of items being hurled around the room. Lady Russell was sobbing. Suddenly the drawing room door flew open. Olivier's footsteps pounded up the hallway and the walls shuddered as he slammed the door behind him. When I finally got the courage to tiptoe out there were pages of a manuscript torn into pieces and strewn across the carpet. The faint whimper of Lady Russell could still be heard from her quarters.

The encounter had been extraordinary but the voice inside my head was telling me it was time to go. I packed up my little bag and moved in with Carol Cleveland. She had been listening to the saga of Lady Russell for weeks and suggested I take the spare bed in a bedsit she lived in at her mother's house in Warrington Crescent in Maida Vale. What a relief to be out of that dank and terrifying environment, although I did worry about how I'd let down Gertrude, who'd arranged it all. That said, once I'd handed in my key it was the last I ever saw of Lady Russell.

At Carol's I needed to share a room but at least I would be with a friend. Safety in numbers, or so I thought. On the first night after getting dressed for bed, I pulled the cord to switch off my wall-mounted lamp.

'Goodnight,' I called over to Carol.

'Night, Lynda.'

Then the weirdest thing happened. Minutes later I was startled to feel Carol's warm breath against my face. She had got up and was leaning over me in the pitch darkness, telling me off.

'Lynda, you forgot to turn the light off. If it's on I can't sleep. You must remember to turn it off.'

What the hell have I got myself into now? I thought. Part of me wondered whether I may have landed in a place crazier than Albert Hall Mansions, but over the next few nights it became clear that Carol was a recurrent sleep-walker. She talked and sang in her sleep, too. And when she and I began working in a burger bar on the corner of Marble Arch to earn some extra money, she'd repeat the orders in her sleep all night long.

'Do you want ice or no ice? That's two knickerbocker glories, one with chocolate, one without . . .'

Our part-time jobs did become another source of hilarity, though. In the burger bar we looked like something out of *Snow White and the Seven Dwarfs*. My uniform swamped my pint-sized frame and Carol's was so tight she couldn't get all the buttons fastened over her generous bosom. One time I turned up with two bright orange handprints across my cheeks. Carol kept an impressive selection of American beauty products but there was one bottle I was under strict instructions not to touch. 'It gives you a suntan. Don't go near it,' she said. Of course, it was the worst thing she could have said to me.

We were also terrible waitresses. Truly awful. On one occasion I confused fish batter for cream and on another I accidentally locked myself in the walk-in fridge. By the time I was rescued I was part-ice-block, part-human.

One summer break Carol also had the brainwave that we should sign up to work as chambermaids at Butlin's Holiday Camp in

Bognor Regis. According to her, the actual cleaning of chalets took around half an hour, leaving us with the whole day to ourselves. There was a swimming pool and we could sunbathe too, Carol promised. Ian McShane and John Hurt were to move into her bedsit while we were away, so neither were too pleased when Carol and I returned less than twenty-four hours after we'd waved them goodbye. As it transpired, we hadn't been allocated any on-site accommodation. Instead, we were shoved into a dingy bed and breakfast with one set of rickety bunk beds plus a single bed, and the strangest girl for a roommate, who sat firing questions at us while we unpacked.

'Why are you here?'

'We're drama students on our summer break. We're going to be actors.'

'Whoa. I could never be one of those!'

'Why not?'

'Well, think of how many times you have to die!'

Carol had to explain that that was the whole point of acting. It was make-believe. No one actually died.

The next day, after our uniforms, buckets and mops were handed to us we began work on our first chalet. By the time we'd changed the bedsheets, cleaned out the sinks and toilet around half an hour had passed.

'How many do we have still to go?'

'Twenty-five each!'

'Ah . . .'

Carol's dream of lounging all day faded fast and we made a dash for it on the next bus back to London, much to the fury of Ian and John.

On other breaks I crewed on yachts around the Mediterranean. I'd discovered this job by chance when visiting Betty, a girlfriend of my brother's, who lived in the Maltese capital of Valletta. She was a lovely girl who rented a wonderfully ornate and rambling house there every summer, the upstairs bedrooms of which were built into the towering sandstone walls of the old city. For me it was an exciting adventure as I'd never been on a plane before or left the UK for that matter.

The romance of Valletta captivated me and Betty's house was like nothing I'd ever seen – marble floors and wrought-iron balconies. After she showed me to my room, I laid out my clothes. I'd also bought a new mascara which I placed on my dressing table, but when I woke the next morning the brush had been removed from its little bottle and each frond arranged in a perfect fan shape. Downstairs, the paintings hanging in every room had been turned to face the wall. Confused, I asked Betty what was going on. 'Nothing to worry about,' she said casually. It was the resident ghost – a monk. Harmless, apparently. But the next night after I lay in bed listening to the chains on my door rattling I made my excuses. I wouldn't be staying for the summer as planned but instead headed to the dockside to find a boat I could work on.

After that I sailed to Italy, France, and Spain – stopping off at places like Palermo, Marseille and Valencia – aboard small sailing boats, often privately chartered by millionaires. I was being paid around thirty pounds a week to cook, clean and serve. It sounds like peanuts now, but I had no rent to pay in London over the holidays, or meals to buy, so I saved a small fortune. Although I do remember one chef in Palermo removing me from kitchen duty when he realised the limits of my culinary talents.

'Is corn beef hash the only dish in your repertoire? I don't fucking believe it!'

Back at RADA, I wasn't cast in any starring roles whatsoever. I suspect most tutors had given up on me and it was obvious who their favourites were. However, one tutor who had been an actor had picked up on my ability to observe scenarios and mimic them effortlessly. It seemed to come naturally to me. During one improvisation class we'd been asked to act out a scene from real life – something that had happened to us during the week. I sat cross-legged in front of an imaginary washing machine and riffed on my fear of the dye running as I watched the clothes tumble around.

Afterwards, the tutor took me aside. 'Lynda, where did you get all that from?'

'The laundromat!'

'And you remembered all of that detail?'

From then on I often found him looking at me with quiet bafflement. After another improvisation lesson he came to speak to me again. 'I can't teach you anything, Lynda. You're the only one. You have it,' he said.

If I did have talent, he was one of the few to notice it. After my early stunt with the name board, the principal had me pigeonholed as a no-hoper. Everything after that became a self-fulfilling prophecy. In the first-year end-of-term play I'd already been sidelined as the maid in Ibsen's *Pillars of Society*. But even that had gone horribly wrong after the costume department insisted I wear a dress too long to walk in without catching my foot in the hem. For the opening night, some bright spark had also presented me with a silver tray filled with china far too heavy to balance with one hand while attempting to open an imaginary door. In rehearsal, the tray had been far lighter. In the end, my grand entrance in Act One got hurried along by a female protagonist who, forgetting about the imaginary door, lost patience and leapt up from her chair to wrestle the tea tray from me. Meanwhile, I desperately tried to kick the dress aside with my little Cuban boots to stop me from tumbling head-first across the stage.

Now as the second-year end-of-term play approached, I became more anxious I'd be left without any acting work to go to once I graduated. The final-year play at RADA was a *really* big deal. Everyone knew the auditorium would be filled with agents and directors waiting to pluck that year's ripe crop of young actors. The play was Gregorio Martínez Sierra's *The Cradle Song* – the story of the foundling Teresa left outside a Spanish nunnery and a very dull play. As the principal's daughter seemed to get all the plum roles and had landed the part of Teresa, I marched bravely to his office to ask if I could act as her understudy. I'll never forget the sneer on John Fernald's face as he looked me up and down with utter distain at the suggestion.

'You have to face facts. You're short. You're not very good-looking. If comedy is your forte, you'll probably be playing maids until the age of forty, when you might land a leading part. That you are even here is both insulting to me and to my daughter.'

No surprise then that I got handed the minor part of a sister with a handful of lines in the first act and even less in the second. In this version I needed to age between acts from middle-aged to elderly. One 'highlight' was that I had to sit at the back of the stage among a circle of nuns and crochet. Seriously? Two years at RADA for that?

When it came to the big night my cue to rise from my seat was the sound of a bell tolling. When it rang I needed to walk across the stage and answer a door.

'The doctor's here, Mother.'

It was the only line I needed to say.

I have no clue what was going through my mind but, when I think about it now, my audacity was mind-boggling. When my moment came I simply thought *fuck it* and launched myself into the part of an arthritic, dementia-ridden nun with such mawkish theatricality I even surprised myself. In rehearsal, I'd done nothing of the sort.

It took me at least a few minutes to rock myself up from my chair. Then I hobbled across the stage so torturously that when I did eventually reach the door the audience were so exasperated they burst into impromptu applause. I shuffled back.

'The doctor's here, Mother . . .'

'Well, show him in.'

Off I staggered again. Now the girl whose lines followed didn't have time to deliver them before the curtain came down. Afterwards the director approached me, furious.

'I have worked at the Royal Academy for ten years, but I have never seen anything so disgusting in my entire life. You have destroyed this play.'

I stood rigid, holding back laughter or perhaps even tears. Suffice to say my performance didn't blow anyone away, not even with my demon-crocheting technique. I exited RADA under a cloud and no agent contacted me.

However, rather satisfyingly I did get my own back on the principal some years later. At the time I was at the Liverpool Playhouse playing the lead role of Lucrezia in Machiavelli's satire *La Mandragola*. After the show, there was a knock at my dressing-room door.

'Someone's here to see you – a Mr Fauld or something . . .' The doorman shrugged.

'Could you please show him in?'

When I saw Mr Fernald's face I could barely believe it. He was smiling at me with such affection that I could have been his own daughter.

'My darling girl. You were wonderful. Absolutely incredible!'

Stamped in my memory was that moment in his office when he'd told me – such a young actor – that I'd never amount to anything. Quite extraordinary to me that someone who had been so contemptuous now had the nerve to stand in front of me effervescent with praise.

'Fuck off. Just fuck off,' I snapped.

As I brushed Mr Fernald out of the room, he was visibly taken aback. With hindsight it taught me why I should never take no for an answer – a lesson that has stayed with me throughout my career.

Chapter 4
Calamity Jane

I can't recall whether I outstayed my welcome at Carol Cleveland's bedsit or I left of my own accord but by the time RADA spat me out, I was living in a flatshare in Platt's Lane in Hampstead. I'd answered an advert in the *Evening Standard* and moved in with three girls completely unconnected to the acting world.

I myself was close to giving up on that world, and in the grips of a depression. My parents hadn't a clue what I was doing in London. Part-time work as a barmaid was keeping me afloat financially but I was terribly clumsy with the glasses. Meanwhile, I was writing to every agent with a pulse to ask if they would represent me. Most hadn't replied.

One day when I was walking home a workman repairing the road stepped out of his tarpaulin hut and spoke to me. I must have looked completely adrift because he asked, 'Are you all right?'

'No, not really,' I replied tearfully. 'I've just left drama school and I don't know what I'm going to do.'

'Cheer up, girl. Things always come right in the end.' He smiled.

I always think fondly about that piece of advice, because it turned out to be true. A few days later I received a letter from Eric Goodhead – an agent on Old Bond Street, long gone now. 'I saw your performance in *The Cradle Song* and I looked at it in disbelief. I would very much like to meet you,' it read.

Even then, I had no passion to see my name in lights at the National Theatre or to join the Royal Shakespeare Company. I was just happy to have been noticed. And when my new agent suggested I change my name to Lynda Marchal – apparently Titchmarsh wasn't going to get me very far – I went along with it. I also went to an audition for the part of Lady Cynthia Hardcastle in a play called *One for the Pot,* a production running at the Whitehall Theatre. It was the resident theatre for Brian Rix's Whitehall Farces, a series of popular comedies headed by the actor–manager Brian Rix that had been running since the 1950s.

The audition was very short. All I needed to say was, 'Can I pour your tea, Auntie?' and act holding a teapot.

When I finished, Brian Rix nodded. 'Next!'

Other than RADA it was the only audition I'd been to. I was so nervous that when I left the stage I mistakenly stumbled through the wrong door.

Christ. I don't recognise a thing, I thought. Then, I pushed another door which I thought might lead me to a passageway under the stage, but it didn't. Instead, I found myself in an inky-black corridor and a dead end where I got showered with soot. From the stage I could hear girl after girl auditioning.

'Can I pour your tea, Auntie?'

Christ. I'm going to have to go back the way I came.

After half an hour of waiting, I'd had enough. *It's now or never,* I thought, opening the door and launching myself across the stage.

'Sorry! I'm so sorry! I've been down there ages, and I don't know how to get back. I need to get out,' I said, wiping the soot from my eyes.

From the auditorium, Brian Rix's voice called over.

'What part did you read for?' he asked.

'Lady Cynthia Hardcastle,' I said, flustered.

'Let her read for the maid,' he said, signalling for me to stay.

Winnie was a very comical part, and when I read the lines Rix smiled.

'That was fantastic!' he said. 'It's yours if you want it.' I couldn't believe it. It was regular, well-paid work at around fifty pounds a week.

Audiences howled with laughter at the Whitehall shows. Certainly my parents viewed it as the pinnacle of my career. Many of the farces appeared on TV until well into the 1970s and it's probably the only popular culture they watched. In their minds, Lynda had made it. I may as well have quit there.

But at eighteen years old I had no awareness that the Whitehall Farces were sniffed at by critics and the acting fraternity alike as 'low comedy'. Quite the contrary, I learned so much. Fellow cast members had been on the boards for years: music-hall old-timers and masters of physical comedy with the generosity of spirit to take me under their wing. Double takes, double trips, pratfalls: each move got perfected down to a single beat. I'd be attached to a drawer on an invisible string that would open as I walked away from it.

'No, Lynda. Wait. Wait one beat, and then move,' they'd say and I'd practise the trick over and over. Timing was everything.

So too was the interaction with the audience: understanding how to grab an audience, take them with you, knowing when to delay a line or how to stop a laugh. Although I picked up the techniques quickly, each one needed to be learned and honed.

Actors were naughty, too. As the maid, I'd regularly have to pour tea into china cups. There were nights when some joker would have placed a toy frog at the bottom of one. It took every sinew in my body not to corpse on stage – that uncontrollable laughter that renders an actor useless – and I often failed miserably.

Earning a decent wage also gave me some freedom. In the afternoons I spent every penny I had taking myself off to the little cinema in Hampstead. I'm often asked if my later TV work was influenced by the new wave of British realism – films like *Look Back in Anger*, adapted from John Osborne's kitchen sink drama. I can't say that it was. Instead, I got hooked on foreign films. A poster outside must have drawn me in but I discovered François Truffaut's *Jules et Jim* and the 1964 Swedish noir epic *Dear John*. And I devoured anything by Ingmar Bergman, whose films I adored. That brooding cinematography struck me as so fresh and fearless while the characters were sophisticated and multifaceted.

I began an awakening of my own. A year or so after joining *One for the Pot*, the production went on tour to regional theatres. When we finally reached the Liverpool Playhouse in 1964, not one member of my family came to see me perform but watching on that first night was the theatre's repertory director. After the show an attractive man in his mid-forties with a stubbly beard appeared at my dressing-room door and introduced himself as David Scase.

'You're a great physical comedienne. Your timing is superb. But you're wasted. When the run is finished, write to me. I want you to come to the Liverpool Repertory to do some classics. Trust me and come,' he said.

When the tour ended, I wrote to David and within weeks I'd relocated to Liverpool to learn under one of the best theatre directors I've ever worked with. David also agreed to pay me an equivalent wage to that I had been earning in London on the proviso that I keep my mouth shut. He had great faith in me, but he was no pushover. He stood on stage, brow furrowed, dragging furiously on his cigarette: 'Come on. I want energy! More energy! Get your balls out. Get your fucking back into this.'

David could be ruthless, too. He weeded out time-wasters at lightning pace, but if he thought you were good he used you as an example. Because of my farceur experience, I came into my own in productions like Noël Coward's *Blithe Spirit*. During rehearsals, he'd say to the other cast members, 'OK, watch Lynda. Look at her timing. She's demanding the stage, demanding attention.' And I'd learn from other actors in exactly the same way.

To a large extent, though, David taught me to unlearn much of my farce training as I had a tendency to overplay certain roles. 'Use what you have, but don't flaunt it,' he warned me. And then there were the great leading roles that I got handed such as Ibsen's *Hedda Gabler*. To bring out the complexity of Hedda, trapped in a dull marriage and whose manipulation and mental unravelling define the play, required far more subtlety, economy and emotional range than in my previous roles.

In my view, David Scase was a dynamo whose talent was squandered in repertory theatre, but the list of young actors under his tutelage who went on to become huge stars speaks for itself. At the Liverpool Playhouse, I met Anthony Hopkins who was such a dominant force even then, albeit drunk a lot of the time.

On each play we had a three-week turnaround. Rehearsals lasted all day, then we'd perform whatever was on the programme each evening. Saturdays were our only proper day off as Sundays were often spent learning lines. Mostly I stayed in a rented room in town during the week, but late on a Friday night I'd sometimes travel home to see my parents in Crosby and bring Tony with me.

'That Welshman's here again, Lynda! I told you I did not want him sleeping on the sofa!' my mother would complain as Tony lay open-mouthed and snoring like a filthy coal train. He'd get so drunk he'd pass out.

On another night she interrupted a young John Thaw, also paralytic and wobbling on one knee, proposing marriage to me.

'Marry me, Lynda! We're made for each other!' John and I were never together but given enough alcohol he proposed to anyone and everyone back then.

On stage, Tony was also competitive. In the J. B. Priestley comedy *Mr Kettle and Mrs Moon* he played the punctilious bank manager George Kettle and I his housekeeper Monica Twigg. In the story George Kettle abandons his straight-jacketed life after an affair. Every night I came off stage to a round of applause. Tony, failing miserably to get any attention, was enraged.

'What do you do? Why do you get a round of applause every night? I go on and off the stage and I get nothing – only a trickle. Why?'

That's where my training at the Whitehall Farces gave me the edge. Those comedy masters had taught me that a sure-fire way to take an audience with you was to give them permission to laugh.

'Give them a sign. A slight look. A gesture. Something as simple as a raised eyebrow,' I told him.

'Show me!'

I showed Tony and he practised and practised.

The next night I watched as he paused, raised an eyebrow and teed up the audience. At that moment, he had them in the palm of his hand. From then on Tony got the applause he craved.

I also recall him blazing with fury when he failed to get a recall after his first audition to join Laurence Olivier's then embryonic National Theatre Company back in London. Other actors we worked with such as John Hallam did. In fairness, Tony was a better actor than all of them and my feeling was that he knew it. Why he didn't knock them dead is anyone's guess. His real strength lay in his ability to mimic. He could copy anyone, both verbally and physically. Finally, when he did get a second chance, Olivier himself was there to watch.

'What are you going to do for me?' Olivier said.

For weeks Tony had been perfecting an impersonation of Olivier himself performing Othello, which he did.

'I will sleep well tonight,' Olivier apparently uttered afterwards, and within six months Tony had left us behind and moved to be one of the National's leading players.

Two other male leads shone out for me. David Scase had the balls to bring in Steven Berkoff at a peak in his acting career. He'd recently wowed critics in Edward Albee's two-hander *The Zoo Story*. At Liverpool he took the role of the rebellious private Bamforth in a wonderful Second World War play called *The Long and the Short and the Tall*.

I was irresistibly drawn to Steven's creativity, and even had a brief fling with him. Even now, I believe he is one of the most underrated powerhouses of British theatre – a magnificently provocative actor and equally inspiring writer and director, never afraid to play by his own rules. It was no surprise to me that ten years later audiences were queuing around the block at the Edinburgh Festival to see his play *East*, a coming-of-age story set in London's East End that crackled with raw energy.

In Liverpool, Steven rented a flat and the actor Bruce Myers lived in his basement. I adored Bruce, who was a lead at the Everyman Theatre. It had not long opened and, under the directorship of Terry Hands, was a far more edgy and contemporary company than the established Playhouse.

Although I greatly admired his acting talent, as a boyfriend I found Steven uneasy and temperamental and I recall one night after we'd had a row I waltzed downstairs to see Bruce for a chat.

'Steven's going to kill me!' Bruce said nervously, and I could see his buttocks clench when an hour or so later there was a loud knock at the door. Bruce opened it gingerly and Steven loomed into view.

'She'll be needing her toothbrush,' he said, thrusting it towards Bruce.

After that Bruce and I became a bit of an item. He made me laugh so much. One weekend we set off in a Triumph Herald for a holiday in the Lake District. En route we visited a perfumery where Bruce picked out a musky scent called Tarn Hows Otto for me. Hilariously, a few years later when he was dating Helen Mirren I read an interview where she said, 'The thing I love about Bruce is the perfume he gives me. Tarn Hows Otto – it's his favourite.' I never did tell her that I'd been gifted the same.

Bruce went on to become a staple at the Royal Shakespeare Company and after that, when he left for France to work with the director Peter Brook, I didn't see him again. Sadly he died recently, but his humour still makes me smile. And the last time I saw Steven Berkoff was a few years after Liverpool. I attended a couple of his acting masterclasses in London but in the end he refused to teach me. 'You just can't take anything seriously, Lynda,' he said. On one trip I dropped in to see him at his home in Islington.

'Yoohoo,' I called out after being let in.

Steven's voice thundered up from the bowels of the house. 'I'm down here. I can't move!'

When I peered around the basement door, Steven was pinned against a wall. He'd been painting the floor and had literally painted himself into a corner. He was trapped for three hours watching paint dry before he could get out.

If only your adoring students could see you now! I thought. It was such an un-Berkoff mistake to make.

He was right about me, though. Just like at RADA, I didn't have it in me to take the acting business seriously. Back in Liverpool the actor Sara Kestelman who I appeared alongside in *Life Worth Living* described me as a complete nightmare – always in trouble with the management.

'Lynda, did you take a fox fur from the costume department and drape it over the dog and bring it on stage?'

'Erm . . . I may have . . .'

'For goodness' sake, Lynda. The play's a tragedy!'

Competition was also fierce between the Playhouse and the Everyman, and we had bets running between us. During a performance if a match got left on a table you'd have to sneak in a comedy jerk to your scene. If the match was left on the floor, it was your cue to perform a double trip. We'd clock up our numbers and compare scores. After a while it escalated to outrageous proportions. Bruce Myers was double- and treble-tripping as Richard III! At the Playhouse we were constantly told to behave ourselves.

Other actors I met at Liverpool have remained in my life. I worked alongside the adorable Jean Boht before she went off to join Joan Littlewood's theatre in Stratford, and many years before she made her name as the matriarch Nellie Boswell in Carla Lane's brilliant TV sitcom *Bread*.

Jeannie was probably one of the most generous-hearted women I've ever met – a real mother-earth figure and bursting with fun. For all her fame, she always stopped for people, gave them autographs and had time to talk.

Very sadly, both she and her second husband, the composer Carl Davis, passed away within weeks of one another while I was writing this book. But they had the most wonderful marriage. Several years after meeting Jeannie, she asked me to be chief bridesmaid at their wedding. She was heavily pregnant at the time, and dressed in a maternity smock as big as a tent.

'Are you the bride?' the registrar asked me as I was stood beside Carl.

'No, she is.' I pointed to Jeannie who was waddling around the registry office ordering guests where to sit as they trickled in.

'Ah,' the registrar replied, raising an eyebrow.

It's a story I wanted to tell when Jeannie appeared in 1989 on the ITV show *This is Your Life* with the host Michael Aspel, but my slot got dropped. Beyond belief to me that a story about Jeannie being heavily pregnant on her wedding day was deemed unacceptable, even in 1989.

Jeannie always made me giggle, though. When we were at the Liverpool Playhouse together she bagged an audition for the part of Queen Margaret in Shakespeare's *Richard III*. Not long before, I'd been gifted some very high-quality pearls by an admirer.

'Could I borrow your necklace? Queen Margaret has to look regal. She needs to look incredible,' Jeannie asked before she set off.

'Sure! But please take care. They're quite valuable,' I pleaded.

When Jeannie returned she was over the moon. 'Lynda, I've got the part!' she cried.

'That's wonderful, Jeannie!'

'Yes, they said they'd never seen the grief scene played so convincingly.'

'And my pearls?' I asked. I couldn't see them around her neck.

'Well ... I clutched at the pearls in the throes of anguish, but they broke. The scene ended with me scrabbling on the floor, trying to pick them up. I was crying because I knew how angry you'd be,' she admitted, sheepishly handing me a small bag filled with the loose baubles.

I loved Jeannie for that. She was a walking danger zone.

Years later when I had my son, Lorcan, she'd turn up at Christmas with sacks of toys and carrier bags filled with past-its-sell-by-date Marks & Spencer food.

'Oh, just eat it, Lynda. It'll be fine!'

And she bought the craziest of houses. One house she purchased in Redhill had no garden, only a gargantuan lake. And the walls of another in Barnes collapsed on account of her knocking through so many other walls.

'I'm having an arch here, and an arch there!' she announced if ever I dropped by: Jeannie could defy all laws of physics.

Jeannie was ninety years old when I last visited her. She had been suffering from dementia for some time and couldn't recognise me. I felt sad about that, but I could still see flickers of the old fun-loving Jeannie shining bright.

'I used to know a Lynda La Plante,' she said just as I was leaving. 'She was very slender.'

Clearly, I'd turned into a pudding, but I didn't take offence at all. In fact, I found it rather touching.

* * *

As much as I enjoyed my time at the Liverpool Playhouse I didn't want to limit myself to being a big fish in a small pond. Yet trying my luck back in London was harder than I'd expected. In auditions I reeled off a list of lead roles I'd played, but I may as well have said I'd been swinging from a trapeze in Hyde Park.

'Liverpool? Oh no. We didn't make it there to see that . . .'

Directors didn't step a foot outside of London. If you weren't in the West End, nobody knew you. Instead, I juggled some early TV work with stints in repertory theatre wherever and whenever I could.

One early TV appearance was in the cop drama *Z Cars* where I played Marlene, the daughter of Mrs Nesbitt played by the magnificent Hylda Baker. It's still one of the highlights of my life. Like all comics of her generation, Hylda had begun her career in music hall theatre, ultimately becoming top billing in a comedy duo which consisted of a four-foot-nine Hylda and a six-foot-tall stooge-in-drag called Cynthia. Double entendres and malapropisms were Hylda's stock in trade, delivered in a gravelly Lancashire accent. She was also a superb physical comic. Absolute perfection.

When *Z Cars* director Michael Ferguson first auditioned me for the part, he didn't think I was right for it. Then I read a part of the script mimicking Hylda's voice. At that he walked out of the room and brought in the show's producer.

'Listen to her,' he said. 'Right, we're done. She's got it.'

The producer nodded.

However, a word of caution was whispered in my ear. 'Don't go into rehearsals and mimic Hylda. Ask to learn from her,' Michael told me.

Given that this was around 1966 and I was in my early twenties, I naturally agreed, but I did worry about who I was going to meet. I needn't have. From the outset Hylda had me and the whole crew in stitches. During one rehearsal she was eating a fish supper and had laid out the episode's getaway car scene with her chips.

'Oh, I've just eaten a lorry!' she said, popping a chip into her mouth.

Another time I was with her in the queue in the BBC canteen when the dinner lady dared to scrimp on Hylda's portion.

'Counting the peas, are you?' Hylda said bitingly. Her gags arrived like bullets. And if she ever dried in a scene, she simply made it up. Every improvisation turned out to be funnier than the original script.

During that period I got to know Hylda quite well, and would even visit her in her flat just off Goodge Street, filled with old-fashioned mahogany furniture and a pet monkey whom she'd taught to clean its teeth. Hours would pass while I listened to Hylda talk about her life. It was then I realised that she was much older than I'd initially thought. She was probably in her seventies at the time, and had so much experience behind her. Mostly I laughed with her, but I felt a pang of guilt because it was hard not to laugh at her occasionally.

Hylda had once been a heavy smoker and I remember looking on with utter incredulity when once she reached for a miniature wooden replica of a Swiss chateau. It had several storeys and a snow-covered roof. When she pressed a lever on its side, the song 'Edelweiss' tinkled away and out of every window, door and even the chimney a cigarette glided out. She took one, pressed it to her lips and lit it.

'Worth a lot of money, that,' she said, completely deadpan.

Another regular TV slot I was given started in 1969 in the BBC soap *The Doctors*, set in a drab North London surgery. I played the part of Molly, the receptionist, who sat behind her desk with a buzzer. I'd have to press it and send in whoever was waiting in reception. One of the main differences between theatre and TV was the sheer amount of hanging around actors had to do in the latter, waiting for their scene to be filmed. I found it extraordinarily boring.

One highlight was that sometimes I'd be allowed a little creativity.

'Lynda, can you stretch your lines out a bit?' the director would say when the front-of-set action required a longer run-time, and I'd have to ad-lib a few more buzzes and calls in the background. Virtually catatonic with the tedium of it, I began mucking around.

'Marylin Monroe, the doctor's waiting for you. Do go through.'

'Gloria Swanson? The nurse is ready to see you now.'

Weeks went by and no one noticed who the hell I was sending in to see a medic, so I became far more cavalier.

'Margaret Thatcher. If you could provide a urine sample and deposit it back with me. Thank you.'

Then I got the call from the show's big cheese.

'Lynda, who did you send into the waiting room in last week's major episode?'

'Erm . . . I can't remember.'

'Did you send in Mickey Mouse?'

'Yes . . . Perhaps I did.'

'You do know we'll have to go through each episode and wipe those parts!' I wasn't let go, just reprimanded. Instead, the hammer finally dropped when between us, the cast decided that the scripts were more wooden than a row of telegraph poles and that we needed to do something about it.

Of course, it was me who had the bright idea.

'What we need to do is go one by one to the producer and tell him we're not working if the scripts don't improve. Do we all agree?'

There were nods all round and, buoyed by the support, I marched in first.

'If these don't improve, I'm quitting,' I said, clutching that week's episode.

'Thank you very much, Lynda. We can't wait for you to go.'

No cast member followed and I got replaced. So much for collective action!

Despite the odd sacking, I was rarely out of a job but that didn't always work to my advantage. Few actors who had been through RADA mixed and matched like I did. Instead, like Tony Hopkins, they ploughed one furrow and kept at it until they got to the top of their game. I doubt anyone else would have contemplated appearing in a musical. The usual route for that career would have been a dance or performing arts school. You were either a straight actor or you weren't. But when I was offered the role of Jane Canary in *Calamity Jane* at Sheffield's Crucible Theatre, I went for it. For me it had the potential to bring together my comic- and straight-acting experience.

The director of the production was Colin George, who was also ambitious about raising provincial theatre out of its slumber to compete with the West End. Primarily he saw me as having the right comedic talent to bring to Jane's character – the plucky sharp-shooting heroine full of chutzpah.

One problem was that no theatre in the UK had staged the musical before. The script had been adapted from Hollywood screenwriter James O'Hanlon's original 1953 version starring Doris Day and Howard Keel. As far as I was concerned, it had less life in it than a cadaver. So bad, in fact, that from the outset I began ad-libbing in rehearsal – adding new lines and jokes and mainly discarding the script that had been handed to me. I developed Jane line-by-line as if she were my own, and I was the only actor Colin let take charge of my own material.

What Colin had overlooked in the audition was that while I could act, he'd never questioned whether or not I could sing. When the musical director came into the frame it seriously knocked my confidence. Robert Mandell was a bully. I found him an objectionable man. On his first introduction to the cast he proclaimed in his American drawl, 'I don't care who you are or what you've done in the past. I just care about voices.'

Mandell also had a stick he loved to use. At that same meeting he lined us up in a semi-circle, pointed his baton at each actor and asked us to sing.

'Wonderful baritone!' he said to one.

'Good soprano,' he continued around the room.

When he got to me, I puffed out my chest and hollered out a few lines.

'No voice,' he said and moved on to a girl who had the voice of an angel.

'Ah. You must be my Calamity!' he fawned.

'Actually, that's me . . .' I said, raising my hand.

'Dear God, no. You can't sing.'

I almost died that day.

After that, I began to take a back seat. As soon as it came to rehearsing a big number, Mandell's stick would skip past me and he'd point it at the 'voice of an angel'.

'You. From the top.'

The worst thing was I let her sing for me. The more it happened the more I choked with nerves. To everyone, it was becoming increasingly obvious that I wasn't going to be able to hold the show.

Had it not been for the piano player in the chorus I may have given up entirely. He had been watching Mandell undermine me day in, day out.

The piano player took me aside. 'You *do* have a huge voice, Lynda. I've heard you, but you're not listening to the notes. You need to step up. Let me help you.'

He took me for some extra tuition. Gently, he nudged me to find the most comfortable way I could embrace those big beefy show tunes so that I could build my confidence.

In the next rehearsal when Mandell's stick got pointed at the voice of an angel I took a deep breath and stepped in.

'No. I will sing it,' I said boldly, even though I felt like a mouse inside.

'Really?'

'Yes, but I'd like to sing it my way.'

The song was 'Secret Love' and I wanted to sing it more quietly to give it more emotional depth.

'*Once I had a secret love, that lived within the heart of me . . .*'

After I finished, I could feel Mandell's eyes on me. 'We can work on that,' he said.

If anything, the whole episode taught me to have the courage to stand up for myself. I would need it in years to come, and I have much to thank that piano player for.

When the show finally opened in 1974, word got around that it was the hottest ticket in town. By that point, I was playing fast and loose with Calamity, and gags grew organically on stage during the run. My costume was a striped flannel shirt, a coat that consumed me, boots and a floppy hat with a large arrow through it. One night I was stood next to the folding screen Adelaid used to change behind. Suddenly the arrow flipped out from my hat. With split-second timing I noticed a fox fur draped over the screen and improvised an entire routine where I rolled onto the floor and wrestled the fur, pretending it had attacked me. It brought the house down. So the next night I got one of the crew to clip the fox fur onto the back of my coat. And the next night onto my shoulder, each time tweaking the routine.

In another scene, I had to rummage around in my pocket and bring out a photo of Adelaid. During one performance I panicked when I realised I'd forgotten it. My heart raced. *Fuck. I don't have the photograph. I didn't pick it up.* Stalling for time, I rooted around in the other pocket. Then, my farce training kicked in. One flicker of an eye let the audience know that I knew what I was doing.

'All right, it's a very small photograph,' I said, pulling my hand from my pocket and holding up absolutely nothing between two fingers. It was spontaneous and it got the laugh. Myself and the voice of an angel even became a bit of a comedy duo. I'd pretend I couldn't hit a high note. I'd wink at her and throw her the line and we'd volley back and forth.

Calamity Jane became a barnstorming success. Local press gave it five-star reviews. *The Yorkshire Post* called it, 'A gun-toting, rip-roaring triumphal blaze.' Meanwhile, Sheffield Radio said, 'Lynda Marchal has just created the definitive *Calamity Jane*. She had the Crucible in the hollow of her hand.' Following Sheffield, the production transferred to the Belgrade Theatre in Coventry for a longer run. In those days moving a big show like that took some effort. Transporting the scenery alone was a Herculean task. On stage there was a Wild West stagecoach secured by chains with two mock horses up front. My glorious entrance was to jump from its roof to be caught by two guys. As part of our training, a circus performer had been brought in to ensure the catch ran smoothly: a dangerous stunt that could result in a fatality if it went wrong.

During one of the early shows in Coventry I launched myself head-first from the Stagecoach trusting that I would be caught, but I landed at an angle and slipped like slick oil through the guys' hands, crashing to the floor and twisting on my shoulder. The often crippling neck pain I now suffer may date back to damaging the nerves in my spinal cord during that fall, but it's impossible to know for sure.

The Coventry run became even more popular than Sheffield's. Tickets were like gold dust and there was a rumour that the production would transfer to the West End. I don't know exactly how far talks got but I believe the company were close to agreeing a deal. Only there was a catch. The unknown Lynda Marchal couldn't possibly carry the show on a West End theatre stage, I was told. *Calamity Jane* could only go ahead if I was replaced by big-name Barbara Windsor.

That stung me hard. I'd re-written parts of Jane and I'd developed her, performance by performance. Audiences and critics loved it. I'd kicked Calamity up the ladder only for someone else to roll the dice and see me slide back down. 'You can't have her, because the script and the routines are mine,' I said to the management, and afterwards all talk of a transfer simply faded away. But the victory felt pyrrhic. To me, it was as if I were back at square one.

Chapter 5
Performance

As a jobbing actor I rarely refused roles, but there are some turn-downs I look back on with no regrets whatsoever. I was at the Windsor Theatre playing Honey in Edward Albee's *Who's Afraid of Virginia Woolf?* when the play's lead Nicolette Roeg asked if I would meet her brother, Nicolas.

'He's making a film, Lynda. There's a part you'd be perfect in.'

Nicolas Roeg was casting for the film *Performance*, which was to star Mick Jagger and be set in London's criminal underworld. Of course, the film is now considered a cult classic, but at the time it was just a low-budget movie where East End gangsters collided with 1960s London bohemia. The part Nic wanted me to play was that of a girlfriend of Mick Jagger – a role eventually taken by Anita Pallenberg. He explained that the film was rather experimental – a heady mix of violence, three-way sex and drug-taking. 'You'd have to appear nude,' he told me.

Nic seemed surprised by my response.

'I'm sorry but that's not for me,' I refused. Now I look at young female actors who take on similar roles but essentially end up doing porn without even realising it. Even in my mid-twenties, I was certain I was not taking my knickers off for anyone.

I can't say I've ever had a #MeToo moment, and the demands of the casting couch seemed to pass me by. One night at The Ivy restaurant, the director Trevor Nunn's hand mysteriously made its way up my thigh, but it quickly shot back when I asked him, 'Do you know your hand is on my leg?'

The closest I probably got to feeling under pressure was with the director Max Stafford-Clark. He was directing at the Hampstead Theatre Club in the early 1970s, a smaller affair than it is today, run from a portable cabin in Swiss Cottage. The play, David Edgar's *Death Story*, was set in a clinic and I'd have to walk around starkers in some scenes alongside the actor Carol Drinkwater.

'I'm very sorry but I won't be doing that,' I announced during the audition.

Max Stafford-Clark looked puzzled. 'Really? Why ever not?'

'Well, I'm just not doing it.'

'Do you have a problem with your body?' he continued.

'No. But I do have a problem with being in a very intimate theatre and the front row looking up my fanny. I just don't fancy it, that's all!'

Stafford-Clark would not let it go. He went on and on about me having issues with my body and said that I needed to deal with them.

In the end I became exasperated. 'Oh, for God's sake! I don't have a problem!' I said, yanking up my T-shirt to expose my breasts.

Max Stafford-Clark almost lifted out of his seat.

'No-no-no need to strip!' he stuttered.

I did get the part, but while Carol Drinkwater was happy to strut around the stage nude, I appeared in my underwear.

As for drugs, I was always on the periphery of that world. I tried most things once or twice – imbibed, shall we say – but I never got sucked into it all. I don't feel in the slightest bit sorry that I didn't go down the strung-out route of the Anita Pallenbergs or Marianne Faithfulls of this world. If I smoked marijuana, I simply felt sick. Moreover, it gave me terrible nightmares. As for hallucinogens, I did take half a tab of LSD once and lost a shoe. The rest I can't remember. At heart I was always straight-laced Lynda. I was then and I'm still like that now.

Cars were my guilty pleasure in those days and continue to be so. Once I started properly earning in TV and in commercials I bought a white Mini Cooper only to find out later that it was an exceedingly dangerous car. When I took it to a garage to have the steering rebalanced, the mechanic revealed it was in fact two halves of two Minis welded together, the newer half having been in an almighty smash-up. I traded it in for a bright yellow VW.

I spent a small fortune on clothes, too. Mini skirts; knee-length boots from Courrèges. I adored the brand Biba, and dressed in short bold-print dresses and flares. Many years later I got to know its founder, Barbara Hulanicki. Friends also joked that if I went out for a pint of milk, I came back with two fur coats. And we'd have regular dress-swap parties at friends' houses. If I was performing in repertory, say in Sheffield, I'd drive back to London that evening and bop around at parties and nightclubs like the L-Room in fashionable Soho or Alvaro on the King's Road. That was hot stuff.

Life got even more fun after I met the actor Lynda Bellingham who was a dear friend right up until her death in 2014 after a very public battle with cancer. We got to know each other in Oxford while acting in the most preposterous version of Aristophane's *Lysistrata,* a bawdy comedy about a sex strike imposed on Greek men by their wives that forced them to negotiate a peace settlement during the Peloponnesian War. To direct it, the Oxford Playhouse had flown in Minos Volanakis – a flamboyant fruitcake from Athens who swept past us every day with his jet black hair and a long suede coat draped over his shoulders.

We knew the play was heading towards disaster when the set designer interrupted him halfway through an early rehearsal.

'Excuse me, Mr Volanakis . . .'

'Yes, wvat is it you are wanting?'

'Well, I've been given dimensions to build an ear.'

'Yes! An Ear. Tventy-five-feet high!'

'So, just an ear . . .'

'Yes! This is a problem?'

An hour or so later the designer returned with another sketch.

'I have further instructions about a nose.'

'Yes!' Volanakis boomed.

'And would you like that the same size as the ear?'

'Of course! Why would you have a nose not matching the ear?'

Our costumes were ridiculous: bright blue with huge rubber tits and a bulbous bottom that we had to strap on, plus leggings, clumpy shoes, a Japanese wig and, to top it off, a Kullu cap and stick-on beards.

The actor Lesley Joseph was very self-conscious about her breasts and spent a lot of time in tears, refusing to wear her blue tits. I tried to make light of it by drawing an eye on one. When that got a laugh, I drew another on the opposite side and moved my shoulders up and down so it looked like they were winking.

Jenny Logan, who went on to become the face of Shake n' Vac carpet freshener, tried to persuade us all of Volanakis's sanity.

'Look, I'm sure there's a perfectly reasonable explanation why he's insisted on us wearing these.'

She was singing the show's opener – a boisterous number calling together all the citizens of Athens. Her tune changed quite rapidly when she returned from the costume department with her outfit.

'I'm not fucking walking on like this,' she said, holding up a horse's head and a strap-on bodice with six nipples. With the head on, no one could hear her sing.

The opening night was calamitous. You've never heard the crash of so many seats going up in your life, but as a group of actors it bonded us. Lynda Bellingham, or Bellie as I called her, had me in stitches. She was such a generous and warm-hearted character, but over the years I felt sad that people took advantage of that side of her personality, especially men.

The only time she and I ever had a problem in our relationship was after she married her second husband, the Italian waiter Nunzio Peluso, who she picked up in La Famiglia, a restaurant we used to eat at in Chelsea.

She ended up buying him his own restaurant and I'll never forget standing behind him at the opening night cocktail party. I overheard that horrid little man boasting to guests that he'd got the whole venture off the ground himself, but I knew that wasn't true. Lynda's hard-earned money had paid for everything. I couldn't bear to listen, so I tapped him on the shoulder.

'You were a waiter. Where are you getting these lies from? That lady has done an awful lot for you,' I said, pointing to Lynda.

He must have told her, because after that Lynda was a bit off with me for a while. Then I found out he was beating her. The abuse was horrendous and eventually she had to have a restraining order placed on him. The joy got knocked out of Lynda for quite some time.

One of my favourite moments with Bellie was around 1980. She'd arrived at my home in a terrible state, bawling her eyes out.

'What on earth's the matter?' I said, seating her down on the sofa.

'I've lost the film part I was destined to act!'

'That's awful news, Lynda. I'm so sorry.'

'No, you don't understand. It was my part. Stolen from me!'

'Well, who stole it?'

After a moment, she wiped the tears from her cheeks. 'Meryl Streep!'

It took all my effort to keep a straight face. The part was the lead in the film *The French Lieutenant's Woman*.

'Well, Meryl Streep may have had the edge on you,' I said, trying to cushion the blow. Honestly, the madness of actors! But Lynda did make me smile right up until the end. She would often ring me then.

'I'm getting all this publicity, and I'm still not dead,' she joked. 'It's going to be very embarrassing if I don't go soon!'

Brave Lynda. I miss Bellie and all the good times we had together.

* * *

Back to the 1970s. Bellie and I would often meet at Country Cousin – a cabaret club on the King's Road in Chelsea that had become incredibly popular as an after-show venue. High camp on steroids, and a club packed with the likes of Elton John and Ian McKellen. Several of us, including Lynda and the actor Christopher Biggins, featured on the bill as amateur artists rather than headline names, and from that time onwards Chris and I also became life-long friends. The club was low-lit with a runway surrounded by dining tables. Performing there felt far more nerve-racking compared to theatre. It was horribly exposing and it gave me a real appreciation for stand-up acts. Dying a death as a company was tough but bearable. Facing it alone was torturous. And, unlike theatre, the crowd would often talk throughout the performance, which I found rude and off-putting. Worst of all was the pick-up of the microphone from the taxi rank next door. The walls were paper thin. Mid-song, you'd hear, 'Driver 42. Driver 42. Drop off at Victoria. Come in driver 42.'

Nevertheless, I threw myself into my acts. For one sketch I'd written a song called 'Tallulah', and in another skit I dressed as a tart in a gown and a feather boa. One night I was strutting down the runway belting out the song 'Shanghai Lill'.

'I've covered every little Highway, I've been looking high and I've been looking low . . . Looking for my Shanghai Lill.'

Now and then I threw out a funny one-liner to the audience.

'Hey, you on your own tonight? Well, you should be!'

One night, out of the corner of my eye, I saw a group arrive late and shuffle noisily to their seats: two girls and a guy who was wearing an eye patch. I may as well have been invisible judging by the racket they made.

'Waiter, can we have the menu?' the guy raised his hand and shouted.

Then there was a kerfuffle about the seating arrangement. 'I don't want to sit here!' one girl with bright blonde hair complained loudly.

I kept on with my song, but it was impossible not to feel distracted.

'Well, where would you like to move to?' the guy shouted.

'I don't know. Just not here!'

My fury rose from zero to sixty in seconds. The girl had her back to me and I strutted to the edge of the runway, paused my song, and booted her hard in the back with the sole of my shoe.

'With a voice like that, you shouldn't be here!' I roared.

'How rude!' the guy called out.

'Listen, One Eye. Keep your remarks to yourself,' I said, flicking my feather boa with a dramatic flourish.

When my act finished, I marched off stage still boiling with rage.

The next day, my agent rang. By now I'd moved to be represented by a rather hot agent called Kate Feast. She was new in the business, energetic and ambitious for her clients. In the months I'd been with her, she'd lined up some lucrative work for me, especially commercials for which I got paid repeat fees every time the commercial aired. Of course, I'd often tell the most outrageous lies to get the work, like I'd just been offered the part of Ophelia at the National Theatre. Nobody checked, and if I'd admitted I'd just come from a summer season doing stand-up or a run in repertory, noses would go up.

I'd been the face of the Little X Bra – an excruciatingly awful advert when I think about it now. I played a nurse hoisting up the broken leg of a man into a harness while he lay in his hospital bed. As I struggled with the leg, my breasts almost popped out from my uniform. Cut to the next scene where I was saved by my Little X crossover. Now I could swing his leg around, bend over, cartwheel around the room if I'd wanted to, and retain my dignity.

From there I'd been invited to advertise the Little X girdle, one of the first underwear garments to be made using the wonder material Lycra. I had to leap into the air as the voiceover promised, 'Won't wrinkle, roll over or ride up.'

This time, Kate called me with a biggie. The cereal giant Kellogg's needed someone to star in an advert for cornflakes. This deal was a buy-out which equalled big money. I'd have to sign an exclusivity clause promising not to appear in any other breakfast cereal commercials but the fee was in the thousands with ongoing income from repeats.

All I had to do was turn up for an initial chat with the casting director.

'Thank you for coming, Lynda,' she said when I arrived.

It was always a good sign if a casting director knew your name and thanked you for coming. If you were offered a cup of coffee you knew you were the favourite, but a warm greeting was just as reassuring.

After a few words, she asked if I would meet the director.

'Sure, I'd love to.'

As I was led into a separate room, a man swung round in his chair. My blood froze. It was the guy from Country Cousin with the patch over his eye – a director called Robert Bierman, working in commercials at the time but who later went on to make several films including *Vampire's Kiss*.

I gave a tepid smile.

'This is Lynda Marchal. You're going to love—'

The casting director could barely get the line out before he interrupted her.

'I know who she is and I do not want to work with her. Get her out!'

Her jaw almost hit the floor. I spun on my heels and sashayed out of the room. I didn't want to give him the satisfaction of seeing me humiliated.

The process of auditioning and appearing in cabaret gave me a carapace. A hide like a rhino. As well as appearing at the Country Cousin I was playing end-of-pier summer seasons in seaside towns like Southport as a warm-up act for comics like John Slater, a very kind person, who took farce to holidaymakers and down the country. John had also started his career in Brian Rix's Whitehall Farces many years before me. I met Tommy Cooper there, too. A large man, always sweating and rather a loner. I spent hours with him, transfixed at how he used his props.

'I don't like people coming to see me between shows,' he said.

'Oh, I am sorry. I'm just fascinated.'

'Well, I don't mind you coming, but not as often as you have been . . .'

Around 1975 I also became one of several warm-up acts for the comedian Max Wall. He'd spent years in the entertainment wilderness after the press outed him as having an affair with Miss

Great Britain. His career had never fully recovered but he made something of a comeback with his one-man show at the Greenwich Theatre, *Aspects of Max Wall*.

Max was a malevolent, awkward character. Every evening he'd scuttle in through the stage door to his dressing room. Head down, he didn't smile or utter a word to anyone. Yet watching his show was mesmerising, especially his character Professor Wallofski. Dressed in clown-like shoes, black tights and a green waistcoat, he peacocked around the stage like a double-jointed hobgoblin. His comic piano routines became legendary.

One night the audience were as cold as a dead fish. My warm-up character was based on the old music hall luminaries. I'd recite a poem called 'There are Fairies in the Bottom of our Garden', once a children's rhyme but most famously performed by cabaret star Beatrice Lillie in the 1920s and filled with double entendres. I was elegantly dressed but I'd pretend to be paralytically drunk, taking an age to get to the microphone, swaying back and forth with a glass of champagne in one hand and a huge feather fan in the other. When I came off, I lingered around to watch as the next warm-up act barely managed a smattering of applause. Then out of the shadows I became aware of a body looming over me. When I turned, Max Wall was standing in full costume. He looked me straight in the eye.

'Watch me,' he said leeringly.

When the last act left the stage Max strutted on. I heard a single titter from the audience. He stopped, acknowledged it, played with this crumb of appreciation and within seconds the rest of the audience were on board, cheering and clapping before his act had even begun. After that I watched every night as he adapted his act over and over. The respect I had for him was immense. None of us could get that from the crowd.

In between acting I was also dabbling in writing. Musicals mainly and the odd play, which is how I ended up marrying my first – and, thankfully, only husband – Richard La Plante. He and I had been introduced to each other at a wedding hosted by the wealthy entrepreneur and theatrical benefactor Laurie Marsh. Laurie had a sumptuous house in Virginia Water with a pool and tennis courts and I often went for open weekends to enjoy the company of a motley crew of guests.

Richard was from Philadelphia and had flown over to be the best man at this wedding, having been at university with the groom. He was the most extraordinary looking man. Odd, rather than dashing, with long ivory-white hair and incredibly high cheekbones. That day he had on a velvet suit, no socks and Mexican sandals with black-tyre soles. We danced and he asked, 'What do you do?'

'I'm an actor,' I replied.

'Can I come and see you in something?'

'I doubt it. I'm working in Coventry at the moment,' I said.

We parted company, and I thought no more about him.

At the time – the mid-seventies – I was, in fact, appearing as Regan in a production of *King Lear,* also starring Paul Jones who had been the front-man in the rock group Manfred Mann. He and I hadn't seen eye-to-eye, mainly because I couldn't stop giggling. In the war scenes I had to wear thick woolly dresses and furry boots and a helmet with a nose guard. I looked like a gonk. And Michael Gough who was playing King Lear, kept calling me Cordelia by mistake. There were some nights when I had to turn my back on the audience to hide my snorts of laughter. Paul approached me in one interval to tell me how embarrassed he was.

'I saw you in rehearsal and thought your portrayal of Regan was really quite moving, but now you do nothing but titter. You are destroying this play!' he said.

I blushed with shame, but it did little to stop me corpsing throughout most of the run.

One night, the doorman tapped on my dressing room door. 'Lynda! There's an archangel here to see you . . .'

That turned out to be Richard. Sure enough, he'd driven all the way from London to meet me at stage door. We went on a couple of dates and gradually became an item. Richard seemed sincere. More than that he was so unusual. Free-spirited, a hippy, and a complete mystery to me.

The musical I'd been writing was about the outlaw Billy the Kid. I'd become obsessed by him after reading a book about his life. Then I'd seen Sam Peckinpah's biopic and been incensed at how little resemblance it bore to the actual story. First off, Billy the Kid had been tiny in height and a cross-dresser – not the hulking adonis portrayed by Kris Kristofferson in the film.

Eager to discover more, I jumped at the chance when Richard offered to take me to New Mexico one summer to carry on my research. Richard knew that part of the world very well. He didn't have a job as such but he'd been buying up artefacts such as pottery from the Mexican outback and selling it on. He was also dealing in leather goods as well as contraband Harley-Davidson motorbikes – moving them across the Mexican border without complying with any of the import regulations.

America for me was an overwhelming adventure. I couldn't have imagined how expansive it was, or how long we'd have to drive to get to Mexico City. We criss-crossed Louisiana and Texas, and Richard had a superhuman ability to drive for hours. Fourteen-, fifteen-, sixteen-hour stretches with very few breaks. We fought like hyenas. The boredom got to me and I sang in the truck just to pass the time.

'*Ten green bottles, hanging on the wall . . .*'

'If you keep singing, I'll throw you out!' he complained.

In New Mexico, Richard did throw me out and he would often leave me on roadsides for hours to wait for him while he ventured into the villages to do his deals. Whenever I did tag along, I noticed how the locals treated him like a god whenever he drove into their village.

'Riccc-arrrrrrrr-do!' they would shout and run towards the truck, arms open wide. People were drawn to Richard, like he was a shaman. With some research under my belt we headed north to Philadelphia and Richard took me to meet his parents, the most bizarre people I had ever met. Their house was on the city limits, not a large affair but there was money in the family.

His mother, Adelaid, was referred to as The General. It didn't take me long to understand why. She was the boss, overbearing and also the source of their wealth. She was an antiques dealer and the house was filled with curios and clocks, cabinets and mirrors. Nothing was clean. I was appalled to discover that it wasn't a shaggy rug on the floor of my bedroom, but a layer of cat fur that had lain untouched for years.

Roy, her husband, had been a virtuoso violinist but he'd stopped performing and didn't have a bean to rub together. Although he was immaculately turned out and, at first, a polite, adorable man, once he'd had a couple of martinis he transformed into a lech and a bit of a groper.

Richard's grandpa, who was around ninety when I first met him, was even more eccentric. His house was in Eastern Pennsylvania. I was fascinated by it, and him. In the hallway there was a wooden statue of a Native American, the kind you saw outside tobacconist shops across the States. It stood in full headdress and saluting. The walls were covered in deities and idols, and antiques burst out of every cupboard.

Among it all, his grandpa sat in his chair with greasy food stains covering his shirt and balancing a lopsided wig on his head. He was famed for driving his Lincoln car backwards to save on petrol.

It wasn't on that trip that Richard and I got married, but it wouldn't have been long after. The marriage happened rather on the spur of the moment: as I recall some fear that Richard's grandpa was on his last legs, even though he ended up living for several years more. We married just before Christmas 1976. The ceremony itself took place at Richard's grandpa's house. No guests were present other than Richard's parents, his brother, also named Roy, and his grandpa. I wore a fine, pure wool red dress, an outfit I'd picked up at a dress-swap party. Long sleeves, round neck. I looked as prim as Miss Jean Brodie with a sprig of holly in my hair.

The service was abysmal. Richard's dad had been doing some charity work for a man called Lou Solomons, whom he loathed with a passion. Every single day Roy came home with a Lou Solomons story.

'Well, you'll never guess what Lou Solomons did today!'

There were yarns about Lou Solomons getting stuck in a lift, Lou Solomons being rude in meetings. The vengeance with which Roy spoke of this man reached epic proportions.

That day the priest began the ceremony with the opener, 'I'd just like to say a few words on behalf of Lynda Titchmarsh.'

'Who the hell is Titchmarsh?' Roy Senior called out.

'It's me!' I half-raised my hand. 'Marchal is my stage name.'

'Titchmarsh? What kind of a name is that? Who's ever heard of a Titchmarsh!' Richard's grandpa butted in.

The priest cleared his throat to quieten the outburst.

'OK, now we've sorted out the name of the bride, I'd like to read a passage from the Book of Solomon.' When I glanced over at

Roy Senior, he was open-mouthed and scowling. The General and Richard's brother were practically rolling around the floor in hysterics. I stood still, watching the madness unfold. *Why am I doing this?* I thought. In fact, it's one of the most unfathomable aspects of my personality. So often I just go along with things, no matter how crazy they seem.

The wedding may as well have never happened. None of my family were present, and although I remember someone having a camera I have never seen a single photograph. There was no wedding cake and no honeymoon. Instead, Richard booked a nearby motel for the night and not long after we flew back to England. Incidentally, in the late seventies my musical about Billy the Kid did enjoy a limited run at the Belgrade Theatre in Coventry. Very limited. The director Willy Russell saw it and took me aside after one performance. 'There are two minutes of sheer, theatrical brilliance,' he told me. 'The rest is absolute rubbish.'

By now, I'd used my savings to put a deposit down on a flat in Maida Vale. Richard moved in, but from the outset he was often off travelling. At times the living room was piled high with all the goods he was selling – 8,000 leather hats stacked in boxes. I'd begun working at the Royal Shakespeare Company as well as continuing with various TV work. For the majority of actors, the RSC may have been the pinnacle of their career. For me it was the beginning of the end.

The offer to join the RSC had come about after I'd been scouted performing in lunchtime theatre. In the 1970s these were regular 1 p.m. slots that started out in the BBC studio theatre but often graduated to the Bush Theatre in West London if they proved popular. It was a way to showcase actors and up-and-coming playwrights and they were mainly attended by students. In 1975

I'd been starring in an outrageous play written by the wonderfully talented Snoo Wilson called *Soul of the White Ant*. What a cast! Simon Callow starred alongside me, as did Clive Merrison and Nick Ball. I played the housekeeper Myrtle who murders her Black servant during the era of Apartheid in South Africa, to be visited by a racist biologist who returns from the dead to offer her atonement. Throughout the play I had to gradually morph into an ant. A ludicrous piece of theatre but highly subversive and hysterically funny.

No one even told me I'd been nominated for a Best Actor in the Theatre Awards, but word of mouth had brought the RSC's associate director Howard Davies to see the play. From there, he invited me to the RSC. *At last!* I thought. It had been nothing but a hard grind to achieve any kind of recognition. Yet the shine soon wore off. One of the first plays I appeared in was Eugene O'Neill's *The Iceman Cometh*, but that turned out to be a baptism of fire. Frightening, in fact. During the previews the lead actor Ian Holm had frozen on stage. We looked on, agape, as he turned to the actor Patrick Stewart.

'Pat . . . Pat . . . rick . . . Patrick,' he stammered.

His eyes glazed over. None of us knew what the hell was going on. Then he turned to another actor, Norman Rodway.

'N-n-n-n-Norman,' he said, barely able to get the word out.

It was some time before the curtain was brought down and Ian was helped to his dressing room where apparently he curled up on the floor and cried. The audience was told he'd had a bad asthma attack but in fact he was in the throes of a nervous breakdown. He didn't step foot on a stage for another eight years.

Quickly taking his place that night was the show's understudy. Not the most accomplished of actors, but he did a damn good job considering the panic backstage. When the show finally ended, I was in the wings after taking my bow. As the understudy took his, I burst into applause. I couldn't help thinking how terrified he must have been to go on, and how he'd done his very best. I put my hands together and managed a couple of claps, but the artistic director, Trevor Nunn, beckoned me over.

'We don't do that here,' he said firmly.

Really? You don't thank an actor who's just saved a show? How very strange, I thought.

It was a taste of what was to come. At the RSC I found actors who took histrionics stratospheric. Many of them spent longer wringing their hands and refusing to perform than they actually did on stage.

Just get on with it! I wanted to say. I suppose because I'd arrived at the RSC via an alternative route I was less inclined to pander to the soap opera of it all.

One of the last straws was when I appeared in *Naked Robots* at the Donmar Warehouse in the very early 1980s. The play by Jonathan Gems had a young Trudie Styler playing the part of Desna. I'd been incredibly irritated by Trudie. She'd been having an affair with Peter O'Toole and was always in a high state of anxiety. During the play O'Toole had finished with her but Trudie oscillated between being hysterical about it and rather manipulative, in my view. I was also friends with O'Toole's ex-wife, the actor Siân Phillips, so I knew he had form when it came to putting it about a bit.

One night Trudie came to see me. She seemed very upset and didn't know what to do. Peter had given her these pre-Colombian beads and she didn't know whether to hand them back or not. I didn't know what advice to give her, although I did say that, if they were pre-Colombian, they'd be very valuable.

A couple of nights later I was with Siân and happened to mention the beads.

'Did you know Peter gave pre-Colombian beads to Trudie Styler?' I asked.

Sian threw her head back and gave a hearty laugh.

'Oh, those bloody rocks. He picks them up in Mexico for ten dollars. He gives them to every girl he gets his leg over,' she said.

Trudie seemed to recover quickly from the heartbreak. The next minute the musician Sting was loitering around stage door, and in the corridor she was never off the phone to him, telling him she was on her own and needed help to get over the affair.

I had also known the actor Frances Tomelty who was married to Sting at the time and heavily pregnant with their second child. In truth, I found the whole affair faintly disgusting, but perhaps it also touched a raw nerve for me.

Just before I'd married Richard I'd had a brief, but rather serious relationship with the actor Nicholas Jones who'd courted me obsessively. He'd moved into my flat in Maida Vale but the actor Angharad Rees who, unbeknownst to me he'd been seeing behind my back, kept calling my landline. She was married to Christopher Cazenove at the time.

'Could I speak to Nicky, please?' she'd say, as if I were the maid answering. She sent gifts, too. Beautiful blankets. Then one day Nicholas came home and announced, 'I do care for you, Lynda, but I'm not in love with you.' So I asked him to leave and listened to Melanie's 'Ruby Tuesday' on a loop to drown my sorrows.

I later confronted Angharad Rees when I spied her sitting alone by the bar at the BBC. The betrayal had left me really quite heartbroken: a feeling of rejection I'd never experienced before. I tapped her on the shoulder.

'You broke my heart. I hope everything painful that could ever happen to you happens,' I said.

Her reply?

'I beg your pardon. Who are you?'

She hadn't got a clue. That people could tread over others with so little care astonished me. As far as Trudie Styler was concerned, far be it from me to get involved but I did urge someone very close to Sting that perhaps they should warn Frances that Trudie was making moves on her husband. That suggestion went down like a cup of cold sick. The next thing I knew Sting had left Frances and he and Trudie were together.

The play, *Naked Robots,* was equally troublesome. During it I had to run on stage at a hell of a pace just after a scene where a pile of coat hangers got strewn across the floor. I didn't have to be Einstein to envisage the scenario.

'Please be careful and throw the coat hangers to one side,' I asked the cast, knowing that if I tripped I could do myself a serious injury.

As soon as I said it, eyes rolled as if I was being some kind of diva. When my request got ignored, I reminded them again. 'Please. Do you mind throwing them to one side? Otherwise I will stop and pick them up.' Nothing happened. And that's when I got so pissed off that I inadvertently broke the fourth wall. Halfway through a performance, I ran on and stopped dead at the pile of coat hangers.

'Ladies and gentlemen,' I announced. 'Do bear with me one minute while I pick these up.'

I cleared the coat hangers to one side.

'I do apologise. I'll now go back and do my entrance again.'

Everyone looked rather stunned.

What I hadn't known was that Trevor Nunn was in the audience that night. Afterwards he approached me. 'You stopped the play.

You came out of character to move scenery around. At the Royal Shakespeare Company!'

'I'm sorry, but I'm not breaking my neck for anyone!' I snorted.

Nunn looked at me with contempt. 'I can't believe it.' He wandered off, shaking his head.

I could. I'd had enough. I'd been in the acting game for nearly twenty years and I felt wrung out and worn down by it. *Naked Robots* was one of the last stage plays I ever appeared in.

Chapter 6

Widows

British TV in the 1960s and 1970s was far less exciting for a female actor than theatre ever was. Meaty roles were few and far between and a handful of actors dominated, like Felicity Kendal of *The Good Life* fame. Towards the end of the seventies, I starred in *The Sweeney* with John Thaw and Dennis Waterman. Writers of the cop show had shaken up the cosy *Z-Cars* format, and created a fast-paced, gritty crime drama. Yet women still played long-suffering wives, dutiful daughters and, in my case, prostitutes – a role I was offered time and again. I was mouthy with a bonfire of red hair, a shoo-in for a sex worker. In that episode I played Eve Fisher: a former good-time girl harbouring a criminal boyfriend accused of shooting a detective. I had a Scouse accent and screamed lines like, 'You bloody bastards. You've murdered him, you pigs!'

Some scripts were just ludicrous. In 1980 I featured in one episode of *The Gentle Touch* starring Jill Gascoine as Detective Inspector Maggie Forbes. Aside from DCI Forbes and the character of Juliet Bravo in the BBC series of the same name, there were no female police leads on TV.

In *The Gentle Touch* I played a mother whose son had been caught watching pornography. DCI Forbes paid me a visit to talk mother to mother. Her son and my son were school friends and she feared her son was being exposed to hardcore material. I was very well-to-do, living in suburbia with the name Juanita Shervington. *What? Juanita?* Unbelievable! Who in their right mind would call a character Juanita Shervington?

When it came to rehearsals, Jill and I had to repeat take after take.

Our script read like this: 'Our sons are such close friends, we shouldn't need to be so formal, Mrs Forbes. Should I call you Margaret or Maggie?'

'I don't think the occasion calls for cosy informality.'

'Very well, Mrs Forbes, but do call me Juan—'

Jill only needed to glance at me and my lip started to wobble.

'Juanit–' I tried again, but now Jill was doubled up. 'Juanit—' I erupted with laughter.

By the time I got 'Juanita' out she and I had tears rolling down our cheeks. In the end the line got dropped.

'Who the hell writes this rubbish?' I said.

'Why don't you write an episode?' Jill suggested.

At first I brushed it off, but the thought lingered. *Why don't I?* I thought. After all, I'd been writing theatre scripts and developing characters, but only ever for the stage and never for TV.

The truth is I didn't know where to start, so I asked around. Seemingly I didn't need to submit a complete script, just what was called a 'treatment' – a synopsis of an episode, no more than two pages long. I submitted four story ideas to the series editor, essentially writing myself into every lead part. Lesson number one: when a show already has a successful leading lady, there's no room for another. I received a polite thanks but no thanks.

However, across the top of one story called 'The Women' someone had scrawled in pencil: THIS IS BRILLIANT. Who wrote it, I have no idea. It could have been the cleaner for all I know, but I felt encouraged by the comment and started to rework it. I'd based the premise on an article I'd picked out of the middle pages of the *Evening Standard* – one of those news-in-brief stories about a woman up North who'd been charged with armed robbery after a bungled attempt to hold up her local Post Office. She'd worn a distinctive hat and the postmaster had recognised her. The story fascinated me. Why did she do it? What drove her to that extreme?

In my developed treatment I wrote that four men had died after a failed heist on a security van. They'd left behind four widows. The guy who had planned the raid was called Harry Rawlins. His wife, Dolly, adored him and, believing him to be dead, cajoled the other three widows into finishing the job their husbands started. I listed the names of the characters, the dates when the key action took place and changed the title to *Widows*.

This time, instead of sending it to London Weekend Television, I sent it to Euston Films, a subsidiary company that made programmes for the network. Euston had commissioned and produced the crime-comedy *Minder*, plus *The Sweeney* and *The Professionals* (which I'd also briefly starred in the same year as *The Gentle Touch*).

At its helm was Verity Lambert, Euston's chief executive, and previous head of drama at Thames Television – ITV's weekday production franchise. I'd met Verity several times before in casting for TV shows but I didn't *know* her. Only that Verity's reputation preceded her. During the 1960s when she'd been at the BBC, she'd been the founding producer of *Doctor Who* and instrumental in commissioning its futuristic music. Verity was terribly posh. Roedean educated. And, by God, she was a force of nature. Numero uno in the business.

But Verity was complex, too. Bull-headed beyond belief when she wanted to be. Around that time she was embroiled in legal action. In the mid-1970s she'd been pitched an idea for a groundbreaking drama that followed the female rock band, Rock Bottom, by the actors Annabel Leventon, Gaye Brown and Diane Langton, whose real-life three-girl band the series would be based on.

Verity had pursued the idea but after some debacle or another had replaced the actors with Julie Covington, Rula Lenska and Charlotte Cornwell, renamed the series *Rock Follies* and took it to BAFTA award-winning success. What she hadn't banked on was Rock Bottom suing the network for breach of confidence, and eventually winning at the High Court. Throughout, Verity had maintained that the format hadn't been plagiarised.

As far as she and I were concerned, I always felt Verity had my back. She was fabulous in seeing potential in others and drawing it out. Did she care that my story was written by a woman at a time when there were so few of us in front of the camera and even fewer behind it? I don't think so. All Verity cared about was the material. And having led the charge in male cop dramas since the late 1970s she had the vision to see what might be coming down the line.

Euston Films rented offices at 365 Euston Road and when I got a call to meet with Verity, I agreed. As I walked in, her receptionist looked me over.

'Oh you're Lynda La Plante?' she smiled. 'We've been laughing. With that name we expected a transvestite trucker!'

Well, thank you very much, I thought. And when Verity looked up from her desk, she couldn't believe it either.

'Lynda?' No one knew me as La Plante, only by my stage name Marchal. 'Your story leapt off the page. I love it,' she continued. 'Have you actually written any of it?'

I hadn't. Actually, I didn't think I would get that far. And because I was such an inexperienced writer, Verity had a proposition.

'As you haven't written anything of this size before, I'll commission you for one episode,' she said. 'If you're unable to do it, or the quality of the work is unacceptable, would you agree to me bringing in another writer?'

I sat for a while in silence. Not because of Verity's suggestion, but because I had no idea what the word 'commission' even meant.

'Of course,' I agreed before getting up to leave.

'Oh, and Lynda . . . Can you start straight away?'

'Sure . . .'

'And how long do you think it will take?'

I haven't a clue, I thought. *I haven't written a fucking word.*

'Not long, I expect!' I feigned an enthusiastic smile.

Perhaps it was my initial panic, but I approached the writing of *Widows* in exactly the same way as I've approached every other TV script or book I've written since: I went out and I researched. To build the characters I knew I'd have to get deeper into London's underworld, but where to start? Sure, I'd played numerous street girls, but I'd never met one, talked to one, understood one. At the same time, I had a guillotine over me. If I didn't get it right, another writer would land in my shoes. I had to get it right, but more than that I *wanted* to get it right.

I began my search around King's Cross Station. Not today's gentrified neighbourhood, but a grimy red-light district filled with greasy spoons, pushers and prostitutes. I spent weeks approaching girls who looked like they might give me the time of day.

'Excuse me, I'm writing a TV episode and I wondered if you would be—'

'Fuck off, love!'

I got smarter. These were working girls. Time is money.

'I'll pay you,' I offered. 'If you'll have a coffee with me.'

Bingo. I began to build up a rapport.

As I sat and listened to the details of these girls' lives, I built pictures in my mind. Some of these women were drug addicted; some were not. Some had been in prison; others had escaped abuse. There was darkness to their lives, but also humanity and a blistering humour.

When I asked one girl how much she charged for sex, she didn't draw breath: 'Going rate. Fifty quid.'

Immediately a voice piped up from another table.

'Oh she's a liar. She never gets more than twenty-five!'

The more I talked to the girls, the more I became consumed with shame. In playing these women I hadn't even scratched the surface. My one-dimensional characters said things like, "Ello darlin', lookin' for somethin' for the weekend?' I hadn't understood these women. Besides, I'd been to elocution lessons and RADA, for heaven's sake. I had no clue how they spoke other than in clichés.

Next on my list were police officers. I'd never really had any dealings with the police before – only once, years before, when I'd bopped a parking attendant on the nose for handing me a ticket. I ended up escaping a fine but did receive a stern ticking off from a court magistrate. Now, I persuaded a couple of officers to drive me around in a patrol car, pointing out the back alleys where women worked from. On one wall the girls had daubed in paint the name of a well-known judge with a huge arrow above so everyone, including the police, knew where he picked girls up. Years later, when Melvyn Bragg filmed me for *The South Bank Show*, I took the film crew to that exact spot. The name and arrow were still there, but it never appeared in the final film.

As I continued to make inroads, other leads started to form. Given the casual nature of the work and the black-market trade in props, the prop department of any film company was usually home to a handful of ex-jailbirds. I asked a guy I knew called Micky if he had contacts with any big-time criminals.

'Yeah course, who'd you want to meet?' he said. From there, I'd go to pubs, mainly in the East End, and listen to men, some of whom had just come out from doing time.

I was in the Thomas A' Becket on the Old Kent Road one night when one gentleman I met with asked, 'So who are you interested in? Bank robbers, getaway drivers, anyone like that?'

'Well . . .'

'D'you remember that bloke who was suspected of handling bodies and feeding 'em to the pigs?'

'Oh yes, that one.' I smiled. I had no clue who he was talking about.

'Oi, George – that's him there – come over 'ere, mate . . .'

Others knew where to get me a shooter, should I need one. Several asked if I wanted protection.

From the outset, I never took a notepad with me or pulled out a tape recorder. I needed to build trust, work my way into their world, not place any barriers between us. Concealing a tape recorder was also too risky. If I got caught that would be that. No second chances. Instead, I absorbed their stories and wrote notes when I returned home.

Some contacts I found in more bizarre ways than others. Whenever Richard was home, he spent his waking hours working out in the gym or practising karate. He was a seventh dan black belt, or something like that. Richard's body was his temple. I, on the other hand, rarely got out of bed without a Silk Cut cigarette hanging from my lip. Goodness knows how we ended up together: Bruce Lee to my Fag Ash Lil.

Yet through Richard's karate club, I met a guy who knew another guy who, rumour had it, was more than a bit dodgy. He had a completely reconstructed face. Surgery after a car crash, allegedly, but I never discovered the full truth. I have never revealed his identity, and I never will.

He was a wealth of information. He'd done robberies, heists, all sorts. But I'm not sure I could have gone face to face with him had I not been an actor. I was good at putting on a front. Courteous, interested, never judgemental and never vulnerable. I knew I'd be toyed with if any of those men ever sensed a defenceless core.

After we met a few times I even got calls from him. 'Got some lovely lampshades straight outta Harrods, you wan' 'em?'

'Oh gosh, thanks but no thanks.'

Through him and others I was able to enter prisons to talk to family members or acquaintances inside. None of it was legit, but going through those contacts was my only way in. Sometimes I'd pretend to be someone's sister-in-law. Yet there was no such thing as a free lunch. I couldn't take, take, take but never give. No one asked me directly for payment. It wasn't their style. Besides, I wasn't permitted to pay prisoners anyway, but I learned the code. I got round it by offering to make a donation to a boxing club that someone's henchman or kids sparred at or by buying a fridge or a cooker for a prisoner's wife. At meetings of prisoners' wives I also brought cakes and gifts. I never paid serving police officers and I never have. Nor experts. But everyone else received something, however small. And although I mainly visited male prisons, I became a regular at Holloway women's prison, where I began to teach writing.

My main breakthrough, however, came via the antique markets in West London. I'd always been a browser and buyer at stalls in Portobello Road or Ladbroke Grove. Never a seller. But now I was writing I couldn't take up acting jobs. To support myself I worked the markets when I could. My stall was mainly junk, but I learned so much from the other traders.

I'll never forget one passing by to tell me that I'd never sell anything. 'What you want, love, is something interesting on your stall to bring in the punters,' he said.

'Oh really?'

Days later I stumbled on the perfect attraction. Sat in a pet shop window was a Myna bird in a massive cage. It was rather old and had a twisted beak, but charming nevertheless.

'Hello, hello,' it repeated.

'How much for the bird?' I asked the owner.

'Fifty quid, love, but if you buy 'im you can't bring 'im back.'

For most people that would have rung alarm bells, but not me. I planned to position the bird front-of-stall.

Ah. One unforeseen problem . . .

At home I was clearing a space for the cage, when all of a sudden a torrent erupted from the living room.

'Fuck off you cunt! You bastard! You piece of shit. Open your legs, hee-hee-hee.'

'Stop it! Stop it!' I shouted.

'Stop it! Stop it!' it repeated. No word of a lie, that bird could mimic me, the doorbell, cats, dogs, telephones. Its previous owner must have been called Pete, as it shouted that name incessantly.

'Pete! Pete!'

After weeks of listening to this vile creature, I had to have him taken away. I didn't dare take it onto my stall and that remained largely unvisited. Still, I got to know nearby stallholders quite well.

On one bric-a-brac stall, there was a woman called Alice. She knew I was an actor.

'Not doing any acting at the moment, love?' she asked one day.

'No, I'm writing for TV, actually.'

Behind the scenes I was, in fact, in a state of near hysteria. Time was ticking on and Verity kept calling.

'How are you getting on, Lynda?'

'Super, very well . . .' I still hadn't written a thing. I had piles of notes, reams of lists, vague ideas about characters, but no coherent story and no script.

On the market, Alice seemed intrigued by my new career direction.

'What you writin' about?' she asked.

'Well, it's a drama, about these women criminals.'

'Oh, crime is it, love?' Alice tipped her head in the direction of a stall opposite. 'See that woman sellin' fruit 'n' veg. You should talk to 'er. Husband's in for murder,' she said under her breath.

When I looked, there was a short woman in fur-lined boots, stockings, and a long, thick overcoat. On top she wore a woolly hat over a headscarf.

'Ask her, but be careful what you say. She's a toughie,' Alice warned me.

Weeks went by, and I had about as much success with this woman as I first did with the sex workers in King's Cross.

'I hope you don't mind me asking but I'm writing a TV series—'

'Fack off awtov it.'

Then one afternoon, she softened. Only by a fraction, but it was a way in. Alice may have had a quiet word but she straightened her back as I approached and in a flat tone said, 'Writing for TV, are you?'

From her pocket she brought out a piece of paper with an address written on it. 'Come Sunday morning. Round eleven. Coffee,' she said before returning to her customers.

This woman lived in a tower block in London's East End. I'd become more familiar with that territory, having met criminals in pubs there. But it still felt like a forbidden side of London: run-down, industrial, dark.

That Sunday, I was let in through the downstairs buzzer and took the lift. As I got closer to her door, I could hear opera drifting out. Kathleen Ferrier singing 'What is Life?' from Gluck's opera *Orpheus and Eurydice*. The only reason I recognised it was because my grandmother Gertrude used to play it. I knocked, and watched the outline of a body move towards the glass. When it opened, the fruit and veg lady with the boots and the headscarf had disappeared. This woman was dressed in a black suit. Tailored and rather expensive by the looks of it. Her hair was perfectly coiffured. She had on make-up and neat stilettos.

'Surprised, are you?' she said with a half-smile.

I was gobsmacked. The woman on the stall was a blunt stereotype; the woman in front of me challenged all of that. Even her voice didn't sound the same. No dropped consonants or stretched-out vowels. As I made my way through to the living room, I couldn't help but notice the framed artwork on the walls, the fitted carpets, the nested tables.

The conversation itself wasn't so helpful. Perhaps I was expecting her to reveal everything about her world. She did tell me that she loved her husband, no matter what he'd done, and that she'd longed for a child but had suffered many miscarriages. I stayed for around an hour. After that I paid her a couple more visits. On the market she blanked me completely, as if we'd never met.

Soon, another stall holder tapped me.

'There's a chemist. Ladbroke Grove, towards Marylebone. Think you'll find something interesting in it,' she said.

When I walked there it looked ordinary enough, but in the window I noticed a bust of a Marilyn Monroe-type figure. Pretty eyes and soft bobbed hair. It was Yana, a torch singer from the 1950s who'd fallen into relative obscurity. It took me a while to make the connection but standing behind the counter was the same woman. Older, still as striking, but now with peroxided hair scraped off her face and tied into a bun. She was chatting amiably to a customer. I hovered around, pretending to look at some lipsticks.

Seconds later a voice, as rough as a Brillo pad, yelled out, 'Look, love, if you're not buying, no handling. All right?'

It was the same Yana, now scowling and shouting across the shop floor.

'Terribly sorry,' I apologised and took the lipstick to the counter. As she finished serving me, she glanced down.

'Come 'ere, Wolf,' she said, beckoning to a pet poodle that had wandered in from the back room. It jumped up into her arms.

And that was it. From those two women I knew I had my series' leading lady, Dolly Rawlins. Suddenly, she was three-dimensional: a childless woman, never without her poodle Heidi. A woman crazy enough to cajole three other women into a heist, yet smart and sophisticated enough to get away with it. She was refined but powerful. If crossed, more dangerous than her husband Harry. Piece by piece, I built her and all my other characters.

Writing that first episode of *Widows* took me around six months. I was terrified to hand it in. It was my first script but also, being acutely aware of my dyslexia, I needed it to be perfect. In all the years I'd acted, I'd got someone to read through scripts with me so I could learn difficult words and memorise them. It didn't stop me from mixing letters up – Hippolyta regularly became Hippopotamus – but it helped. Spelling was a real bugbear, so I asked a friend to make corrections before it reached Verity.

I've always referred to Verity Lambert as my mentor, and there's good reason for that. After she'd looked through it, she sat me down.

'OK, Lynda, this is great. But who's your lead character?'

'Dolly Rawlins.'

Wasn't that obvious? I thought.

'Right . . . but Dolly doesn't appear until page forty. And the episode is forty-five pages long. It's running over time, but we can deal with that. The most important thing is to learn to place your characters where you want them.'

During all the time I worked with Verity I never once heard her say that she didn't like something, or that something didn't work. She was encouraging, constructive, and a genius editor – exactly what I needed as a new writer. With her, script-writing became an organic process where I learned and improved and perfected my work.

To my shock, a substitute writer was never mentioned. Verity commissioned me to write the whole series of *Widows*. I'd moved agents by then to be represented by Duncan Heath, who dealt with my contract. Originally, I'd been paid £1,000 to write one episode. Now, I'd be paid a writer's advance of £2,500 for episodes two and three, followed by £2,750 for episodes four and five and £3,000 for the sixth – a buyout deal, as it's known. Around £40,000 in today's money. I began on a learning curve like no other.

* * *

Around the time I was researching *Widows*, Richard decided to move into the property business. With some financial help from his mother, he'd bought a run-down flat on Green Street in Mayfair and refurbished it to rent out. When finished, the flat was exquisite but the rental plan ended in disaster when an American tenant trashed it with cigarette burns across the newly fitted carpets – another of Richard's ventures gone wrong.

Meanwhile, he was also touring the US with a rock band he'd formed called Revenge. Heavy metal, I think. I wouldn't see him for weeks. From the outset, we led rather separate lives, although

I stepped into his family, his karate friends and his rock 'n' rollers far more than he entered into my world. He hated actors, found them abhorrent show-offs, and if they were ever visiting he'd make his excuses and head out to the gym.

But Richard's interest in property did secure our next flat. After selling my little place in Maida Vale we moved into an astonishing apartment in Queen's Gate in South Kensington. There was fierce competition for that property and we were gazumped three times, once by the actor Anton Rodgers, who kindly pulled out at my request. We had our hearts set on it. The clincher for Richard was that the word Revenge was written across the big brass knocker – an omen, he said.

As Richard always pleaded poverty, the mortgage of around £90,000 fell mainly to me. As did the cost of its refurbishment. Even with the commission from *Widows* it almost crippled me. The flat had been designed by the Arts and Crafts master William Morris. It had two bedrooms, a living room with a majestic barrelled ceiling and stained-glass skylight, a dining hall, music room with floor-to-ceiling stained-glass windows, and a minstrel's gallery. Early on, the V&A museum came in to peel off some rare wallpaper for its collection, and beneath the layers of black soot we uncovered fireplaces decorated in ornate pink marble.

As we couldn't move in straight away due to the building works, I wrote part of *Widows* on a typewriter in a flat rented to me by the actor Peter Dennis and his wife, which was largely unfurnished and with no hot water. When renovations were complete I moved to a desk on the minstrel's gallery. It really was the most wondrous place.

One day, there was a buzz at the door. A young man with black hair and a bushy moustache and the most enormous rabbit's teeth was loitering around outside in jeans and a T-shirt.

'Can I help you?' I asked.

'Oh yes, could I come in and play the organ?'

There was indeed a church organ in Queen's Gate, although when it dated back to we didn't know. The flat had been owned by a Russian countess who had married the peer Lord Cook after a scandalous affair. She'd part-financed Diaghilev's Ballets Russes and her beautiful frocks also got left behind. Everyone was convinced the organ room was haunted. There was an icy-cold beam that hit a corner of it, and you'd have to shift position.

'I'm Freddie,' the man said, holding out his hand and looking somewhat perplexed at the Bengal tiger rug and wooden horse's head on a plinth now decorating the hallway.

'Pleased to meet you,' I said, still marvelling at his teeth.

'I'm Freddie Mercury. From the rock band Queen . . .'

I was completely oblivious, but apparently the countess had let this gentleman in regularly.

'Well, I'm terribly sorry but she's died.'

Harsh, I know. But I did consider it cheeky. I didn't want a stranger turning up willy-nilly and tinkling on the organ, never mind if he was a queen, king, or the entire British monarchy.

Paul McCartney came once too, although I thought even less of that. A request had come through Richard that McCartney wanted to bring a camera crew and film a scene for his forthcoming movie *Give My Regards to Broad Street*. I'd known John Lennon vaguely from when I was in Liverpool and frequented the Cavern Club. He was an all right bloke, friendly enough, but I'd never understood all the fuss about the Beatles. As for McCartney coming to the house, I was dead against the idea.

'They'll trash the place, Richard,' I argued, but Richard thought it would be bad karma if we refused. There were lights and cables running everywhere, and I was proved right. Ringo Starr popped a champagne cork and smashed a pane of glass in the William Morris skylight. I was incandescent.

I also found Paul McCartney exceedingly vacuous. Linda was with him and they followed each other around like sand-dancers. I had one conversation with them about Verity's dog Misty, who I was dog-sitting at the time. Only a few words, but it was enough.

'Wha's tha' dog called?' Paul asked.

'It's a Great Dane.'

'Oh yer, I knew tha' . . .'

'It's a Harlequin Great Dane,' I continued, pointing out its pedigree.

'Yer, I know.'

Paul turned to Linda and then pointed at Misty who was sniffing around.

'It's a Harlkin,' he said.

'No, a Harl-e-quin.' I leaned in to correct him. His diction was appalling.

'Yer, that's warra said.'

It wasn't long before I got a housekeeper, too. Quite by chance, in fact. The Christmas after we'd moved in, Richard and I planned an informal party – pizza and champagne for around a hundred friends. But the numbers kept growing and so I thought it best to enlist the help of some students to serve drinks and walk around with slices of pizza. I'd called a couple of agencies but they were fully booked, except one who had a butler it could send.

'I don't need a butler, just some students,' I declined.

As time went on, no students became available so I rang back.

'Would you like me to send over the butler, Mrs La Plante? He's called Mr Bates. He really is very good,' I was reassured.

Mr Bates was a very dapper man. Black dyed hair, parted in the middle, he arrived carrying a small case.

'Where do I put my belongings?' he said, and I directed him to the small box room by the stairs.

'Right. What are we serving? Canapés?'

'Just pizza,' I said, rather embarrassed.

Mr Bates disappeared into the box room and reappeared in a black waistcoat and white apron, and began polishing the glasses.

During the party itself, he took me aside. 'I would just like to point out that the man in the Hawaiian shirt has brought with him a very inferior bottle of wine and has consumed five portions of pizza.' He tutted.

'Oh, I think it's all right,' I tried to calm him.

But Bates wasn't only an arbiter of perfect manners and good taste, he was also a very efficient gentleman. He could cook, clean, iron, shop, and from then on Bates moved in. I never did interview him, so had no idea where he'd worked before but he'd often drop hints.

'Madam, I've noticed you have some rather inferior cutlery,' he told me. 'Would you like it replaced?'

I do not know out of the back of which lorry Bates found my new dining set, but he brought me the finest silverware, some engraved with royal crests. To this day, I still have that silverware.

And if I did have friends around, Bates took care of everything. At the end of serving a meal he'd always leave the room having lightly sprinkled a tantalising anecdote.

There was the time he had to interrupt Churchill during a very important political meeting. It was strictly against protocol, but Churchill's daughter wanted to see him.

'Well, show her in,' Bates recounted Churchill telling him.

'A little difficult, sir. She's only wearing a tea towel.'

At that, Bates would clear the last plate and toddle off to the kitchen.

Another vignette was about Margaret Thatcher before she was prime minister and who'd once asked him to fetch her some tartare sauce.

'I don't think so, madam, not with veal,' he'd replied.

'Oh, I do beg your pardon,' Mrs Thatcher said. 'I was sure it was fish.'

Bates remained a mystery for the whole time he stayed with me. I had no clue if he was leading some kind of double life. The comedian Benny Hill lived a few doors down and I'd often see Bates in the street chatting enthusiastically to Benny's fix-it man.

Then one day, I was typing away when he appeared beside me, breaking my concentration.

'May I have a word, madam?'

'Of course.'

'I'm afraid I'm leaving. I've been left a legacy and I am returning to family in Ireland.'

I hardly had the chance to say goodbye. The next morning Bates was gone. His box room was cleared, left as neat as he'd found it. There was no trace of him, not even a forwarding address. Later I heard he might have inherited as much as a million.

* * *

Once I'd completed *Widows,* production swung into action. Being on the other side of the table than that of an actor became a fascinating process for me. Once Verity and I edited the script we discussed in depth the four lead female characters: Dolly Rawlins, Linda Perelli, Shirley Miller and Bella O'Reilly.

My feeling was that Verity struggled at first with some of the realism of my writing, but she and I soon hit on the same wavelength.

'OK, Lynda, I've got Dolly Rawlins, I can picture Linda and Shirley. But I can't "get" Bella. Who is she?' Verity asked.

I'd based Bella's character on an amalgam of the women I'd met in King's Cross and also in prison. She was a street worker who wanted a better life. Hard-faced but with a good heart and originally from Tiger Bay, the docks area in Cardiff renowned as being seedy and crime-filled.

'OK. I've got her now!' Verity's eyes lit up.

'She's Black,' I continued. Verity's eyebrow raised. A Black lead was very rare in those days, but Verity seemed to run with it.

'And which part will you play?'

Initially, I'd thought I'd take the part of the feisty, over-sexed but sensitive amusement-arcade worker Linda Perelli, but as I continued to write I'd realised something. I wasn't right for her. I wasn't right for any of the characters I'd created. In that instant, I knew I no longer had any aspirations to be an actor. It was gone. Over.

'None of them,' I told Verity.

'Good girl.' She nodded. Verity's relief was palpable. As the show's writer *and* an actor, I may have been on set daily, micromanaging the production: a nightmare in the making. That said, Verity did what I was later to discover very few producers did. She involved me in as much of the making of *Widows* as she could. The respect she gave me as a writer was tremendous.

The show's director was Ian Toynton – a wonderful man who had a natural rapport with women without ever being lecherous or threatening, as other directors could be. In casting, he put actors at ease and allowed their talent to shine. Like Verity, he also involved me. 'What do you think?' he asked as we auditioned each one, while Verity's dog Misty lay farting away below the table. He worked so hard to understand the narrative I'd created. More than that, he grabbed it, as did other members of the crew under his direction, perhaps because it challenged their preconceptions.

I recall my first meeting with the costume director.

'So, Dolly Rawlins. Lilac Crimplene dresses. Cheap, I'm guessing,' he said.

'No. Jaeger. Classic cashmere. Dolly's nobody you've ever thought of,' I guided him.

When it came to Dolly's home, again there was an assumption it would be a two-up-two-down, or a flat in the East End reminiscent of the Kray twins.

'No. Potter's Bar, Elstree, somewhere where there's wealthy enclaves. And the décor needs to be tasteful,' I said, knowing that since the 1960s big-time criminals had gravitated out to the suburbs on the edge of the M25.

When it came to the heist itself, that took a *lot* of explaining. At first, Verity and Ian couldn't understand how the robbery was going to work. What car was hitting into the back of which truck?

'Look,' I offered, 'would it be helpful if I brought someone in? Someone who's been connected to previous heists?'

'Oh yes, please.'

Ian especially was over the moon, although I warned him that the guy had a reputation. They could never reveal they'd met him. He was the man with the reconstructed face. When I called him he was happy to oblige.

On the day he turned up, the meeting room was filled with Verity, Ian, Linda Agran (Verity's number two producer at Euston Films), and Verity's assistant. They all seemed taken aback when I ushered this gentleman through. He was tall with shoulder-length hair and wearing a long leather jacket with a heavy fur collar.

Ian gulped. Everyone else seemed afraid to speak, so I skipped past the pleasantries.

'Would you like him to run through the robbery with you?' I said, breaking the silence. 'If you would, please.' I gestured to him.

'Right-o.'

At that he opened his leather jacket, visibly bulging on one side. As he reached in everybody opposite recoiled, pinning themselves to the backs of their chairs. Ian's eyes widened. Verity looked aghast, clearly imagining a shotgun was about to be drawn.

'So . . .' he continued, bringing out a colourful selection of dinky toy cars one by one and neatly lining them up on the table. 'This is your hit car. This is your driver's car. This is your block car.'

I could feel the tension in the room soften as he demonstrated the robbery in the minutest of detail, right down to how to cut off the underpass where it would take place. The whole thing was astonishing.

'Right, I'll be off,' he said when the meeting wrapped up. I only ever saw that man once more. He asked if I could handle some forged banknotes. I declined his generous offer.

When it came to casting, I couldn't have dreamed of the talent that walked in. Ann Mitchell, who ended up playing Dolly Rawlins, bounded through the door. I'm sure Ann won't mind me saying this, but she was overweight with terrible permed hair and very badly dressed. Initially, I couldn't envisage her as Dolly at all but I couldn't have wished for someone with a better understanding of the character.

'This is my part. I've been waiting for it all my life. I know who she is,' she told us. Ann had grown up in the East End. Dolly was all the women she'd ever known. My script had resurrected a bygone world for her. Ian admitted afterwards that she'd scared the pants off him when she did a read-through for us. And in so many ways, Ann was a step ahead. While I was still dumbfounded that *Widows* was even being made, I think Ann knew it would make her a star.

By the time it came to filming, she'd shed two and a half stone. The perm had gone. She'd taken Dolly to a different level, deconstructed her and pieced her back together with all her complexity. Now she was Dolly – the woman that hid so much, including the burning, smarting pain at the moment she suspects her husband Harry is still alive and has betrayed her. Ann's voice took on the exact flat tone of the real inspiration for Dolly, but viewers would know so much was going on under the surface. She was quite simply brilliant.

Maureen O'Farrell as Linda Perrelli and Fiona Hendley as Shirley Miller happened relatively easily. The chemistry between them just worked. The part of Bella O'Reilly, taken by Eva Mottley, took more of a leap of faith. Bella was a part-time sex worker and exotic dancer. When Eva arrived at casting, she'd not long been released from Styal Prison – inside for a relatively minor offence, drug possession – and she wanted to begin an acting career.

Many years later, I heard an interview with the late Humphrey Bogart when he said that whenever Lauren Bacall was in an audition she had a habit of never looking a person in the eye. Instead, she bowed her head and glanced up shyly. She admitted feeling sheer terror whenever auditioning for parts. I'd never thought about it until Bogart said it, but Eva had that exact same look. Face-to-face she was bashful, almost timid, but when she read in character, Eva was raw power – a lightning strike of talent. I loved her, so did Ian. Verity needed a little more persuasion. Given Eva's background she was a risk, but eventually Verity agreed: 'OK, let's go.'

I never knew much about Eva's life. Off set she was private and while productions are intense, hermetic environments, none of us socialised together. Occasionally Eva would go AWOL, but not for long. And the cast and crew loved her. But one evening she turned up at Queen's Gate to see me, apologised for not being in touch, and said she had something to tell me.

'I'm sorry, Lynda, I can't play Bella.'

Filming was just about to start on a strip scene and Eva needed to undress down to a bra top.

'Why ever not?'

'I just can't do it,' she repeated.

I couldn't contemplate replacing her. Everyone worked so well together. Besides, no one else could have brought what she did to the part.

'Are you sure?' I asked.

'I'll show you.' She dropped her head.

Very hesitantly, Eva unbuttoned her shirt and turned her back to me. She had lines of scars running across the top of her back and odd stretch marks further down. I couldn't bring myself to ask her how they got there.

'I can't do it,' she repeated.

'It's fine, Eva. We can work on that,' I reassured her.

After some thought, I redesigned Eva's outfit for that scene. A black leather bra with a long fringe attached to the hem. Whatever had happened to Eva it was hidden from view and she carried on. She was extraordinary.

The male lead in *Widows*, Harry Rawlins, was also a tough nut to crack. In my mind, he had to be unknown – not a recognisable star. Not an actor people thought they knew. His eyes needed to be piercing, his looks dark, sculpted but rough-hewn. After all, this was a man capable of extreme violence, but also a man Dolly had loved obsessively since the age of seventeen. Nowadays, finding actors all happens online but back in 1982, we flicked through pages of faces in the industry address book called *Spotlight*. Nobody leapt out at us. I'd taken to eyeing up men on the street, but I finally found the actor Maurice O'Connell after watching an advert on TV.

God knows what the advert was for, but Maurice was playing a trumpet. *That's him,* I thought. Striking and enigmatic. I made Ian and Verity watch it.

'Just look at him, look at his face,' I said. Both agreed he had potential, but there was something about his voice that was unexpressive. 'It doesn't matter,' I argued. Harry Rawlins had very few lines in the first series of *Widows,* or appearances for that matter. For the most part he was assumed dead.

'It's his face we want,' I kept on.

When Maurice came in, the decision was unanimous. Finally, we had our man.

When *Widows* screened in March 1983, I had no concept of how it might capture the public's imagination. All I knew was that I owed so much to the team who had painstakingly seen the story through my eyes. I was proud of it, terrified of it airing, but also incredibly excited. In Queen's Gate, Richard's parents were staying.

'Do you want to watch something Lynda's written?' Richard asked them.

'Sure!'

We all sat around to watch the first episode. Five minutes in, I looked up. Both Roy and The General were flat out, comatose and snoring on the sofa.

Chapter 7
Widows' Revenge

These days, it's easy to forget that hardly anything on TV airs in real time. Netflix, Amazon, Sky, iPlayer: we choose what we want to watch and when, but when *Widows* first screened in 1983 it drew in audiences like no other. Unbelievable to think that Channel 4 didn't exist then, just two BBC channels and ITV. At the time I was oblivious of the viewing figures – the writer-for-hire wasn't party to those discussions – but Verity did tell me that streets up and down the country cleared on the night of episode five: the climax of the series when the widows carried out the raid. People legged it home just so they wouldn't miss it. Eighteen million watched that night, knocking *Coronation Street* off the top spot. I couldn't have predicted that. Not bad for an untried writer and a cast of unknown actors.

Ann Mitchell, especially, became an overnight star. And it was bizarre because Dolly was no conventional heroine. It was also rather glorious. Ann was in her mid-forties, yet if you walked down the street with her it was like stepping out with Marilyn Monroe. It terrified me! But men loved her. Young men, in particular. They chased her down the street.

'Dolly! Dolly!'

She couldn't pass a building site without workmen downing tools and shouting, 'Go for it, Dolly, you get 'em, Dolly!'

None of the younger actors were mobbed like that. Ann couldn't step on a bus or do her shopping without being surrounded. She was dumbstruck, but I think Ann also enjoyed every minute of it. She owned that part.

Dolly Rawlins' name was even graffitied across walls. At some of the boxing clubs I'd sponsored in the East End, they'd had the word *Widows* printed on the backs of their hooded robes. The show didn't need any publicity. Like a runaway train, it built up a momentum all of its own.

The following year the consensus was that *Widows* should have swept the board at that year's BAFTAs. Ahead of its time, many critics said. But the establishment wasn't ready for *Widows*, it seemed. Richard and I did attend the ceremony. By Christ, it was boring and Richard spent most of it desperate to go home. And *Widows* didn't win. That year, *Kennedy* took Best Television Drama – a British–American mini-series about the Cuban Missile Crisis starring Martin Sheen. When the winner was announced, boos spread across the room. I was disappointed, but not crushed. I'd not set out to win awards. I'd set out to write my first ever TV show with integrity and I did believe that had been achieved.

What I hadn't realised was how spoiled I'd been as a writer. As a rookie my experience had been with Verity and Ian, and a superb cast and crew. As well as being present in casting, Verity had also made sure I was in the editing suite most evenings when the rushes came in – the raw, unedited footage from that day's filming. Through being there, I watched and absorbed the editing techniques from the hotshots working beside me.

I remember one night I'd been in the suite by myself running through a finished version of episode five – the episode where Dolly's poodle, her child in essence, is accidentally killed. I couldn't stop myself from bursting into tears. An editor poked his head around the door.

'You all right, Lynda?'

Christ Almighty, I was more than all right!

'It's just how I've written it. It's the best thing I've seen on TV,' I sobbed.

When *Widows* was commissioned for a second series, I was impatient to get started. I'd considered carefully the ending of series one. Yes, these were women, and, yes, they had compelling reasons to carry out the heist. They'd got away with it. But *Widows* series two gave me the chance to explore the aftermath, the fall-out from pulling off that magnitude of crime – would it justify those reasons? What kind of people would it turn them into? And then there was the unfinished business of Harry Rawlins. I had reams of material I'd learned from male and female prisoners, and prisoner's families, collected over the course of my research, plus a bulging contacts book.

One aspect that had been recurrent was the depth of betrayal that wives and girlfriends of criminals felt. Some weren't aware of the extent of their partner's crimes, but many also found out the men had mistresses or secret love-children, as Harry Rawlins had in the series. Their partners were con men in every sense. I asked one woman what it felt like when she found out about her husband's mistress and child. She stared at me, stretched out her forearm and scratched her fingernails along her skin, as if that pain had no words. It was such a haunting, visceral moment that I wrote it into Dolly's script.

The success of *Widows* not only elevated the cast but also benefited Verity. She was now being offered big-budget productions – films too – and her time became divided. In 1985, she left Euston Films to start her own production company, Cinema Verity. I had built up an emotional attachment to her as well as a deep respect. When she handed *Widows* series two to her number two at Euston Films, Linda Agran, I wanted the transition to feel seamless.

Linda had always been the front-woman at Euston. Big hair, big mouth, bouncy and confident. She excelled at the 'Hello, dahlings' and the 'mwah-mwah' of TV, while Verity beavered away in the background. I got on OK with Linda but I never considered her as having Verity's talent or attention to detail. Once she took over, we simply got off on the wrong foot. Under her command Ian Toynton was off the show. A travesty, in my view. Instead, the director Paul Annett was brought in. Linda thought him marvellous and had wanted to flex her muscles in her first major project. She also brought in the show's producer Irving Teitelbaum.

I'd never met Annett before, never really knew what he'd done, and I detested him on sight. A waspish little man. From the outset there was none of the spirit of collaboration that Ian had fostered. He didn't ask me to explain anything about the script I'd written or my thoughts on casting. In the second series there would be new roles to fill, and I could already see the danger signs up ahead.

The initial action in *Widows* series two was set in Rio – although in reality it was filmed in Portugal – and followed Linda, Shirley and Bella after the heist. As the heat died down, they were making a new life for themselves until they could return to London. Dolly had stayed on and stashed the cash from the raid. Harry Rawlins, presumed dead, was alive and after his money.

'There's going to be a problem,' I told Annett.

'Problem? What problem?'

'Well, it's rather obvious, isn't it? There's going to be a problem with the part of Harry Rawlins . . .'

The four women had signed on for the second series. Maurice O'Connell who had so brilliantly played the inscrutable Harry Rawlins had too. But Maurice would feature more heavily this time around and, while he had the perfect looks, I felt his delivery of a more substantial speaking role was weak. To mitigate, I'd created the character of Micky Tesco, a sidekick to Harry: hot-tempered and impetuous and a strong counterpoint who could sweep up much of Harry's dialogue.

Whoever took the part needed to be striking. Blond, against Harry's swarthy complexion. Loud, against Harry's quiet menace. Several actors were auditioned for the part, but none of them were right. I did my usual flicking through the pages of *Spotlight*, keeping my eyes and ears open, trying to track down a terrific unknown. Like kismet, he appeared.

I'd been at the Dorchester Hotel. Another actors' awards ceremony that, as usual, had dragged on far too long. Outside, the cabs were lining up to take guests home and I was hanging around the portico waiting for mine. A couple swung through the double doors. Exceedingly beautiful, which immediately caught my attention. He was tall, blond, wearing a white tuxedo, and when he turned, the most incredible ice-blue eyes switched a light on in me.

He had a wit, too. When a white Rolls-Royce pulled up he joked with the queue. 'Right, everyone, I think my chauffeur will be able to drop you all off.'

The car was obviously meant for guests far more important.

It got a laugh, and he ran with it. Smiling and fooling around, he moved towards the rear door of the Rolls, as if to open it.

'Fuck off, guy. Don't you touch that car!' The chauffeur waiting beside lurched towards him.

And that's when the white suit turned. His eyes widened, a volcano of anger surged through him. Within seconds he was squaring up to the chauffeur.

'You wanna fucking come at me? Come at me! C'mon!'

It was an exhilarating moment. *That's my Micky Tesco*, I thought.

The actor's name was Bruce Payne. At that time he hadn't done anything notable, but the previous year Steven Berkoff had cast him in his play *West* at the Donmar Warehouse, where he'd played a member of an East End gang. As soon as I found out Steven Berkoff was his mentor, I knew this actor had some pedigree.

'I think I've found our man. Bring him in, try him,' I went back to Linda and Annett and told them. My enthusiasm was not shared. Apparently, Annett had already lined up the actor Andrew Kazamia. Dark in looks, just like Harry Rawlins, and dreadful in the part. Flat, lacklustre, none of the fire that character needed. Had Verity and Ian been there, they may not have ultimately chosen Bruce Payne but at the very least they would have auditioned him.

I argued my case, but I was overruled. Kazamia was a very close friend of Annett's, I understood, and even though Linda was in charge she deferred to Annett every time. Because the actor was so bad, the lines that Micky Tesco should have spoken got cut and more lines ended up being handed to Maurice, the very actor who needed less to do.

Then I overheard Linda talking a little too loudly.

'The only reason Lynda wants Bruce Payne for the part is because I think she's having a scene with him.'

An affair? Beyond belief! Nothing could have been further from the truth. I recognised talent and I wanted to give the guy a shot.

By that time, though, other problems were starting to unravel on set. The beauty of the first series of *Widows* had been its powerful undercurrent of violence – always present but never overdone.

One scene seared in my memory from the first series happened in episode one and featured Harry Rawlins' rival gang the Fisher

Brothers – a sequence where Arnie Fisher and his brother Tony argue over whether or not the desk in Arnie's office had been properly reconditioned. I remember it so well because it was lifted word-for-word from my own life.

Back when I'd just started out as an actor, Carol Cleveland and I had gone to a cocktail party. I must have been around nineteen at the time and it was in the 1960s when lots of men were body-building and emulating the Kray twins with their slicked-back hair and sharp suits. The venue was in a very narrow mews just off Marble Arch. Carol would have had no clue most of the guests were criminals, but I sensed something sinister not long after we arrived.

Of course Carol, being a former Miss Pasadena, got whisked off for drinks immediately, while I perched on the edge of a smart settee in a slightly frumpy dress I'd sewn myself. A man sat next to me with Brylcreemed hair, wearing a grey shiny suit.

'Would you like a cocktail?'

'Em . . . Yes, please,' I said.

At that moment, a head popped round a door that led into a back room.

'It's about the desk,' the head said to the shiny suit, subtly rolling his eyes.

'Sorry, love, I'll be back in a minute,' the suit apologised.

There was something about the exchange that intrigued me. I shuffled along the settee so I could peer through the half-opened door. Inside a few men were milling around but one guy, a boss-like figure, was speaking.

'I told you I wanted this French polished. And this is not French polished,' he said.

The shiny suit answered back defensively, 'It is, it's French polished. I told the guy to French polish it.'

'No, it's lacquered.' The boss was now bending over a large mahogany desk and running his fingertip across it. 'This is fucking lacquer,' he growled under his breath. Then he took a pen from his pocket and ripped it across the surface.

'Fucking lacquer.'

The threat of it terrified me. These were dangerous people. I'm not even sure I told Carol I was leaving, but I upped and ran out and hailed a taxi. Years later, when I recreated that scene for *Widows*, the actor Jeffrey Chiswick who played Arnie Fisher did so sublimely. There was no brute force but that vicious criminal underbelly was never in doubt.

By contrast, Paul Annett wanted to deviate from the 'less is more' direction entirely.

'Needs more oomph, Lynda. You know, drama. Give viewers drama!'

We simply didn't share the same vision. Annett wanted punch-ups. Endless scenes of men squaring up to each other. Actors slapping each other around. Blood. Lots of blood. He was busy creating a cartoonish abomination. If *Widows* series two was another learning curve for me, it was never a positive one. As a writer-for-hire I was learning how to be slapped down and shat upon. Nothing Paul Annett wanted had anything to do with my script.

But the worst was yet to come. Annett was so corrosive, he'd managed to rub many of the cast members up the wrong way. Eva Mottley, in the part of Bella O'Reilly especially, bore the brunt of his ill judgement. I'd already heard complaints trickle in from cast and crew members and then it reached tipping point. In one scene set in Rio he'd insisted Eva wear a white outfit, but she had refused. She was the only Black woman on set and she'd sensed a racist overtone. She felt abused by him, something that was anathema to every single person who had worked on the first series.

Apparently, Annett had been with her in the costume department when he made the comment, 'I like Black women in white.'

Eva had reacted, 'This Black woman does not wear white to match the colour of your skin.'

'Well, you should,' Annett had replied. 'And as I'm the director, I'm telling you that you will be wearing white.'

Until Annett apologised, Eva had walked out and refused to come back on set. And when Eva walked, I walked.

I'd written the part for a Black actor partly because that's how the character appeared in my mind, but also I'd worked with so few when I was an actor myself. I felt strongly that needed to change, and racism in any form sickened me. To have Eva, who was dynamite, on set should have been a gift to be nurtured. Granted, she was not the most stable of people. She was vulnerable, but Ian Toynton had so skilfully harnessed that for the good and built her up. Paul Annett's sulphurous handling of anyone who disagreed with him lost her. It lost everything.

Before any whiff of a resolution was found, Eva was quickly replaced. I tried calling her phone. Repeatedly. Ann Mitchell did too, as I'm sure other cast and crew members did. But there was never any reply. Eva simply vanished. By the time the first episode of *Widows* series two screened in April 1985 Eva Mottley was dead – discovered in her flat in Maida Vale after having overdosed. She was thirty-one years old. To this day I have never watched *Widows* series two. I simply can't – not without Eva.

The wound deepened further when I became the last to know about Eva. Certainly Annett, perhaps others, had known of her death but the fact it was a suicide had been kept from everybody else involved in the production. Not only that, but with the publicity gearing up for series two's debut episode, cast and crew were told Eva had died but were under strict instruction not to pick up the phone or answer queries from the press about her. No one called me. The first I knew of Eva's death was when I opened a newspaper. I remember speaking to Ann around that time, who told me, 'They've cremated her, Lynda. The funeral's been and gone.'

None of us got the chance to pay our respects. Instead, myself, Ann, Maureen O'Farrell and Fiona Hendley made our own journey to the cemetery where a small plaque had been mounted on a wall for Eva. We took a heart-shaped wreath and privately said our goodbyes. What a foursome those women had made. For it to end in such tragedy is something I've never been able to reconcile. Paul Annett and I never spoke again. The only back-and-forth correspondence I had was with the show's producer, Irving Teitelbaum, who had blithely enacted every disastrous instruction Annett had proclaimed. I found the following letter recently. It brought back all the anger I felt over the series, over Eva's death, over everything:

Dear Irving,

Well, well, well. You show your true colours at long last. I thank you for your letter, which I found so hysterical, I have had copies made, and the original will be framed and placed in the toilet. Alongside the copy of my original letter to you. May you and Paul Annett go hand in hand into the non-talented void your blurred visions direct. Creatively, together I am sure you will manage to destroy a number of other writers' work, not to mention actors and actors' performances.

My lesson was simply never to work with either of you, or have my work tampered by either of you ever again. To also ensure that I have casting and director approval. Perhaps Irving, you should be aware that far from an 'unhelpful habit' of writers being in close touch with actors during filming, it should be an imperative. I have kept in close *contact not only with actors but editors and I am fully aware of just how much work the editing department had to do to try to make something of Annett's filming. My work by no means was improved. It was stitched together by artists who made what they could of a wretched, cheap piece of work by a totally inept man.*

Please don't feel you have to reply to this letter. Throw it into the waste bin. Frame it. Stick it up your ass. Whatever you care to do. I have not the slightest interest, you see, in your rudeness. Your arrogance is met with total discourtesy from me. The only thing I care about is honesty, both in my work and in my relationships with other people.

Yours sincerely,
Lynda La Plante.

Linda Agran and I have also never spoken. The last time I saw her was across a crowded street. It was in 2022 and I had been invited to the unveiling of a blue plaque in memory of Verity who died from cancer in 2007. The plaque had originally been erected in 2014 but had been in storage while London's Riverside Studios were redeveloped, the location where Verity had worked on *Doctor Who* for the BBC. I noticed Linda from afar but I couldn't bring myself to walk over.

A little while after when I was speaking at one of those 'Women in Film and TV' functions, Linda Agran and a few others sprang to my mind when I told the audience how sad I found it that women didn't always support other women. In fact, my experience had often been different. There have been several times in my career when I've been kept down or moved aside by a woman for reasons beyond my understanding and often to appease others. Some women in the audience didn't like what I'd said. In particular, it seemed to upset a Scottish daytime host.

'Och, don't listen to her. She's drunk!' I heard her call out from her table.

I wasn't drunk. Neither was I shooting from the hip. I just wasn't prepared to stand up and be dishonest about the reality of my own experience. And if that wasn't a politically correct thing to say then I couldn't give a hoot.

Chapter 8
The Legacy

The remedy to all my problems has always been work. It's damaged me and saved me in equal measure, but it's consistently been a rich source of nourishment for my mind. I'm a self-confessed workaholic and I'm also an insomniac – probably the worst combination. Nowadays, I'm at my desk by 7 a.m. having already had a swim and an Epsom salt bath to ease the pain in my neck. I'm finished by mid-afternoon and in bed by 8.30 p.m. with a mountain of reading. Either that or I'm propped up against the pillow chattering away to myself, rehearsing symphonies of dialogue for an upcoming book. Anyone listening in would think I'd taken leave of my senses. But when I look back at my late thirties I don't know where I got the stamina to fit all of that and more in. I was always on the go.

Yet as a writer, I didn't have to fend off the same kind of feeding frenzy that happens today, say, to actors. These days all roads lead to *Doctor Who*, and once you've reached that pinnacle you'll get so over-exposed you'll become dried up. It also means that actors often get chosen for roles, not because they're the best choice, but because they're a recognisable face. A celebrity. It's the same with ideas. There's a 'If you enjoyed this, you'll love *this*,' recycling of content. Where's the risk? When does TV break new ground? Who opens the door to drama that shifts the dial? When does TV grab the big debates of the day by the balls? In my view, it happens less and less.

It's not an altogether new phenomena. I experienced something of that clone mentality following *Widows*. Opportunities trickled in, but there was a snag: the only projects that network commissioners rang me with were carbon copies of *Widows*.

'We've had this idea about a bank robbery, we think you'd be perfect.'

'Oh really?'

I didn't want to hear about the bank robbery, the Post Office robbery or the jewel heist. 'Been there, done that!' I said. I had no interest in re-hashing *Widows*. I mean, what would be the point? Instead, I pitched an idea about a drug squad – that hadn't been seen before – but it got rejected. So did several other ideas. It all made me feel rather jaded.

My experience on *Widows* series two had been so bruising. The only thing I felt proud of was that I'd walked away. Where I got the bottle to do that I do not know. It could have signalled the end of my career – I was hardly in a position of power – but I felt so strongly that I needed to fight for my original concept to appear on-screen.

Certainly I didn't have anyone buoying me up or inflating my ego at home. Richard was mostly in the gym or off on tour. I'm not even sure my parents saw *Widows*.

'If it's clashing with the football, Lynda, I won't be watching it.'

My mother repeated that line about most of the TV series I wrote.

Did it bother me? Probably, somewhere deep down, but I'd learned not to expect praise. God forbid there would be anything like adulation. A good thing, perhaps, but sycophancy didn't ever encircle me.

Since marrying Richard, I'd also been trying to get pregnant. Very unsuccessfully, I might add. Some years before we moved to Queen's Gate, I'd seen a gynaecologist in Maida Vale. A portly man, and rather to-the-point.

'The reason you can't get pregnant is because you're late,' he told me.

I had no idea what he was talking about.

'Late? I was here on time and I've been kept waiting!'

'No, your periods. Very late. My dear, you won't get pregnant because you've begun the menopause.'

I must have been around thirty-four years old.

'Right. Thank you.'

After I left his office, I walked down the corridor still trying to process what had been thrown at me – the finality of it. *Wait a minute,* I thought, before turning back and knocking on his door once more.

'Come in!'

I smiled insincerely as I poked my head around. 'If you see anyone else my age and you tell them they have no hope of having a baby, I suggest you rephrase how you say it,' I said.

He looked at me as if I'd grown two heads.

In any case, I ignored his dire protestation and began taking fertility drugs at a very high dosage. Too high, as it turned out. The tablets made me feel bloated and horrible. I did get pregnant on several occasions but I suffered miscarriages very early on in those pregnancies. Heartbreaking, yes, but I can't say I let it consume me. If there was an emotional void to be filled, work filled it. Keeping busy became my way of coping. I just kept on trucking.

After another appointment at a clinic in Chelsea, I found myself caught between a rock and a hard place. On one side of the waiting room in the gyno ward sat mothers-to-be, flicking through *Woman's Own* and rubbing their space-hopper bellies. On the other side young women were lining up for an abortion. As ever, I never quite fitted in.

On that occasion I came away unable to remember whether the doctor had told me that Richard and I needed to have sex that evening before my next-day tests, or the next morning. Richard wasn't impressed.

'Could you find out, Lynda, because if it's this evening I won't have time. I'm at karate.'

When I rang the clinic to double-check, a man eventually picked up.

'I'm terribly sorry. My name is Lynda La Plante. I spoke to the gynaecologist earlier. I have some tests tomorrow and I can't remember whether I should be having sexual intercourse tonight or in the morning.'

'Well, if I were you I'd do both,' the voice on the other end replied. He did sound strangely flippant about the whole thing.

'Sorry . . . are you a fertility doctor?'

'No, I'm a painter and decorator. The phone kept ringing so I picked it up.'

When I appeared on Welsh radio not long after, the producer had asked beforehand if I could think of a funny personal anecdote. That's the one I chose. It was a graveyard slot and in Wales, for Christ's sake. I didn't think anyone would be listening. But news travelled fast in the 1980s despite us not having mobile phones or the internet. Someone at Richard's karate club had heard it and Richard came home furious over why I felt the need to broadcast our private business.

Richard never did have much of a sense of humour.

As far as work was concerned, that momentarily took a more bizarre twist. On the back of the first series of *Widows* I'd been drafted in to warm up a few scenes in a script for a big-budget British horror movie called *Link*. The production starred the American Elisabeth Shue and the British actor Terence Stamp. However, its real star was to be a chimpanzee who turned violent on its masters as they attempt to have it euthanised. I'd never before sat around a table discussing the casting of a primate.

'How far have we got finding a chimpanzee to play the part?' the director Richard Franklin enquired. Not very far was the answer. However, Clint Eastwood had starred with a very talented chimp called Manis in the role of sidekick Clyde in the hit film *Every Which Way But Loose* in 1978.

'Excuse me!' A hand raised and somebody pointed out that Clyde was in fact an orangutan and that male chimps could be very dangerous on set.

'What's the difference?' Franklin asked.

'Well, the colour for starters – an orangutan is orange and it has much smaller ears.'

I sat in astonishment as he and the make-up department discussed how they could fly over Manis at considerable cost from the States, dye his hair black, and have a prosthetics company fashion new ears to be attached with animal-friendly glue. *I don't quite believe what I'm hearing*, I thought. Until then, I'd been used to ITV round-tables where we debated whether it was safe for Dolly Rawlins to own a pint-sized poodle. Suddenly, I was getting a taste for the absurdity of the film world.

In the end I believe Manis was flown over and with his hair dyed jet black had made a very convincing chimp. But his starring role got curtailed when he wouldn't stop detaching his £2,000 prosthetic ears and eating them. After that he was replaced. Absolute madness!

In the months following it was hard to know which way my career would turn. Just when I was at a low ebb, an editor at Pan Books (now Pan Macmillan) approached me with an offer. That editor was Sonny Mehta, at the time a new kid on the block. Sonny was a fierce intellect, who went on to become a towering figure in the industry, moving to the States to head up the esteemed publishing house Alfred A. Knopf. One of his editors, Caroline Upcher, had read some interviews I'd done on the back of *Widows* and wanted to commission me.

Just as I'd known very little about writing for TV, I knew even less about the book publishing industry, but I was interested.

'Could you write a novel?' Sonny asked.

'Yes, all right!' I agreed, not having the faintest idea where to start.

'What would be good is if you can send us an idea.'

Thankfully, ideas were something I was never short of.

One of the stories I'd come across while researching *Widows* had been about the Kray twins. I'd never been overly interested in their brutality itself, but I was fascinated in how they'd become such big gangsters. I'd heard that their father Charles Kray Snr, a rag-and-bone-man by trade, may have been a Romany traveller, known as a Kairengo – low-down in status within the Romany community because he lived in a house.

What intrigued me most was how on earth their mother Violet would have met and married him. Apparently, he'd disappear for months on end. He was a violent man and he boxed too, a sport that loomed large in the Kray family narrative, from the travelling fairground boxing booths to the boxing clubs of the East End.

Other than my uncle Stanley's mother apparently descending from gypsy lineage, I knew nothing about Romany gypsy life. I needed to find out. Well, that was probably my first mistake. I didn't stop 'finding out'.

Someone had told me about a large gypsy camp in South Wales, near Cardiff. Gypsies also travelled through the Welsh valleys, from coal pit to coal pit, buying ponies for next to nothing, then bringing them back to health to sell on. I visited and talked to people. Gypsy communities were never too welcoming to outsiders due to being highly discriminated against. They humoured me, but

I gathered what information I could and also went down several mines to understand how the operation worked.

The more I discovered, the more obsessed I became. I felt an enormous freedom, too. Researching a novel seemed to give me this tremendous release. If there was a hard-and-fast deadline, I don't recall it.

'See how you get on,' Sonny had told me.

Absolutely the worst thing he could have said! One thing led to another. And another. My original story about the Kray twins flew out of the window and I allowed myself to be pulled in all directions.

As peculiar as it may seem, I'm a huge believer in fate. Superstitious beyond belief. While I was in Cardiff, a professor got chatting to me in a cafe and he just happened to be studying gypsy life. A coincidence? I don't think so. Then, I'd been rummaging around in a second-hand bookshop, sifting through the assortment of titles in a tray outside, when I stumbled across the most precious treasure. Tied up in string was a thick, faded manuscript, part-typed, part-handwritten. On the cover it said, *The History of Romany Gypsies.* Unbelievable! As I flicked through I felt an overwhelming sadness that it had been abandoned. Someone had painstakingly documented a compendium of gypsy customs: their clothes, jewellery, there were even diagrams of how they erected their homes. Neatly listed at the back was a glossary of words. Wonderful words like 'wongar' meaning money; 'stir' meaning prison – where the saying 'stir-crazy' derives from. It's where I learned the word 'dukkerin' – in old Romany language, a woman born with the skin fused over the vagina, but more recently used to mean fortune-teller.

Whatever information I needed, I took it down in note form. It didn't feel respectful for me to keep the manuscript. It belonged to Romany people, so back in London I took it to Stable Way, the only travelling community I'd heard of with a designated site under the flyover, The Westway, near Shepherd's Bush. The community is still there to this day, but much reduced and populated by Irish travellers, I believe.

'What do you want?' one man greeted me at the gate in clothes fit for a scarecrow. Like so many of the places I'd been before, building up trust was difficult. I never arrived expecting people to talk to me.

'I have something for you,' I said, holding out the manuscript. He looked far less impressed than I'd hoped, but he did lead me to a small trailer. 'I want to discover more about fortune-telling,' I told him.

'If you want stories, there's camps in Cornwall. You'll meet dukkerin there.' He nodded. He was absolutely right.

Over the next few months I'd set off in my little car. I headed towards Penzance, or coastal towns like Fowey. Gypsies were on the move through that rainswept landscape but in one camp I found what I was looking for. An elderly woman, eighty perhaps, in a grubby trailer that stank of pee. She was dark-skinned. Her heavy black dress embroidered with floral motifs had seen better days. She had long, grey hair, studded with rose buds. I'd bring her 200 cigarettes or a bottle of whisky and she'd gift me little trinkets of jewellery, and so much insight. It was there that I first saw the technique of ghost palmistry. She'd drip a paper-thin layer of hot wax into my upturned palm then peel it off slowly to reveal the impression. Then she'd place a tea light behind the sheet and read it. When she finished, she rolled the wax up into a ball.

'Never leave the imprint of your hands behind,' she warned me. Back luck, apparently. Curses, too. This dukkerin could inflict every level of curse. Locks of hair and twigs burned in sand got thrown into the mix, sometimes with birthstones. If the gem became clear in the middle, the curse was lifted. To see that with my own eyes: it was impossible not to be drawn by the power of magic.

When it came to writing, I'd mapped out a sprawling family saga that followed the fortunes of Evelyne, the daughter of a miner from the Welsh valleys who falls in love with a prizewinning boxer called Freedom Stubbs, wrongly accused of murder. His character was based on a real fighter. By then I had an electric typewriter, and I could not stop tapping away. Pages were spewing out of me. A secretary I employed took away each chapter and cleaned up my spelling. Strangely, when the deluge got too much I noticed she had a relative who'd died suddenly and a request to take time off.

Meanwhile, Simon & Schuster in the States had also made an offer to buy the book based on the synopsis. It was big money, too. Around a quarter of a million, I think. For a first-time novelist that gave me such a boost, so I kept going . . . and going . . . and going. As well as researching Romany life, I also drew in some of my own experiences.

When I'd been an actor, I'd known another actor called Virginia Balfour. Virginia was horsy and vivacious and had starred briefly in the 1970s comedy *The Rise and Fall of Reginald Perrin* with Leonard Rossiter. I didn't know much about Virginia other than there was a sadness about her. She lived alone and was a religious fanatic. Holographic Jesuses jumped out at you if you walked around her mews house. Tragically, she'd been diagnosed with cancer while I knew her and the disease was terminal.

'What would you like to do before you die?' I asked her once. First on her bucket list was a formal dinner with ten eligible men. I had been living in Queen's Gate when I arranged that, although finding ten attractive singletons proved very difficult. When they did turn up there were long, awkward silences. None of them knew her or each other. But Bates had been living with me then and had organised the most delectable menu. And Virginia looked beautiful in a floaty purple silk dress I'd lent her for the occasion.

Next she wanted to see the play *The Liars* in the West End. The production starred Mary Millar. Physically, Virginia was really quite fragile by then. Emotionally, too, poor thing. After we'd visited Mary in her dressing room, I lost Virginia momentarily outside the theatre. When I turned around she was resting her head on a framed billboard photograph of Mary. 'I should have been cast in that role, but no one ever asked!' she said wistfully.

The most troublesome request was when she was nearing the end of her life. Then I would visit her in hospital. No one seemed to be there for her regularly so I tried to go as often as I could.

'I'd like a pink nightdress, Lynda,' she requested.

'Sure, I can do that!'

The next day, I went out and bought her one. Marks & Spencer, I recall. Long, dusty pink and Winceyette flannel to keep her warm.

When I pulled it from the bag, Virginia looked horrified.

'I can't wear that. It's an old ladies' nightgown,' she exclaimed. 'Could you please change it?'

I carried out Virginia's request, but still she was unsatisfied.

'Fine, I'll take it back and choose another,' I agreed. Three nightdresses later and I was beginning to wish I'd never offered. In a last-ditch attempt, I tried a shop on the Fulham Road called Night Owls. It sold the most exquisite night gowns: diaphanous and silk and astronomically expensive. I picked one out for her in the secret hope she might reject it and I'd get my money back. It cost a small fortune!

I sat with her on her bed while she opened the box. Her arms looked so thin that they might snap as her hands moved the tissue paper aside. When she held it up a glow spread across her face.

'At last, Lynda. At last!' she said, and put it on. It did look beautiful.

Virginia had one more request.

'When you leave today, Lynda, I want you to walk down the corridor and don't look back. It's unlucky. Please promise: you won't look back.'

'I won't,' I agreed. And when it came time to leave I did as she asked. I got to the end of the corridor but ... well, what can I say? Curiosity got the better of me. I couldn't help but turn.

Through the half-opened door I watched Virginia in her pink nightdress. She was gently waving her arms, like a ballerina swan whose wings were gracefully rising and falling. She looked child-like and happy, at peace with the world. 'Goodbye,' she was mouthing. 'Goodbye.'

When I next called the hospital, Virginia had died. I felt such sadness, and that scene played over and over in my mind. It was so powerful that I used it in my book to describe Evelyne's death. I wanted it immortalised on the page: 'Goodbye, Evie, Goodbye.'

By the time my novel was complete, it ran to almost two thousand pages. My secretary delivered a clean copy to Sonny at Pan, who seemed very excited to receive it.

That was on a Thursday.

'I can't wait to read it. I'm hoping to have completed it by Sunday lunchtime. Why don't you come over for a bite to eat around then?' he offered.

When I called that Sunday morning to double-check we were meeting, Sonny sounded rather flustered. 'Lynda, could you make it mid-afternoon?'

'Sure, no problem.'

At around 1 p.m. I received a call from Sonny. 'I think an evening dinner out would be better.'

Is he trying to cancel? I wondered. His tone was rather uptight for a man who'd had been so calm and encouraging.

When I arrived at Brown's Hotel in Mayfair, Sonny looked as though he was hanging to a life-raft by his fingernails amid a squally sea of paper.

He pulled languorously on his cigarette, smoothed his dark goatee beard and spoke slowly. 'I don't know what to say,' he confessed.

'You like it?' I smiled nervously.

'Lynda, most people writing a novel control around thirty characters, at most. Your novel has eighty. They are all wonderful characters, but I'm drowning. I haven't been able to come up for air. A window opens and a new character comes in. A door opens and there's another.'

'Right...'

Could he give me any encouragement? I thought.

'This is Dostoyevsky on LSD,' he continued, shaking his head. 'It's got to be cut, Lynda. Cut. Cut. Cut.'

Sonny passed on my epic to the very experienced Caroline Upcher. For protection more than anything else, I took along to the initial meeting my secretary who'd so diligently cleaned up my work. Caroline pulled no punches. Across the desk, my gargantuan telephone directory of a manuscript had been marked up in red pen.

'Look at this.' She tutted. 'There are pages about Mrs Williams and her Jack Russell dog, and the basket it takes to the butcher's to have filled up with sausages. It's beautifully descriptive, Lynda, but it has nothing whatsoever to do with your story.'

At that moment, my secretary piped up. 'Excuse me!' she said. I was all ears. In the months of her correcting my work she'd never expressed an opinion about any of it. Not once.

'It's the best part of the book!' she cried.

In the end it was agreed that while much did need to be jettisoned, the book should also be split into two: the first instalment to be called *The Legacy* and a sequel *The Talisman* to be released a year or so later.

When a manuscript reached Simon & Schuster in the States the welcoming committee was less sympathetic. In fairness, one editor wrote telling me how much she'd loved it. Pure Dickens, she opined. Shortly after I got a memo informing me she'd been sacked for alcoholism.

Instead, I got passed to an editor called Michael Korda, who'd recently had a bestseller with his own book *Queenie,* loosely inspired by the actor Merle Oberon. We met at the Four Seasons hotel in downtown New York where he kept a table.

'There's so much work needed on this,' he said.

Throughout lunch, I listened to Michael deliver his truths. He had rodent-like features and a soft, clipped voice.

'If you want to read a one hundred per cent successful novel, read mine,' he said rather smugly.

'I've read it,' I replied. 'What does that have to do with anything?'

I didn't mention it, but I'd also read some of the reviews. Quite devoid of great characters or interesting dialogue, according to some.

Nothing Michael Korda said helped me. I just felt belittled. And his subsequent notes on my book turned out to be hair-splitting. Edits that went on almost as long as the story itself. Some were preposterous! Words like limousine weren't acceptable. It had to be limo, and so on. Mine was a book set in the 1920s and '30s! No one said the word limo then! He obsessed over the modernisation of the language.

Weeks went by where he and I communicated back-and-forth by fax. I received a salvo of changes, more finicky than the last.

I'd fire off my missives. *Right back at you, ferret-face!* I could only assume this man was engaged in some kind of private war, albeit using passive-aggressive tactics.

It felt like bullying beyond belief.

'I refuse to use his notes,' I told Pan in the UK. 'Not only that but if Simon & Schuster wish to publish my novel, I will let them but only if I can publish Michael Korda's ridiculous notes alongside it.'

'Calm down, Lynda, just forget it.'

An attempt was made to sweep the whole debacle under the carpet.

In the end Simon & Schuster refused to publish *The Legacy*. Worse, I feared they'd make me return the advance paid to me, but that never happened despite some vague threats – a relief seeing that I'd spent every penny of it. I had to be thankful for that.

The Legacy celebrated its thirtieth anniversary in 2017. For all my inexperience in the publishing world, it is a book that remains close to my heart. I always say to people, if you want to know the real Lynda La Plante, read *The Legacy*. I may not have been the most accomplished of novelists, I may have had much to learn, but it has all of me seeping from every page. And it's still selling all these years later.

As for Michael Korda, I quietly exacted my revenge upon him using a rather unconventional technique.

After both *The Legacy* and *The Talisman* had eventually been published, I happened to be in New York meeting with a woman who would go on to become a trusted editor in the States for a brief time – a magnificent lady called Jeanne F. Bernkopf. I'd been introduced to her through a very well-known agent. More of Jeanne later, but during the meeting her phone rang.

'I'm so sorry,' she apologised. 'I'm going to have to take this. It's Michael.' As the conversation went on, I started to recognise the robotic voice drifting out from the earpiece.

'Was that Michael Korda?' I asked as she replaced the receiver.

'Oh yes. Michael, I adore him. I'm editing his new book,' she gushed.

'Oh really?'

I couldn't help grinding my teeth.

Back in the UK, I paid the dukkerin a visit and asked her to put a curse on Michael Korda. Nothing too dramatic. I didn't want him to suffer anything like a heart attack or death. I wanted something prolonged. Excruciating. Continuous throbbing pain. Like toothache.

Some months later I was back with Jeanne in New York.

'How's Michael's book coming along?' I enquired.

Jeanne's nose wrinkled with an expression of loving concern.

'Poor Michael. Poor, poor Michael,' she said.

Now, I became *very* interested.

'Poor Michael?'

'Yes. He's been desperately ill with impacted wisdom teeth. Can't work a day!'

I'm not proud of it at all, but a guilty smile spread across my face.

'What's wrong, Lynda?'

'You have no idea how funny that is,' I replied.

I told Jeanne about the Romany gypsy and the dukkerin curse, and how I'd found Michael Korda so disagreeable I'd placed one on him. Jeanne frowned disapprovingly and pursed her lips. She was utterly horrified.

'Lynda, I don't think you should tell anyone about this. It's deeply unpleasant and it should never be repeated, be it true or not.'

That same day I had a meeting with the agent who had introduced us. Jeanne must have called her as I tootled across town. Over coffee she spoke in a hushed tone.

'I know all about Michael Korda and his teeth,' she confessed.

'Oh, you do?'

My face flushed. I felt like a naughty child and really very ashamed.

'Yes, I do,' she continued. 'And I agree with Jeanne. It must not be repeated. You must not tell a soul about this.' She paused before leaning across the table. 'Can I ask a question, Lynda?'

'Yes...'

She gave a faint, self-conscious smile. 'Can you do this for anyone?'

Chapter 9
Civvies

Just as my novel-writing career was taking off, I decided it was time to move. The flat in Queen's Gate had been a wonderful home, but I needed a change. Neither of us had planned to move outside of London but, when Richard and I came to see the house I still live in more than thirty years later, I fell hopelessly in love. It was an easy commute to central London and on the edge of Richmond Park. Yet what I fell in love with all those years ago would have been hard to imagine at the time.

I doubt an inch of work had been done on the property since the 1950s. It had once been home to the actor Joss Ackland, who had a small army of children, yet for all its bedrooms it had only one bathroom. On its north side there was an annex that had been sealed off by a brick wall. Sitting tenants lived behind it, in utter squalor, and it took me several years to remove them and knock through. The whole place was filthy. In the kitchen there was an Aga, untouched for years, and a rug in front covered with an inch of congealed fat.

It had been the building's main sitting room that had drawn us in. Even though it was covered in dusty tasselled lights from Woolworths, the drama of its wooden panelling took our breath away. Rich burnished pine from floor to ceiling: originating from Windsor Castle, by all accounts. And, throughout, its baronial fireplaces and arched stone door-frames were reminiscent of a Scottish castle.

To buy it I had needed to take out a bridging loan from the bank. Queen's Gate hadn't been as easy to sell as I'd expected. For all its magnificence, its lack of bedrooms made it less attractive to prospective buyers. It all felt rather precarious. The loan amount was based on my earnings. More terrifying was the repair work that needed to be carried out on our new house.

We'd been shown around by its then owners who, it became patently obvious, were paralytically drunk. Then, as the sale was going through, a section of the roof blew off. A gas explosion, if we listened to officials; quite deliberate, if we spoke to neighbours. Suspicions were that the couple were bankrupt and it had been an insurance job. Some of the upstairs rooms had been damaged. We proceeded but our moving-in date became delayed.

One afternoon I was at the house when a gentleman arrived, believing it to be a previous residence of Field Marshal Sir Douglas Haig, Commander-in-Chief of the British Expeditionary Force during the First World War. This chap was a sort of amateur historian who'd dropped by unannounced.

'I really don't think so,' I told him.

However, when we pulled back the floorboards we found weapons: three guns, a shooting stick with Haig's initials carved into it and a set of swords. Sadly, they all got stolen while I'd been taking them to an antiques dealer in Portobello Road. I'd only left them for ten minutes wrapped in cloth on the back seat of my car. When I returned, they'd gone. I couldn't believe it!

Initially, we employed a local builder, John, to carry out the repairs on the roof. He was a talkative chap – said he'd been in the Black Watch, the infantry battalion of the Royal Scottish Regiment, but he'd built his own successful business once he'd come out from the armed forces.

'Not everyone's as fortunate!' he commented.

'Really, why's that?' I was curious.

'Some of them can't get work. No one will touch them. Ex-paratroopers. Terrible reputation. They'll fight, cause problems.'

John had friends in exactly that predicament: soldiers who'd returned from the Falklands War after 1982, unable to adjust to civilian life or find work. They'd been members of the airborne forces, dropped out of the sky and into bloody ground-combat.

'Could you help?' he asked. Some of them had wanted to set up a security firm, but no bank would loan them the money. 'They're in real trouble. Thought you might know a thing or two about security and protection, what with you writing *Widows* and everything.'

Hilarious! Maybe they'd like advice on a heist, too?

'That was fictional!' I impressed upon him.

'Well, would you agree to meet one?'

I promised I would consider it. Between thoughts of work and the upheaval of moving I felt rather overwhelmed, but the story did pique my interest. I had no clue whatsoever about what life was like after military service. Don't the army look after soldiers? Don't they get a big pay-off or a generous pension or something?

'Why don't you bring your friend to the house?' I said when I next saw John. I was dividing my time between it and temporary accommodation in Edith Grove in Chelsea while initial works were completed, so we set a date.

That was to be the start of an unforgettable ride.

When Jim Morgan – as I have chosen to call him – stepped through my door he would have been in his late thirties. Dark black hair, bulging muscles. He had the strangest facial hair I'd ever seen. Not a beard, as such. Instead, he'd grown his body hair right up to the line of his chin, like a kind of werewolf.

'Never allowed a beard in the army, so I grew this,' he explained. A mini-rebellion against the orders of his superiors. It looked ridiculous, but I understood the sentiment.

Jim was courteous. At first, he called me Mrs La Plante. 'Lynda, please,' I said. We talked a little about his life. He'd been a sergeant but since exiting the forces things had been tough. Really tough. Work had been sporadic but employers weren't willing to take on ex-paras, so regular income was scarce.

'Can't you claim some kind of benefit?' I asked.

I assumed that having served their country, some help might be available.

'Yeah, the dole, but none of us will.'

'Why not?'

'That's for poor people,' he said proudly, flexing his chest.

There were seven men in total – all ex-combatants from the Falklands. Some of them had also served in Northern Ireland after the British Army established a presence there in the 1970s. Now, what they really wanted to do was to start their own business. Only investment was non-existent.

In truth, I liked Jim from the off. Furthermore, I felt sorry for him and his mates. These men wanted to work, so why couldn't they? Was his story entirely legit? I didn't know, so I did some digging around. I rang up a number of security firms. Could they offer guys like these work?

'Doubtful. Ex-Paras. Too institutionalised,' the firms said. Besides, ex-soldiers could seldom hold down a job. Many had criminal records.

'OK, understood.'

It was a complete revelation to me that these barriers existed, but what I found the most surprising was the chasm of support. I began thinking. If these guys needed a cash boost, I could secure a loan. I discovered that seven ex-soldiers could legally form a company and, with the sale of Queen's Gate, the bank would agree to an amount and I could put up the finance, around £30,000. By the time repayments were due, the business would be on a sure footing and they could repay it. Admittedly, hope got the better of me.

In exchange for helping them, I wanted to pitch a TV series based on their story. Did I have a burning desire to write *Civvies*? I can't say that I did. But I did feel passionate that their story should be told. As far as I knew, it never had been. Not on TV, anyway. War was about patriotism and heroism, battlefields and victories, never about the aftermath. Never about a family waving a man off to the frontline and welcoming him home a different person. Never about the gruelling adjustment to civilian life. Nobody talked about that!

The drama was pitched to head of drama at BBC Wales, Ruth Caleb. She was based in London but oversaw the regional arm. The team there loved the idea. It was fresh – a powerful subject with an upbeat finale. 'Go for it, Lynda,' they said.

Jim agreed that he would talk to me about his experiences and little by little, the other men agreed too. As for my investment, it was a risk but I had a good gut feeling about where these men were going. They had a plan to run a chauffeur service at first, and then branch out into security work. *Good luck to you*, I thought.

Months later, the new offices of The Sentinels opened on Putney High Street and the local press loved the story. I can't recall exactly the headline: 'Falklands heroes turn Sentinel saviours'. Something like that. And underneath there was a photo of the men in smart suits and caps in front of the signage. That my money was bankrolling the venture was never revealed, but I couldn't help feeling secretly proud and excited! I put the word out, too. Most of my friends started using the firm as a taxi service if they ever came to visit.

Jim and I met regularly. Mainly, he'd come to the house and we'd sit in the middle of the building site. He'd talk and I'd jot down notes. We spoke about the Falklands: the fire and the gunshots that still kept him awake at night, drenched in sweat. The visual flashbacks that could overwhelm him at any time. The smell of burning flesh that remained in his nostrils six or seven years later.

He'd also struggled living with his wife and two children. The slightest noise could anger him. And there were little details I noted down, like being unable to remember the layout of the kitchen or where his wife kept the sugar.

His wife would like to meet me, Jim told me after a while. 'Sure,' I agreed. One night they both came for dinner. Jim's wife was a large lady: rather dominant, I suspect. But she also seemed very nervous. I served whole fish. Trout, I believe, but I could see her hesitate as I placed the plate in front of her. These were not people who went to dinner parties, I realised. I sensed that she may have felt intimidated.

'She's very embarrassed. She doesn't know what to do with the fish,' Jim stepped in and spoke for her.

Well, if there's one thing my education at Streatham House School had taught me it was how to fillet fish.

'Would you like me to take the head off and bone it?' I offered.

'Oh yes, please.'

The evening was awkward at times. Polite chit-chat and then they left, but slowly I gained a trust that allowed me to hear more experiences. After that, Jim brought stories from the other men. I visited some of them too. The majority lived relatively locally and I might meet them in a pub or get invited to their homes. Some talked of the depression they suffered. Most of them drank heavily. Very heavily. Others battled suicidal thoughts.

I was beginning to build a picture of a complex issue. Military hospitals might help put soldiers back together physically, but I couldn't find any evidence that the psychological aspect of post-combat life was ever considered. After all, this was the late 1980s. In fact, research into veterans' mental health didn't begin until the late 1990s in the UK following the first Gulf War, and then only because of pressure placed on the Ministry of Defence by Falklands veterans. They wanted recognition of what was known as post-traumatic stress disorder (PTSD). They claimed it could and should have been treated, and they wanted compensation.

Paratroopers' wives also agreed to talk to me, and it was with them that I probably got closer to the heart of the story I had set out to tell. Domestic violence had become present in their lives. Sometimes, these women didn't recognise the husbands who had come back from the war – they were broken men. And now these were broken families.

Then, there were the stories Jim brought me that I decided not to include. He described the shortage of food and equipment that soldiers had experienced on the frontline. Of how decorated war heroes had unnecessarily led men to their deaths. He showed me pictures. Dead Argentine soldiers, stripped naked and bloodied with target-boards painted on their arses, so that the British could take pot-shots. War crimes, clearly.

He wanted the full horror of the war those men had been through exposed. After some consideration, I decided that was not my story to tell. That was the work of investigators or journalists. I'd set out to tell a human story. 'I'm not writing a drama about the rights and wrongs of what went on in the Falklands,' I drummed into Jim repeatedly. 'I'm writing a story about how you don't have any support adjusting to civilian life, and how war has traumatised men like you.'

Jim looked at me, often utterly blankly.

It was then that I realised that he didn't recognise what trauma was or even that he may be suffering from it.

Away from our regular meetings I had been piecing together the background. I started to research the thousands of soldiers who had returned from the Vietnam War who had experienced the same and also found help unavailable. PTSD was being discussed far more openly in the States than in the UK. Nevertheless it had only been officially recognised as a mental health condition there in 1980. Before that time, symptoms would have been called 'shell shock'. I sifted through medical reports, testimonies, books, whatever I could find, in whatever library, some housed within the Imperial War Museum and dating as far back as the First World War.

I also knew I was going to have a problem setting the series in the Falklands. I couldn't reveal these men as the source of my research. For that reason I built the drama around the Troubles in Northern Ireland.

One man had been shot in the throat and could barely speak. I kept that character in but made sure that there were other soldiers who had suffered the same injuries so that no soldier could ever be identified. I changed everything about those paratroopers, apart from their underlying experiences.

As the script developed, I read it aloud to Jim. He liked it. Loved it, in fact.

'Do you know, Lynda, you've given me everything I wanted in life,' he said.

'What do you mean?'

'In this you've made me the father of two boys. I always wanted boys.'

Jim took the script away for the other men to read, and it also met with their approval. At last they felt their story was being told. The wonderful thing about it was its feel-good ending. These men would turn their lives around.

I sent it to the BBC and waited. And waited . . .

If *Civvies* was too daring or raw or harrowing, or just not what the BBC were looking for, I never found out. Whatever the reason, it got shelved. Just like that. I wasn't even called into a meeting.

Only a message sent through my agent, Duncan Heath. The script got shoved in a drawer, I assumed never to see the light of day. I felt crushing disappointment. Jim and the other men did too. In fact, telling them was dreadful. And it would be another five years before *Civvies* got dusted off and revisited.

Chapter 10

Meeting the Mafia

Civvies' cancellation was a rejection that took time to recover from. A year's worth of work now languishing in Broadcasting House. What felt worse was that my track record had given me no security whatsoever. Moreover, the project had felt fresh. Without sounding too grand, it had also felt important. Now that story wouldn't be told.

With *The Legacy* and *The Talisman* released, I turned back to novels. Crime had been a part of both of those books, but not the sole focus, and I'd felt like an uncaged bird writing them. Yet with hindsight I hadn't exorcised the simmering anger I still felt over *Widows* series two. It kept returning to my mind. An echo that I needed to expunge. I needed a means to write it out of me.

On spec I took a flight to Atlantic City. Initially I'd wanted to scope out whether I could write an American version of *Widows* (one mini-series was eventually released in 2002). I'd not offered it to any network or spoken to anyone about it, but I had some leads. Mafia ran like rats underneath Atlantic City and a close associate of the Kray twins I had befriended during my research for *Widows* knew people who could help me.

'Make two strips of passport photos,' he instructed me. 'Keep one. I'll take the other and send it to my contact. When you meet, if he produces a picture you'll know it's safe.'

Okey-dokey.

There was another avenue, too. I could also go through the American film unions who had lists of police officers willing to assist writers and researchers, so I faxed over a request. I also arranged an assistant. Someone who knew the city, where and where not to go.

On my arrival, it struck me that I was more at risk in Atlantic City than I'd ever been in the East End of London. Behind the neon lights, glass-fronted casinos and Vegas-style hotels that lined the boulevards, there was a far darker side. Money had flooded into the city since the legalisation of gambling in the late 1970s. Crime was rife: murder, robbery, mob warfare. Always tell someone where you're going; wear bright clothes so that you can be seen easily – I bought a green chequered coat; take a bodyguard if needs be. These were techniques I learned on-the-hoof. No drama is worth coming home in a body bag.

Frustratingly, my initial contacts didn't get me far. The assistant turned out to be next to useless. And the hot-shot gangster I'd been directed to from my contact in London turned out to be a bit of a damp squib. Officers from the police department had agreed to drive me around in a patrol car to give me a feel for the city's underbelly, but I sensed they didn't really want me there.

'If we get into a situation and I say get down: get down. Get your head down in the car,' I remember one officer instructing me.

'Sure,' I agreed, but what's the point if I couldn't see anything? It made being on patrol exceedingly boring. Most of the time I tried to decipher the messages coming through the police radio, but that was very confusing.

'Blackmail. Blackmail. 42–44 East side.'

That's all they seemed to say. I assumed 'blackmail' was some kind of code. The reality soon became clear.

One afternoon we were driving downtown when word came through:

'Suspect on the fire escape. Blackmail. Blackmail.'

All of sudden the cop driving put his foot down on the accelerator. 'Get down,' he screamed. 'Get down now under the dashboard!'

In seconds we were swerving round corners, screeching to a halt. I could hear the radio crackling as sirens wailed and patrol cars heaved into view.

I felt compelled to look. Every time I tried the cop pushed the back of my head: 'Down, get back down!' he shouted. But I did turn momentarily and managed a clear view. I could see the figure of a Black man dressed in jeans and T-shirt, surrounded by police snipers on the steps of the warehouse building. Ah. Black male. Black male.

'Freeze!' one cop was shouting.

Seconds later, the suspect reached into his pocket and I clearly saw a handgun. A shot sounded. Bam! I watched his head jerk back, then his body keel over the metal railing, falling like a rag doll before I lost sight of where he landed. My heart was pounding. Such a shocking, but engrossing moment.

Later that day, I ended up offering to give a witness statement to confirm that I'd seen a gun being pulled. What struck me most was how young the guy had been, and also the sniper. From then on, police fell over themselves to help me, given that I'd corroborated their account. They took me to brothels, showed me endless gruesome photographs of murdered prostitutes – something they seemed to take a grim pleasure in. There were patches where bodies had been dug up from under paving stones. All fascinating stuff, but it didn't hit the big-league Mafia crime I was after. Besides, one lieutenant made me feel frightfully uneasy. On his forearm he had a tattoo of an automatic rifle. I was with him when a hooker who serviced the city's high-rollers pulled me aside.

'Don't ever be by yourself with him. Don't go solo, lady.'

I took that advice very seriously.

I wondered whether I should fly home. Then, a peculiar thing happened. Richard had an old friend who lived on the outskirts of the city. Someone he'd been at college with. 'Look him up while you're there,' he suggested. So I did. Mixing socialising with work could slow me down, but evenings in the hotel could also drag. I took a cab over for dinner.

I *say* dinner but it turned out to be nachos and dips with this man and his wife. After an hour or so he took a call. He had some business downtown and he could drop me back. He looked like a young Burt Lancaster and his wife was petite and pretty but unusually nervy. Apparently they had kids but there was no sign of them: their spacious bungalow felt curiously empty for a couple with a young family.

To repay their hospitality I called them a couple of days later. 'I've tickets to see Linda Ronstadt in concert. Would you like to join me?' I asked.

They couldn't have sounded happier.

'Linda Ronstadt? We love her! She's our favourite. Sure, we'll come.'

Linda Ronstadt was playing at the Sands Hotel where I had been staying: a smile-white monolith overlooking the ocean with a top-floor casino. Seating booths circled the auditorium and I waited for them in one. I waited but no one came. Strange for a couple who'd been so keen.

Sitting alone, I began studying the audience. In front of me I noticed two guys in the cheap seats. Casual types, dressed in denim. The concert began. I ordered another drink. Linda performed hit after hit, and then the orchestra got going with an intro to her song 'Falling in Love Again'. From the ceiling a large crescent moon descended onto the stage with a little seat carved into it.

'I'm gonna sing a song y'all know so well,' Linda told the audience. 'And I've got this prop,' she gestured towards the moon. 'It's sure dangerous but management want me to use it!' she laughed nervously before climbing onto the cushion. The moon swung precariously.

By now my attention wasn't only fixed on Linda. My eyes were moving between her and the rows in front. From the moment the song had begun those two guys had whipped out a camcorder and were filming. When it was done, they got up and left. *What the hell are they doing?* I thought. I could only assume they were gathering some kind of evidence. Perhaps Linda Ronstadt had wanted out of her contract, or more money, and her comment was quite deliberate? Why were they filming that song?

Meanwhile, the maître d' had been very attentive towards me from the moment I'd walked into the auditorium. A young man with dark, Mediterranean looks. Harvard-educated, he'd told me. We'd got chatting and I'd explained I was a writer researching in the city.

'Wow, what for?' he'd asked.

'Oh, a new *James Bond*,' I said casually.

A whopping lie, of course, but I found James Bond often opened doors in unexpected places. In fact, it's why he had seated me in a booth. Good old 007 got me into the most expensive high-roller booth. The next time he circled around I waved him over.

'Are you having a problem with Linda Ronstadt?' I enquired.

'What?' Suddenly, he was all ears.

He listened as I told him about the crescent moon and the two guys filming.

'Thank you,' he said, without ever answering my question.

The concert reached its encore, but my guests still hadn't turned up. I headed to my room but on my way back through the lobby I bumped into them.

'Sorry! We're so damn late. Sorry,' the wife said, gasping for breath, without any explanation of why. She was dancing around as if on hot coals.

'Never mind,' I tried to calm them. 'You missed Linda Ronstadt, but perhaps you'd like some champagne?' The husband seemed as frantic, constantly dabbing his forehead with his handkerchief, sweat dripping from his face.

'I'd like to play the tables,' he announced.

'Sure, we can have a drink in the casino,' I suggested, before we headed to the lift and made our way up to the roulette area.

From the start, the evening had felt very dislocated. As the wife and I sipped our drinks, he became more frenzied. At the roulette table, he slapped down his credit card spin after spin. He was betting high, but losing, still wiping the sweat from his face. His hands were shaking.

'He's losing a lot,' I said to his wife.

'I know,' she said, worriedly. Her eyes were wide with fear.

And it was fear. I was sure of it. I'd never sensed anything like it: burning, corrosive fear. I wanted to ask, 'Is everything OK? What's eating you?' but I stopped myself. I didn't know these people, didn't want to overstep the mark by prying into somebody's personal business.

The couple left as hurriedly as they'd arrived. I only ever saw them once more during that trip – a dinner with guests, one of whom was pointed out as the daughter of the slain Chicago gangster Sam Giancana. Something else was going on here, I realised. By then another link had started to form, too.

On the evening of the Linda Ronstadt concert I'd eventually got back to my suite to find a large bouquet of flowers laid outside my door. The accompanying note simply said: '*Grazie.*' It was from the maître d'.

Although I'd ended up ditching my initial contacts in Atlantic City, from that moment on things started to become more interesting. First Richard's friends; then Linda Ronstadt; next the bouquet of flowers. Then a message arrived from the maître d' that his uncle wished to meet with me.

Why? I thought. But, of course, I agreed.

A dinner was arranged. The uncle was first-generation Italian. Small, grey-haired, wearing the finest suit and exceedingly charming. He was incredibly impressed by the non-existent *James Bond* film I was definitely not writing.

'It's an Italian crime,' I said.

'You want crime? Italian crime?' he asked, his eyes flickering.

'I'd like to find out more, yes.'

'Italian crime, eh? Please, go meet with my friends in Palermo.'

'Palermo?'

Christ Almighty! I had no intention whatsoever of scooting off to Italy. But I'd picked up so few scraps in Atlantic City I'd even been contemplating moving the action to Los Angeles, to see if I would fare any better there.

'Goodness, Palermo. Thank you, but I don't think so.'

'OK, Lynda, but it's the place to go,' he said.

'Thank you, but—'

'You wanna go? You call me,' he said, slipping a card into my hand.

Within a few days, I'd abandoned Atlantic City and boarded a flight home.

Back in the UK, thoughts of Palermo started trickling into my brain. Who would have thought a well-spoken Ivy League graduate working as a maître d' in a downtown hotel would have an inroad into the bona fide Mafia? There were so many dots to connect. I called the uncle as instructed, who was more than happy to help.

Palermo was to be an experience that was eye-opening beyond belief. A relative of my new contact would have me stay at his villa with his wife and children.

'You'll be made very welcome,' the uncle told me. In Palermo the Mafia trials were also in full swing – the years-long criminal cases against almost 500 members of the Sicilian Mafia – the Cosa Nostra. So many were being brought to trial after several former Mafia bosses had turned informants. If I wanted to watch, someone could take me.

Just like Atlantic City, in Palermo nothing was ever quite what it seemed. From the airport I got driven to a red-tiled villa. The family were friendly, up to a point. I couldn't help but notice how the women fluttered around the house, polite but servile, especially when the men appeared.

I took gifts, of course. And I smiled and thanked the family repeatedly for their hospitality, but my inner voice told me to be cautious. There was something poisonous in the veins of that household, I knew it. Every morning, before I left the house, I placed my used notebooks in the dresser in my room and trapped one of my hairs in the closed drawer. Sure enough, when I checked every evening the hair had been displaced. And my papers were out of order. Someone had been going through my books.

The Mafia trials themselves were remarkable. I had absolutely no clue what was going on. They were taking place in Carcare dell'Ucciardone, the city's main prison, given it was the location where most of the Cosa Nostra on trial were seeing out their remand. A courtroom had been specially constructed in its basement. It felt overwhelming. Defendants sat in iron-barred cages around the room and witnesses were brought up one by one to give evidence in metal-framed tubes, encased in bullet-proof glass, flanked by Carabinieri police. Bags and bodies were searched endlessly as we entered and exited the prison.

I lost the assistant I'd brought with me early on. She was simply too scared to accompany me and, in truth, her Italian had been less than perfect. I enrolled the help of another interpreter through my hosts but his English turned out to be dreadful. I picked up what I could but mainly I was left watching a very bizarre drama unfold.

Throughout, the men in cages spat out cries in Italian. '*Non Dire Cazzate!*'

Some cages had perhaps as many as thirty men crammed into them.

The judge constantly leapt to his feet and banged his hand on his desk. '*Silencio! Silencio!*'

The whole spectacle was utter chaos: a room boiling over with grown men in the throes of some almighty tantrums.

One guy looked to be aged around sixty. Every day I noticed he was in a cell on his own. He couldn't have looked less interested. Mostly he filed his nails. Every time this man was called to stand up, he looked stiff as if he was wearing some kind of corset. But the antics of his lawyer were unbelievable. He cried and clasped his hands and pleaded with the judge.

'*Per favore! Per favore!*'

'What's going on?' I whispered to my so-called interpreter.

'He's accused of killing four people,' he replied.

'Four?' That did seem rather a lot. I checked the number before writing it in my notebook. 'Four?'

'No, no signora. For-ty. For-ty. Four. Zero,' he half-grimaced.

Crikey.

One evening back at the villa, the head of the family asked if I wanted to go to a party. He was a small man with thick black eyebrows and beady eyes – an almost comical Bob Hoskins lookalike, but someone you knew never to cross. When I'd first arrived in Palermo, he'd taken me aside and spoken quietly to me in his broken English.

'I tell you what you need to know. But careful for me, please. No one must know me. My identity secret, please.'

'I will make sure,' I promised.

When I finally wrote my book *Bella Mafia* the character of Paul Carolla, the mob boss, was based on him. He even gave me the idea for Paul Carolla's name.

The party was a wedding in the grounds of a private villa. 'Go with my wife and enjoy,' he said. It was incredible. I'd never seen so many trestle tables in my life groaning with plates of meat and pasta. Chianti on every table. There were archways of flowers, and the bride was head-to-toe in cascading white chiffon. I sensed people were curious as to who I was, too – I felt a quiet scrutiny.

'Who is she? Why is she here?'

I assumed that was the question being asked because I heard the words 'James Bond' repeated several times.

When I scanned one of the trestle tables it was then that I realised I had stepped into a parallel universe. There, tucking into a plate of veal, was the man from the courtroom who'd I'd watched filing his nails.

My mouth was agape.

'But . . . I saw him in a cage this afternoon.' I tapped my chaperone on her arm and pointed over.

She glanced over and purred coolly. 'Oh you did? Good, good.'

That was the beginning and the end of the conversation.

I was starting to grasp the multiple layers of power, brutality and corruption in Palermo. The main city cemetery told me much of what I needed to know: row upon row of marble mausoleums with small glass cabinets that rattled in the hot summer breeze. Inside were candles flickering and photographs of young men. So many murdered young men.

I was nearing the end of my ten-day trip. I had notes and rough ideas for characters and a story. I'd seen so much. In my mind this was not a TV series but a novel with a family at its heart, torn apart by Mafia violence.

Just before I was about to depart, I had an offer of a visit to see a contessa who lived in a villa in a suburb of the city.

'You want to go, Lynda? She will see you.'

'Yes, please!'

Why her, I do not know. And I have no recollection of who drove me there but it turned out to be a place forever scorched in my mind. In *Bella Mafia* it became the location I was to base Villa Rosa on – the home of Don Roberto Luciano and his wife Graziella, whose family were at the heart of bloody revenge, setting off a chain of events that led the women – the *bella mafioso* – to plot their own reckoning amid a complex web of family relations and mob warfare. The story spanned Italy and the United States.

As we approached, a high perimeter wall loomed into view, giving no indication of what lay beyond. Inside its double gates was a bell. I rang it and waited. After some time a woman in a worn, black dress appeared. She didn't speak much English at all.

'Contessa, she wait for you,' she said, beckoning me in. Along the driveway were rows of marble statues, bodies with heads and limbs broken off and damaged busts on plinths. Two imposing balconies jutted out from each side of the villa and we walked past stables and dog kennels, deathly quiet and abandoned. Further on there was a little door which led to a poky, darkened room. There, hunched over a one-bar electric fire was an elderly, frail woman in a cheap-looking dress with flip-flops and pebble-shaped bifocals. Her long grey hair was tied into a bun.

'Pleased to meet you,' I said, holding out my hand.

I tried to tell the contessa that I was a writer and that I wanted to know more, but her English was as poor as her carer's. I could sense her wanting to explain what she'd been once, how she'd come to live in such faded grandeur. When her pockmarked translation couldn't convey the enormity of her story, she gestured for me to walk around the villa with her. It had to be seen to be believed.

In the cavernous sitting room there were heavy velvet drapes, thick with dust. The chandeliers hadn't been cleaned in years and layers of grime hid their sparkle. Black and white tiles covered the floor and paintings covered the walls. She pointed out a Caravaggio.

'*Originale*,' she said.

The walls were lined with landscapes and portraits and gold Rococo mirrors. Exquisite dressers and cabinets filled every room. As she shuffled around, she waved her hand at the paintings and the furniture.

'Gone.' She tutted. 'Gone. Gone. Gone.'

And that's when it dawned on me that nothing in that villa belonged to her. Beside each of the paintings a red dot had been placed. When she peeled back a rug, even its underside had a small red sticker attached to it. The chapel – my God, the chapel – just incredible! It was crammed with gold icons. A crucifix studded with jewels hung by the altar, but every single thing was marked and catalogued. It was the same in the hallway, where a sedan chair stood covered with a silk canopy. Beside it was a dummy of a woman in a wig dressed in a Marie Antoinette gown with a large trailing bustle. It sent a shiver through me. The Mafia owned it all, just waiting for when the contessa died.

At the back of the property, where the garden stretched back, its fountains were dry. Everything reeked of decay.

'What's in that building over there?' I asked. It was a separate annexe, newly built and appeared incongruous with the rest of the house.

'That's where they come.' She waved her hand in disgust and sucked her teeth. The venom she felt for her masters was obvious. Her eyes narrowed whenever she spoke of them.

'They come there to meet.'

How she used to live, before the Cosa Nostra took everything, became clear when she brought out a set of photographs. Her husband was a marquis, she said. He owned racing cars, had once been a driver and had been killed racing. In one picture they stood together, her in a flowing gown surrounded by a huge pack of Great Dane dogs on leashes, which she bred. Now there were no guards, no men, no dogs anywhere. Just her and her carer in a small room hunched over her fire.

'When did they take it?' I asked.

I couldn't quite make out her reply, but she seemed to say it was in the forties, during the war: a gambling debt her husband couldn't repay.

That's how the Mafia control, I thought.

I came away from Palermo with conflicting emotions of both awe and sadness. Behind the magnificence of its architecture, evil lurked. By this time I'd also done some digging around on the couple I'd met in Atlantic City and found a connection that linked them to Mafia, too. It gave me a sense of how the Mob moved into places like Atlantic City.

As I'd sifted through newspaper archives, I'd stumbled across the family name. As I sifted back further, I found out they ran a laundromat business. Every single restaurant tablecloth, hotel bedsheet and staff uniform went through their network. And it was through the service industry – waste services, dry cleaning outlets, restaurants – that the Mafia funnelled most of its dirty money. As I searched back further, I discovered the family had been city governors who'd voted in Mafia members. Whether that man was in debt or had a bullet on his head, I will never know. All I know is that I'd never seen fear like it. In truth, I've never seen it since. I didn't dig deeper into their story. I became too weary of who I was dealing with. In *Bella Mafia,* Atlantic City became New York.

Some months later I flew out to Italy again, this time to Rome, invited by a contact to attend a large private dinner hosted by the Agnelli family – the powerful Italian business dynasty. Wow. I have never been in company like it – a snapshot of super-sonic wealth beyond belief: women who with one look made me feel like a grain of sand. I didn't have the right handbag, the right shoes, the right anything. Again, the only pass that had got me through the door had been 'James Bond'. But I used much of what I'd seen. I wanted to show in *Bella Mafia* what power on that scale looked like.

When my manuscript was finally complete I did as I had promised: I made sure that the sections that included my host at the villa in Palermo were masked. He and I met on several occasions – mostly in the States, where he regularly flew out to conduct his business.

'I like this, Lynda,' he said. 'But there's a problem. If I am Paul Carolla, no one gonna know who I am.'

I explained to him that that was the point. I'd taken great pains to disguise the identity of everyone, just as he'd asked me to.

'OK, Lynda, but jus' a liddle bit.' He pinched together his thumb and forefinger and held it up to his face. 'Jus' a liddle bit, Lynda. Jus' a liddle people could know, eh?'

Incredible that this man now wanted to be seen. But I didn't change a thing. To this day, whatever story I tell I have always protected my sources.

Bella Mafia was published in 1990. It would take another seven years before it made it to the big screen. Of course, there were many promises. In the States producer Frank Konigsberg had been after the rights for a while. When he finally bought them, he told me the production company would find exactly that villa in Palermo and film there. No expense spared! In truth, I had very little to do with the film's production, but as the months went by and I flew back-and-forth to the US to view edits, it was obvious the location shoots had been pared down to a back-lot in LA.

'I've seen the same donkey in every single scene! Have you only got one fucking donkey?' I remember complaining to Konigsberg.

When I sat beside him in the edit suite and tried to salvage some particularly awful scenes, he seemed surprised. 'You can edit, Lynda? Why didn't you tell me you could edit?' he said.

However, that really was the limit of my involvement – sadly, a taste of what was to come when dealing with US production companies. As for casting, I was not consulted at all. Granted, I did think that Vanessa Redgrave, who played the lead female Graziella Luciano, did a great job, and there were some wonderful moments. However, left to me I'd probably have cast an Italian actor like Claudia Cardinale. But I gave up putting my two-pennies' worth in. *Take the money and run, Lynda,* I told myself. After the film was released in 1997, Frank Konigsberg wanted more of my stories, but I refused. I felt he'd got so much wrong. Funnily enough, my sister brought me over the DVD of *Bella Mafia* recently. To add insult to injury, my name is spelled incorrectly on its cover. Perhaps I shouldn't feel too surprised!

Chapter 11
The Costa del Crime

As a writer, there are stories you search for, and stories that land on you as magically as summer rain. My personal gems – the series I may not be well known for but that I adored writing and making – were stories that materialised when I'd least expected them.

It wasn't long after I'd written *Bella Mafia* that I wanted to pursue a story about British crime abroad. Over the years I'd met many close personal and business associates of the Kray twins. I'd even been to visit them several times in prison. As criminals, the aura they had built up around themselves – even behind bars – was incredible.

Reggie Kray was a person you could have a conversation with, however brief. He was a hard man, but mild-mannered. Underneath all that villainy he seemed utterly lost and wretchedly sad to me. What struck me most about him was his dark black eyes. It is often said about people with gypsy heritage: eyes as black as coal.

Ronnie had exactly the same eyes, but Ronnie didn't seem sad at all. Ronnie Kray was insane: it was a roll of the dice as to which Ronnie you might meet, depending whether or not he'd taken his medication for schizophrenia.

'Hello, Linda. Come to read my horoscope?' he often asked.

In his head I was Linda Goodman, the famous astrologist from the 1960s.

'No, it's Lynda: the writer.'

'Oh right, can't do us a read for Scorpio then?'

'I'm afraid not.'

On other occasions, he was consumed by paranoia: volatile and dangerous.

'Who the fuck are you?'

'It's Lynda: the writer.'

'I don't trust you. What the fuck do you want from me?'

On those occasions, I made a quick exit. In prison, Ronnie called the shots. He had officers working for him. He'd send them out for cakes and pastries, anything he wanted. He also had the pick of young boys, whether they wanted to have sex with him or not. Reggie was no different. I have no memory whatsoever of who passed it to me, but I even have a recording of Reggie Kray on his death bed in 2000, struggling for breath, his wife Roberta by his side. 'I know he went with men in prison, but what do you expect?' she's heard chatting casually in the background. An unknown voice asks Reggie whether thirty-three years in prison was worth it.

'Nah,' he gasps.

Once I got asked if I wanted to write an authorised biography of the Kray twins. It would mean visiting them in prison far more often.

'They'll be upset if you don't say yes, Lynda,' I was told.

'I'm sorry. I won't be doing it.'

I knew enough people connected to the Krays to know that I didn't want to get deeper into their lives. And I didn't want to glorify their brutality either. Observe them, yes. Lionise them, no thank you.

Their network, however, had been very good to me. Through it I'd taken a flight out to the Costa del Sol to meet an enclave of gangsters. The idea for the script had begun back in the UK. Later, it was to become the mini-series *Framed*, which eventually aired on British TV in 1992 and was remade in the States ten years later, rather brilliantly in my view.

It all started with the story of 'The Dancer'. I just happened to be sniffing around a London court when I stumbled across the case of a prison officer being tried. He'd been the last person to chaperone a particular criminal – a mastermind escapee because he could dislocate his shoulder and squeeze through bars and windows. His nickname: The Dancer. Was the officer an accomplice? The prosecution made its case. It got me thinking about the character of a con man, a career criminal, a beguiling chameleon who ends up being in the protection of a young police officer and whether or not that officer could be corrupted. A psychological thriller set in Spain? Worth scoping out, I reckoned.

The southern Spanish coastline was remarkable once you scratched its surface. Sun-kissed marinas. Luxury yachts, marble-floored villas all bought with the proceeds of crime. A madame who ran a brothel there agreed to put me up. She'd been a close friend of Charlie Kray, the Kray twins' elder brother. And, like everyone I met in the criminal underworld, she was ferociously funny, but dark too. From her villa she managed around six girls – so-called weekenders who gravitated to the Spanish coast to service the high-rollers, mainly Arabs who sailed into port. These girls weren't street workers. One was an air stewardess, one worked in a bank. Another was a croupier at a casino. All rather respectable, in fact.

'We can walk away from a weekend with a grand in cash,' they told me.

Another assumed I'd turned up as a sex worker myself.

'Oh, you need to put on a bit more make-up. You're very pasty – need some fake tan, too. Not going to bring punters in like that,' she said, looking me up and down with faint disgust.

'Thanks for the advice.' I smiled politely.

The madame had stories like you wouldn't believe. Once she smuggled into Spain millions of pounds' worth of diamonds, out of Lebanon.

'How?' I asked, imagining some secret compartment in her suitcase.

'Round me neck, love. Made 'em look like cheap baubles.'

The idea that big-money crime was hidden in plain sight seduced me.

One story, in particular, was wonderful. Tetley was a villain who had so many knife wounds he looked like a teabag. He'd been related to a prolific money launderer, but had no police record himself. When suitcases of cash needed to be brought through Spanish customs, Tetley was asked. He wasn't the brightest spark, but they reckoned he could pull off the job. Customs officers in Spain had already been paid off. All he needed to do was get the cash through the UK. He loaded up one suitcase with money, and one suitcase with pork sausages. On the Costa del Sol, good old British bangers were hard to find and his bosses had requested a sizeable supply.

Tetley touched down in Malaga. All had gone smoothly, but an hour or so later he still hadn't appeared through the airport's glass-fronted doors. He'd been apprehended by Spanish customs – not because of the thousands in bank notes stuffed into his suitcase, but for the forty-five packets of pork sausages he'd tried to smuggle through. In the end he had to relinquish those in a deal with the guards. Everyone got two packets each.

I loved the story of Tetley so much and even pitched it to Mel Gibson's film company, Lovell Gibson. It got commissioned and I'd got part-way through writing it when Mel Gibson landed the role of *Mad Max* for the third instalment of the series: *Mad Max Beyond Thunderdome*. While previous *Mad Max* films had enjoyed modest success, this movie catapulted him to superstardom. With deep regret, Tetley never got made.

Mel Gibson, however, had stayed at my home in London when initial talks were underway. What was surprising to me was how shy and private a man he was – not who I'd been expecting at all. I experienced his ability to fade to near invisibility first-hand when he asked one morning if there was somewhere he could buy *The Times* newspaper.

'Sure, I'll walk you to the corner shop,' I offered.

No sooner had we stepped through the door than its owner began accosting me with some headline news of her own.

'You'll never guess which famous person's been in. He just walked in off the street!' she said.

I could sense Mel's body freeze as he loitered by the counter, perusing the newspaper section.

'Go on. Guess!' she continued.

'No, I really can't. I'm sorry,' I said, concerned she was going to whip out a camera and send my guest running for the hills.

'Jimmy Tarbuck!' she screamed.

How funny, I thought. I was unsure rising global megastar Mel Gibson would have even heard of the comedian. Mel paid for his *Times* and the shop owner didn't bat an eyelid.

Back in Spain, I also spent twenty-four hours with the high-profile ex-pat fugitive Ronnie Knight, and his then-wife, Sue. We had a long lunch and then drinks the next day. The casualness of Ronnie was almost surreal – that showbiz persona. That sparkle. Everyone loved him. Such a spellbinding raconteur behind which, you had to remind yourself, was a heavy-duty criminal.

'You'll never believe what the last few days have been like, Lynda. Helicopters everywhere, circling around.' He laughed before sitting back with a cigar, a drink in his hand, and another story. 'You can always tell the undercover cops on the beach, Lynda. Stick out like a bleedin' sore thumb. Always with a white T-shirt on and a sun-tan line at the sleeves. Faces like bleedin' beetroots!'

When I eventually wrote the series *Framed* the police officer Lawrence Jackson, played by David Morrissey in one of his debut TV roles, took on many of those characteristics of a cop abroad that had been described to me. I still think it's one of David Morrissey's finest performances.

In *Framed* my career criminal Eddie Myers ended up being played beautifully by Timothy Dalton. He had been based on an amalgam of people including The Dancer and others I'd been introduced to. One man was unbelievably cultured. As well as the handful of nightclubs he ran, he owned an art gallery in Puerto Banús, high up on a cliff-side. Frightfully good-looking and very, very charming. When we met, he was surrounded by beautiful girls and living the life of Riley.

And it was on my way back from that meeting that the most sad and haunting story I'd ever heard fell from the heavens. A lovely driver had taken me there, English-born but he'd moved out to Spain and was working as a taxi driver. We'd wound our way up a mountain-side on the Sierra Blanca range, where he waited for me as I scoped out the gallery. Afterwards we drove further on to a hut overlooking a steep incline, where we stopped to look at the view.

Beneath the edge there was a huge dip in the mountainside.

Suddenly, my driver broke down in tears.

I didn't know what to do. 'Goodness, I'm sorry. Are you OK?'

'No, sorry. I'm not,' he said.

It took a while for this man to speak. But when he did he revealed that there had been a death at that exact location. Apparently, it was a destination for bikers. The dip was called 'the death ride'. At the top they revved up their engine, rocked the front wheel over the precipice, swooped down and up onto the dirt-track on the opposite side. Lucky riders survived, but some weren't so fortunate.

'My friend,' he said, fighting back tears. 'I was with him.'

'He died?'

'He wouldn't listen,' the man continued. 'We'd been drinking. We tried to persuade him not to do it. We watched him disappear and looked for him on the other side, but we couldn't see him. When we reached him by road, his bike had fallen on top of him.'

'I'm so sorry,' I said. 'To find your friend dead must have been shocking.'

'He wasn't dead,' he corrected me. 'We lifted the bike off him, helped him up. He stood and asked for a cigarette. I handed him a Marlboro, lit it for him and he took a drag. He sang a line from Sinatra's "Fly Me to the Moon" before the ambulance arrived.'

My driver went on to describe how he had followed his friend to the hospital in his car and sat and waited while he was treated.

'After a while the surgeon came out to talk to us. "Did you know him?" he'd asked. We told him we were with him when the accident happened.'

Then the surgeon broke the news, the taxi driver recounted.

'I'm sorry, he's gone. But if it's any comfort to you, he would have died instantly. When we opened up his leather jacket, his heart was completely crushed,' the surgeon said.

But the taxi driver knew this wasn't true.

'No, he was alive. I talked to him. He smoked a cigarette. He sang,' he told him.

'It's impossible,' the surgeon had concluded.

What an incredible story, I thought.

My driver recovered himself somewhat and we drove back down the mountainside. During the journey, the story churned over in my head. Who was this biker guy?

'Did your friend want to kill himself?' I asked.

'I don't know.'

'What did he do?'

'He was a stand-up comic.'

A vicious sense of humour, apparently.

'What else did you know about him?' I asked.

'Not much,' said my driver, 'only one story about his past.

'When he was five, he moved to Atlantic City with his mother and sister. They had a house that overlooked the boardwalk. One morning, he was left in the room and from the window he watched his mother walk into the sea. She was carrying his little sister. Further and further she walked out. He thought they were playing, but she drowned both herself and the little girl,' he said. 'That's all I knew.'

That story stayed with me for years. In 1993, it formed the backbone of the two-parter *Comics* I wrote for Channel 4 and made with Verity Lambert. A perfect pearl of a story, set in London, that followed the washed-up and tortured comedian Johnny Lazar as he became embroiled in a murder mystery. I found *Comics* emotionally blinding to write. Sadly, it's almost impossible to find these days. When the channel's then chief executive Michael Grade saw it for the first time he didn't make a single note.

'There's not a thing I would change,' he said. 'It's wonderful.'

Like stardust, stories are all around us just waiting to be brought to life.

Chapter 12

Prime Suspect

Pitching to network commissioners is never easy, mainly because you never know what TV executives want. So far, I'd gone in all guns blazing: 'Here's my big idea!' But I'd learned a thing or two, and I wanted a commission. I wanted to write for TV again and I was also under some financial pressure. My earnings alone were paying for our house renovations and the mortgage.

I remember sitting Richard down one evening. 'We have a mortgage to pay,' I reminded him.

'We do?' he answered.

'Every month, Richard.'

'Oh, right...'

Reality seemed to sail right past him, and I found myself working like a demented ferret to keep all the balls juggled. At least this time around I was in a more fortunate position. I had amassed some good contacts who supported me in the industry.

At the BBC, I'd met a script editor called Jenny Sheridan. Jenny was quiet and clever. She had loved my writing for *Civvies* and had thought cancelling it without any explanation was an appalling way to treat a writer. When she moved to Granada TV she was kind enough to introduce me to its executive producer, Sally Head. A meeting was arranged between us but this time I arrived with a new strategy. *Don't pitch anything,* I told myself. *Find out what she's looking for, and then strike.* It turned out to be the best weapon in my armoury.

Sally Head was bright-eyed and blonde-haired. She called everybody 'mate'. I warmed to her. She had all the energy of Verity Lambert and, I hoped, the same fearless vision.

'What are you looking for?' I asked.

Sally mulled it over for a moment. 'I'm thinking crime, mate. Murder. Maybe something plain clothes. Female.'

The market-stall trader in me took over. *Sell her something, Lynda.*

'That's so funny,' I smiled. 'That's exactly what I've been working on.'

A monstrous lie, of course. I'd been doing nothing of the sort.

'Really? Do you have a name for it?'

Think quickly, Lynda. Think quickly.

I didn't know a ton about police investigations, but they always had a prime suspect, didn't they? Someone in the frame?

'*Prime Suspect!*' I blurted out.

Sally chewed it over some more and nodded.

'I like that. Mate.'

That day, I walked out with a commission to write a four-hour special.

Fucking Ada. I'd been to the East End, to Palermo, to the Costa del Crime. Now I'd really set myself a goal. *How the hell do I write this one?* I thought. I began with the same process of research, but it didn't start well. High-ranking female police officer. Plain clothes. Exactly how thin these were on the ground only hit me when I made a call to the Metropolitan Police.

'I'm a TV writer. Looking to talk to a detective chief inspector. A woman?'

The sound of tumbleweeds was deafening.

'Well, we have three . . .'

Two were not keen to talk at that time, but one agreed. Her name was Detective Chief Inspector Jackie Malton, and that day began a partnership that lasted several years. I still recall the first time Jackie and I met. She arrived at my home and when I opened the door she bounced in, dressed head to toe in biker's leathers with no motorbike in sight.

''Ello, me duck!' she greeted me.

Jackie had a huge personality, that was obvious.

I explained that I was interested in covering a police murder investigation, but I didn't know where to start. 'I don't have a storyline yet,' I confessed.

'Don't worry, duckie. I can help with that,' she said. 'Ever been to a post-mortem?'

That day my bullshit-o-meter flew off the scale. If I said no, I was worried Jackie would think me too inexperienced to work with.

'Oh yes. Frightfully interesting,' I lied.

'OK, let's get another one under your belt. We'll get you down the labs, too.'

The Metropolitan Police Forensic Science Lab was in Lambeth, sandwiched between Georgian terraces. Blink and you'd miss it. A brutalist building that was as functional inside as out, filled with uniform corridors of sickly cream-coloured walls and Lino flooring. In the preparation area I was handed an oversized green robe, white wellington boots that felt like boats for my size-five feet. I also had a green hat and a mask. I looked like a garden gnome.

The chief forensic pathologist burst through the doors.

'And who is this?' he asked, waving his hand in my direction.

'I'm a writer. Just here to observe,' I replied.

'Well, you're very short. Come closer . . .'

I shuffled a little further forward.

'Come on! Closer. You don't want to miss all the action, do you?'

Now I had a front-row position. A little too close for my liking.

'Right, who have we got today?' The pathologist clapped his hands together enthusiastically.

Whoever this poor person was, he was very, very large. I could see a massive stomach bulging out from underneath the green tarpaulin.

When that got whipped back, I saw he was bloated and his skin a pasty blue colour. My insides turned over like a cement mixer.

'Right, scalpel, please.'

The pathologist started to make a Y incision. One cut from the top right of the shoulder, then the left, then down along the sternum.

'Pfffffbbbbttttt!' Suddenly, a huge raspberry fart filled the room. The corpse sat up, only slightly – but it was as if someone had let the air out of an inflatable. It was more than I could stomach.

The next thing, my legs buckled and I heard the sound of drunken voices swimming around me.

'Is she OK? Can you hear us?'

When I came to, I was laid out on the tiled floor.

'Can someone get her some water and take her out, please?'

'Sorry. I'm so sorry,' I said embarrassedly. I had no idea corpses did that!

Despite my initial car-crash attempt, I persevered. Jackie would drop me off at the lab and leave me there for hours. I sat patiently in a corner with my notebook while ten, maybe fifteen, forensic scientists and technicians worked around eight desks. There were microscopes and petri dishes, pipettes and plastic gloves. The painstaking work of a police forensic lab fascinated me but so did the minutiae of chit-chat among those working there.

For a building packed with morbid reminders of the dead, it could be uproariously funny. I'd be quietly eating my sandwich when a senior pathologist would swing through the double doors.

'Who's got my right foot? I've got a charred victim on the slab minus a foot.'

'Well, I haven't taken it!'

'That foot was in the fridge. I put it there! Now I've only got a shoe and no foot. Come on, which joker's moved it?'

To my surprise, technicians were also incredibly willing to help. Often, I'd lean in and ask them to explain what they were doing. They might be extracting fibres from clothes or analysing a blood or semen sample. Once I sat for an eternity watching a technician unwind a single strand of hair from a button. I left and when I returned an hour or so later he was still there, slowly unwinding. *The patience these people have is extraordinary*, I thought.

'We're hoping for a globule of flesh on the end, so we can get a DNA sample,' he told me.

Of course, DNA as an investigative tool was in its infancy in 1990, and had only been used for the first time in the UK in the case of the double-child murderer Colin Pitchfork, convicted on evidence of genetic fingerprinting in 1988. There was nothing like the DNA database that exists today, and *Prime Suspect* became the first TV drama to even feature DNA. So, in many of the labs I visited, I was still observing old-fashioned techniques.

What struck me, too, was how the pathologists handled the bodies. They touched them. They turned corpses' hands over to look at defensive wounds. I'd never seen that on TV. Dempsey and Makepeace ran around with guns. So did Cagney and Lacey. All adrenaline-fuelled stuff, but it occurred to me that no one had laid bare the reality of dissecting the dead to build a case based on that meticulous evidence.

As well as showing me the labs, Jackie would also pick me up and drive me around in the patrol car. Casually, she'd tell me about her day.

'Christ, you'll never believe it. That guy who's been stealing knickers from washing lines in Hammersmith? Just been brought in. Denies it, of course.'

With Jackie, it was often difficult to get her to be serious. A coping mechanism, was my hunch. As I got to know her better, she revealed more about the pressures of the job. She was openly gay at a time when being an out-and-proud lesbian would be detrimental to your career – she joked that she'd never get accused of sleeping her way to the top. It was also obvious that Jackie had a serious drink problem.

There were occasions when I'd hop in the passenger seat and the car would reek of alcohol. On other occasions, she would be inebriated. No one could accuse Jackie of being a shrinking violet, but I began to tease out of her how hard it had been to rise through the ranks in such a male-dominated profession. Some of the stories she told me were simply unbelievable.

When Jackie had joined CID her initiation ceremony had consisted of two officers grabbing her by the arms while a third put his hands up her skirt, yanked her knickers down and stamped CID on her arse cheek.

When she was promoted to join the Met's Flying Squad and made it to detective chief inspector she had opened the front door passenger seat of the patrol car only to have an officer crush her hand in it. He'd wanted her to sit in the back – unheard of for an officer of her new rank.

I gathered Jackie's anecdotes, all the while checking and cross-checking. Whenever I sat in incident rooms listening to her briefings, I observed the ratio of male to female officers. I listened to the under-the-breath banter, saw the eyes roll. Women were brass-arsed tarts – Jackie herself had been nicknamed 'The Tart'. Either that or most women just needed a good seeing-to.

I spoke with other female officers who confirmed how invisible they were within that culture. Most of the time they felt like abused spouses.

The odious character Sergeant Otley, eventually played by Tom Bell in *Prime Suspect*, was based on an officer Jackie worked with. And the uber-macho character of DCI John Shefford, whose death in *Prime Suspect* paved the way for DCI Jane Tennison, was also based on real men. Unfortunately the actor John Forgeham, who played Shefford, was equally a grade-A arsehole. I remember one actor telling me how the cast couldn't wait until he left the series. 'He dies today,' was a hope rather than a regret.

What I didn't rely on Jackie for was the story arc for my killer.

Jackie had to remain anonymous to the outside world. Not only did I need to protect her as my source, but I simply couldn't risk my narrative resembling any live case that she was investigating or was an ongoing case.

To piece that together, I visited newspaper archives. I took myself off to libraries. Initially, I had in mind a story about a serial killer of prostitutes so I began researching previous cases, criminal profiles, the trophies that killers took from every victim, the rituals they performed.

I also started talking again to the wives of murderers. Gaining trust wasn't easy. One woman I was tipped off about worked behind the nail counter of Selfridge's department store in London. Her husband was inside for a horrific murder. For weeks, I hovered around the counter like a bad fart. 'She's here again!' her colleagues would call out whenever I appeared.

'I'm writing for TV and I'd very much like to talk to you in private,' I'd ventured.

The answer would be 'no' and it remained so for a while. Eventually, she did agree to a coffee. I wanted to ask her what it was like to live with a killer. Did she suspect anything? Did she believe that her husband was guilty of those heinous crimes? Did she lie to herself?

'Ever had acrylic nails done, love? Want me to tell you how to apply them?' she asked. She was planning on setting up a market stall of her own and wanted to drum up some custom, I could tell.

Let's just say, it took a while before I got all the information I needed. And when she was ready, that woman dropped jewels in my lap.

'I was suspicious for a long time,' she admitted. She'd been questioned repeatedly by police, too, but hadn't revealed any misgivings. In truth, she'd been gaslit by her husband for many, many years.

Meanwhile, I got another tip-off from a contact in forensics. They'd been working on a historic unsolved murder – a cold case – of a Black girl who'd gone missing one year during the Notting Hill Carnival in West London. There had been a significant development as a skeleton had been found.

'We've got this technique we want to try. Would you like to see?'

'Yes, please!'

At the time, forensics had dug up the female skeleton and found the skull to be perfectly intact but there was still no positive identification. A medical artist could reconstruct the face using clay, a process that would take weeks. Hair could even be attached to the reconstruction based on what pathologists knew about the body. *Quite remarkable!* I thought. I started to build another story. After a while I began running the research for two scripts together, unsure of which one I might eventually submit to Granada TV. Whenever I wrote something, Jackie came over and we'd read through it.

Jackie never held back in her criticism. 'Well, this is a load of rubbish!' she'd often laugh.

My police interrogations were atrocious, apparently. I'd have a suspect stewing in an interview room with an officer asking, 'Do you have regular place you go to each day at around 4 p.m.?'

Jackie tutted and shook her head in frustration.

'For God's sake, Lynda, what are you dicking around asking this for? Hit the spot. Ask the bloody question. "Where were you at 4 p.m. last Friday? We have a witness who saw you at such-and-such a place."'

It was through Jackie that I learned interrogation techniques: when to press a suspect harder; when to pull back; when an officer over-stepped the mark; what I could and could not ask related to the evidence.

Whenever she read the killer's parts, she'd rub her hands together gleefully. 'Oh, he's a nasty sod, isn't he? I like him.'

That Jackie could handle some of the most gruesome crimes was an aspect of her I wanted to reflect in my female DCI. I wanted a woman to be seen in a light that women had never been seen before.

As I continued, crunch-time loomed. I needed to decide which story I was going to submit to Sally Head, and therefore which script I should plough my energy into. It was a tough decision. The serial killer of prostitutes had been partially written. The second story of the girl's remains, to be set in the heart of London's Black community, had been mapped out. It had the potential to shed light on continuing tensions between the community and the Met Police. It was less than a decade since the Brixton riots, and mistrust, harassment and racism were live issues. Just three years later the teenager Stephen Lawrence would be savagely murdered at a bus stop in South London, exposing a culture of institutional racism within the Met. As I'd seen this with my own eyes, I wanted to tackle the issue from all sides but it would require a seventy per cent Black cast.

Both stories were strong contenders, but in the end I bottled it. I knew that a story portraying the Black experience simply wouldn't get greenlighted. Already, I could hear the response: 'It's just not commercial, Lynda.' It was sad but true that they thought this way.

What's even sadder for me is that thirty years later when I was sitting with a commissioner at a main UK network, pitching a mixed-race lead called Mya, I heard exactly the same nonsense. 'Wouldn't get the cut-through, Lynda. We tried it and viewing figures suffered. We can't run with it.' Seriously? Has so little changed? Hard to believe I was back at square one. *Take the fucking risk,* I wanted to scream.

Back in 1990, however, I put that story in my back pocket, hoping I could bring it out at a later date. Instead, I submitted the script featuring serial killer George Marlow, and the building of a case that may, or may not, convict him.

One of the most difficult aspects of *Prime Suspect* was naming my fictional DCI. That didn't come until very late in the process, way after the initial script had been submitted. One problem was that I wasn't permitted to use the surname of any serving Met police officer, male or female.

'Brownlow?'

'No, that's taken.'

'Cooper?'

'That's gone, too.'

'Tennison? Rather like the poet . . .'

'Yes, you can have that.'

Now I tell writers to think of names as if they were music. All of my names are melodic. In *Widows* there was Dolly Rawlins, Linda Perelli, Bella O'Reilly. Those names have cadence, they slip easily from the tongue. What could DCI Tennison's forename be? Angela? No, too clunky. Elizabeth? No, too prim. Jane? Jane Tennison.

That's it. DCI Jane Tennison. And my first victim would be Della. Della Mornay.

I sent my script off to Sally Head. Writer-for-hire at the whim of the TV executives once again. I waited, but the tip-off from Jenny Sheridan was not encouraging. 'They don't like it, Lynda,' she said when she called me. 'Come to the meeting, but I warn you, it's not good news.'

She was right. Sally didn't hold back.

'We find Jane Tennison heartless. And cold. I mean, she touches the body of that poor girl on the slab. She's not feminine. She's antagonistic. I just don't think we can do it, mate,' she said.

It's what happens in real life, I thought. And I say to writers now: write what you see. Not what you or someone else wants to see. I'd set out to research a drama about a crime and found institutional sexism alongside dedicated teams of people working to solve cases. *Prime Suspect* was *real*. But Sally didn't buy it.

'We're not going ahead, mate. We're running with a cop series set in Spain instead. Sorry it didn't work out.'

I felt numb. All those hours wasted. All that work gone. There was one consolation. In those days there was a system called Flexi-pool. Any scripts that didn't get commissioned were placed in a pool accessible to other broadcasters. If a commissioner picked it up, they could buy the script at a knock-down price. I held out little hope. In a heartbeat, *Prime Suspect* had gone the way of *Civvies* – unlikely to see the light of day.

Then, a very odd thing happened. A few months later I received a call from a Brian Eastman, who ran an independent production company called Carnival Films. I'd never heard of it, but he asked if I would meet with him.

'Sure, what's it about?'

'I have a proposal for you, Lynda.'

Brian did have some big-hitters under his belt, including Channel 4's *Porterhouse Blue,* the adaptation of Tom Sharpe's novel starring David Jason. Carnival was also behind ITV's *Forever Green* starring Pauline Collins. At the time, he was working on a film with Liam Neeson with a working title of *The Key.*

'I'd like you to write a film for me,' he announced when we met. 'A crime drama. Think blockbuster . . .'

Hang on a minute, I thought. It was all terribly confusing.

'OK, but let's start with how you found me?' I said.

Brian frowned, visibly taken aback. 'Don't you know?'

'Know what?'

At that moment Brian bent down, opened his desk drawer and pulled out a pile of paper, which he waved in front of me.

'This,' he said.

It was my script. *Prime Suspect.*

'What are you doing with that?'

'It's like piranhas round flesh, Lynda. There are commissioners tearing each other's eyes out over it. I wanted it, but I can't get it. Granada now say they aren't releasing it. It's bloody brilliant!'

Not a soul had told me, but sure enough, Sally Head got in touch soon after.

'Hello, mate. Look, I've got some good news. We've decided we're going with *Prime Suspect* after all. Do you want to come in, talk about casting?'

'Erm . . . yes!'

I was utterly gobsmacked.

That said, the mind-gremlins had also started to bite. Given my previous experience, I reckoned I might have a battle ahead. I had tremendous respect for Sally Head as a producer. She'd been behind the wonderful *Sherlock Holmes* series starring Jeremy Brett. After *Prime Suspect* she went on to produce the successful detective series *Cracker*. Kudos, too, for admitting she'd got it wrong. In fact, I admired her honesty in doing a U-turn.

But Sally wasn't Verity. She was tough, she was very good, but I didn't feel she wielded the same power. Also, she wasn't the kind of person who would run through scripts or work with me on edits. It wasn't her style.

Yet, what Sally did do was employ a terrific director for that first series: Christopher Menaul. I'd not met him and I was told he was no walk in the park.

'He's rather renowned for re-writing scripts,' Sally warned me.

To avoid any ill-will, she suggested he and I run through any cuts that would be needed.

A good plan of action, I thought. And a good sign of collaboration.

Chris turned out to be tall, white-haired, with a very commanding presence and a sensitivity to detail I had the utmost regard for. Sally had been right about him not being easy. When I first walked into the room he was sat behind two mountains of paper: one was my script, the second was his notes. Notes upon notes upon notes. Now I say that there are directors who read scripts, and then there are directors who read the thin lines in the scripts: the direction. Chris did that and more. But I had to fight for every line.

'Explain this scene to me, Lynda,' he'd say.

'Well, that's when DCI Tennison heads up her first briefing in the incident room.'

'OK, so why do we need this next scene? Bit over-long, isn't it?'

'No, that's really important because in the briefing room she's in control, but underneath she's terrified. We need to see that. We need to see her trembling as she leaves the room and walks down the corridor. It's her first case.'

'OK, I get it. That stays. Next . . .'

Left: My grandfather (whom I never met), my grandmother, Gertrude, and my mother, Florence Isabel Gertrude, as a little girl.

Right: My beautiful sister, Dail Margaret, and my brother, Michael William Henry Reid.

Left: My sister, Gillian Florence, with me and our bulldog Oswold – his claim to fame was that he sat on a mouse!

Right: Gillian, my elegant mother, Michael and me.

Unless otherwise stated, all photos are author's own

Left: Lynda Marchal (me!) in a role described as 'the most beautiful woman in Venice'. The principal of RADA had told me I was unlikely to ever be cast as a leading lady as I was rather short and plain-looking. When he came back-stage after the play to see me I told him to 'Fuck off'.

Right: Anthony Hopkins and me in Shakespeare, at the Liverpool Playhouse.

Left: All my own hair. Funnily enough one of the reviews said I had the longest legs they'd ever seen – it's surprising what you can achieve with a pair of fishnets!

Left: Harold Pinter's play *The Birthday Party*, showing me with Colin Welland who later wrote the script for the wonderful film *Chariots of Fire*.

Below: Me with Cliff Richard (yes, that's really him!) in *Life with Johnny*.

Below: Calamity Jane – my favourite role of all time.

Above: The dreaded *Lysistrata* – this is the play in which I met Lesley Joseph (far left) and Lynda Bellingham (far right). All of us were furious at having to wear huge fake blue tits! I am in the middle at the back.

Left: Me with the stars of *Widows* and the Director, Ian Toynton.

Below: Verity Lambert, me and Ian Toynton filming *She's Out* – we were trying to persuade Linda Marlow to come down from the tree!

Above: The four stars of *Widows*: Ann Mitchell, Maureen O'Farrell, Fiona Hendley and Eva Mottley. They are toasting their individual awards for Best Actress in a series – they all got one. © *Trinity Mirror / Mirrorpix / Alamy*

Above: *Prime Suspect*: Helen Mirren, Tom Bell, Craig Fairbrass and Richard Hawley. © *Everett Collection Inc / Alamy*

Above: Me filming a documentary, learning to fire every single type of gun.

Left: Michael Grade presenting me with the Dennis Potter BAFTA Award.
© *Mark Large/Daily Mail/Shutterstock*

Right: Me with my beloved son, Lorcan.

Left: My wonderful house in the Hamptons (US).

Above: This is where it all happens: plotting, writing, podcasting...

Right: Carol Cleveland and me – we met at RADA and we're still close friends today.

Above: Meeting the Queen at a reception for the dramatic arts at Buckingham Place. This was also where I met Steve McQueen for the first time. © *PA Images / Alamy*

Left: In front of the billboard for *Buried*, my first Jack Warr novel, which was published during lockdown.

Right: Me with my darling friend, Jeannie Boht, and Hugo. Sadly, Jean died shortly after this photograph was taken.

Left: Here I am with Maxim Jakubowski when I received the Crime Writers Association Diamond Dagger Award in July 2024 – it was a wonderful night.

Photo by Gary Stratmann

Right: The last book in my Tennison series. This book ends where the first series of *Prime Suspect* begins...

Left: Hanging out with Hugo.

When it came to other scenes Chris turned out to be spot-on in his judgement, even though I probably didn't agree with him at the time.

'The crushing of Jane's hand in the car door. Too much. Let's pull back. Let's have an officer open the back door for her, but for her to take the front seat.'

On and on it went.

Casting didn't run quite so smoothly. All kinds of names were being bandied around for Jane Tennison. Of course, I wanted a fresh face. Someone with calibre but who hadn't been seen on TV. Helen Mirren, I suggested. She was exactly the right age for Tennison. She was a heavyweight theatre actor who'd done a couple of notable films such as *Cal* and the avant-garde film *The Cook, The Thief, His Wife and Her Lover*. But Helen wasn't big on the small screen. And, by Christ, I had to fight my corner – as if TV executives knew anything about what happened in theatre!

'She's not acted enough TV leads,' became the consensus. Beyond belief!

'Look at her, she's phenomenal,' I said.

Eventually, when Helen did come in to read, she was dynamite. But even she hadn't been overly keen on the part. She needed to be persuaded.

Then, one afternoon I got a call from Sally Head.

'Just to let you know, Lynda. We've cast the lead for Marlow.'

'Oh really?'

As soon as I knew the actor who'd been chosen, I knew he wasn't right. Trust me, when you look up an actor on *Spotlight* and they claim they're five foot eight, always take two inches off. He was too short, too weedy. I dropped everything and jumped into a taxi headed for Granada's offices in Golden Square.

By the time I'd raced up to Sally's office I was gasping for breath.

I could sense the groans: '*Christ, what does she want now?*'

'That actor's not right,' I said.

'What's wrong with him?'

'It's the bodies of the girls,' I said, still panting. 'The killer puts them in thick plastic dry-cleaning bags. He walks out onto the street with them over his arm. He's got to be six foot tall at least, strong as a bull.'

'Oh, I see. Well, everyone thinks this guy is perfect.'

'Look,' I hammered the point. 'If that actor can carry me down this corridor over his arm, by all means have him. My guess is he can't.'

Casting director Doreen Jones got the hint. To her absolute credit, she went out and found John Bowe – at the time a complete unknown – who was absolutely wonderful in the part and went on to feature in many other TV series. In fact, for so many actors, *Prime Suspect* gave them the break of their lives.

That list included Zoë Wanamaker. I have to put my hands up and admit that at first I didn't think Zoë could cut the mustard. She was to play Moyra Henson, George Marlow's girlfriend, a beautician who lived in a council flat. In my view, Zoë was too posh. However, I conceded. And I couldn't have been more wrong, which is testament to Zoë's brilliant acting. She was superb. Yet at times Zoë herself wasn't sure she could play Moyra. Once in rehearsal, she stamped her foot with irritation. 'I just don't feel I've got her,' she said.

'Come with me,' I suggested.

That afternoon, we took a taxi to central London to visit the nail counter at Selfridges. The same lady was behind the desk, still selling acrylic nails.

'Watch her,' I told Zoë. She stood for a while and studied the woman, carefully taking in her mannerisms and demeanour.

'OK, got it.' Zoë nodded after a while.

Zoë also needed a fox-fur jacket. Identical acrylic nails. Once all of that was in place the part seemed to come naturally to her.

Funny some of the things I remember, too. A very young Ralph Fiennes played the boyfriend of another of Marlow's victims. It was his first TV acting gig. He wore a leather jacket that creaked constantly when he sat in the police interview room. He was awkward and unsure. *I'm not sure he'll go far as an actor*, I thought fleetingly. How wrong was I?

As for Helen, she ended up taking DCI Jane Tennison to another level. But that also took some work. Helen is a naturally sensual woman and early on during filming I noticed that when she spoke to male officers she smiled, touched their arms, called them by their first names. 'You can't do that,' I said. 'Forget everything that women do to put others at ease. If you touch them, you're not in charge. In that environment, they'll assume they can fuck you. Smile less, don't touch anyone and wear blouses buttoned up to your neck.' From that day on, Helen owned Jane Tennison.

As filming began on location, Jenny Sheridan became my eyes and ears on the ground. If there's one person who knew how important the script was to me, it was her. And if major scenes looked as though they might get cut or changed, she told me.

In rehearsals, I'd drummed it into John Bowe, playing the killer George Marlow, how he must convince the viewer of his innocence.

'Never show your guilt. Not one sign,' I told him. 'Not until the final interrogation when Marlow confesses.'

Instead, the one scene that would hold all the clues to Marlow's character would feature him and his mother, Doris, played so brilliantly by the ageing but beautiful Maxine Audley. That now-iconic sequence showed only Marlow and her. It was to be filmed at the North Pier in Blackpool. But it very nearly didn't happen.

Chris Menaul called me with the bad news.

'Too expensive. Really sorry. It's going to have to be cut,' I was told.

'What? But it's crucial!' I argued.

The scene needed to be filmed using a camera attached to a cherry-picker crane. Marlow would visit his mother in her nursing home and take her out for the afternoon on the pier. They'd sing Sinatra together and he'd spin her around in her wheelchair. Eventually, the shot would pull further and further back – an expanse of space that spotlighted their loneliness and the claustrophobia of their relationship, how only they understood one another.

'It can't be cut. It's everything!' I cried.

How my fax machine survived that twenty-four hours, I'll never know. There's not a single chief executive at Granada I didn't dash off a letter to.

'You cannot cut that scene,' I stressed. 'If it goes, my name comes off that script.' The fax was still chugging away in the early hours of the morning.

Another crucial scene was when Marlow talked to Moyra about Doris. It was lifted directly from my own life. An actor boyfriend, who I'd dated very briefly when I'd been in repertory theatre, told me that when his mother visited him at his private boarding school, he was standing with several other boys watching from the window when she walked out of the front gates. Suddenly a gust of wind blew, and her hair ended up on the pavement. In all those years she'd been his mother, he had no clue she wore a wig. She was such an elegant woman, but completely bald.

In *Prime Suspect*, Marlow told Moyra, 'Underneath all that glamour she was ugly.'

Moyra replied, 'Who would have known the Rita Hayworth of Warrington turned out to be Yul Brynner in disguise.'

I still remember typing that line.

Soon, though, I had another problem. I opened *The Stage* magazine to read that the new film coming out starring Liam Neeson, the film Brian at Carnival had been working on called *The Key* had now changed title to . . .

Prime Suspect.

What the hell?

Desperately, I rang Sally Head at Granada.

'We have a major problem. It's my title. They can't use it.'

But the reality was they could. I had no rights to it.

'Don't bother about it, it's a film. This is TV,' Sally had tried to pacify me.

'No, I *am* bothered,' I said. 'It's *my* title.'

In the end, Granada did nothing. Instead, I wrote to Brian Eastman myself and asked him, as a gentleman, if he would rename his film. To my surprise he did and I believe the film became the very successful *Under Suspicion*.

With all that going on, it's unfathomable to me that *Prime Suspect* ever made it to the screen, let alone became the success it did. From concept to final product, TV is such a spiky journey and so precarious for a writer.

That said, I was delighted with the final cut and the reaction to it. Rightly so, Helen won the BAFTA for Best Actress the following year and the series also scooped the Best Drama Serial. However, what was tough for me on that occasion was that Verity Lambert was on another table rooting for Alan Bleasdale's drama *GBH* to win. Her company, Cinema Verity, had produced the hard-hitting political series, and she'd been its executive producer. Of course, I understood. In fact, I admired how she always got behind her commissions but it was also a wake-up call about how tough the industry was and how I had to fight for any recognition.

That fight was only to continue. When a second series of *Prime Suspect* got commissioned, no one had bothered to check whether or not I was available to write it. I wasn't. I'd had to keep working, and in the intervening months Anglia had already commissioned me to write *Framed*, the two-parter series set in Spain. Incidentally, *Framed* had been a frustratingly protracted affair. Initially, a treatment had languished on the desk of the producer Judy Craymer for months. She'd contacted me desperate for a project but then sat on it. In the end I got so fed up I offered it to Anglia. 'She won't go far!' I concluded at the time. But, hands up, I was wrong. Judy went on to create the theatre production *Mamma Mia!* followed by its film adaptation starring Meryl Streep and Pierce Brosnan – all multi-million-pound hits.

As far as a second series of *Prime Suspect* was concerned, all power to the writer Allan Cubitt, who took my mapped-out story of the Black girl whose remains had been found, and wrote a compelling drama that explored the exact racial tensions I'd witnessed during my research. And credit to Sally Head, too, who had the balls to show a three-hour special with the seventy per cent Black cast I'd also envisaged. When TV takes bold steps like that it can be exhilarating. And Alan has gone on to become a superb talent. I rarely send fan mail, but when I watched his 2013 series *The Fall*, a gripping crime drama set in Northern Ireland starring Gillian Anderson, I wrote to him to tell him how much I'd enjoyed it.

In 1993, I came back to write a third *Prime Suspect*: a grisly tale of rent boys and sexual abuse. I scooped a BAFTA and an Emmy for it – lovely at the time. I also won the Edgar Allan Poe Award in the States in 1993 for the first series of *Prime Suspect*. I wish I'd realised at the time what a big deal that was – a bit of a joke, I thought at first. I had no idea it was so important! The framed award is now on the wall in my downstairs loo.

After that, however, I bowed out of *Prime Suspect*. I'd heard rumblings that Granada wanted to take Jane Tennison's character in a different direction. She was my character, my creation, and now I was being asked, 'Can you write Jane Tennison this way?'

I can't write by numbers! What writer worth their salt can? In my head, Jane was going to make it to the top position of commander. Challenge after challenge would stand in her way, but she'd do it. But the TV execs wanted to focus on more of her personal life. They wanted Jane to get pregnant and lose the baby; they wanted her private life to become a hot mess. Ultimately, they wanted to turn her into a raging alcoholic, ravaged by the pressures of the job, and worn down by crime and misogyny.

Why? I thought. *Why do that to her?*

Why create an iconic character like Jane Tennison, fighting every inch to claw her way up, thrash through the barriers, and then make her fail? Wouldn't it be more interesting to see the sexism and racism and the closing of rank at a higher level, and expose exactly what she would have been up against?

For me, *Prime Suspect* was all about showing for the first time women in control: women being powerful and interesting to the wider world. Women whose determination and professionalism would triumph in the end. Sure, Jackie's behind-the-scenes life was more akin to the character Granada wanted. At that time she'd not been made public as my source. And it wasn't until after Jackie retired in 1997 that she revealed herself and her own story. And while I took aspects of Jane Tennison from Jackie, her character was never a carbon copy. Throughout my research I'd also talked with one other female DCI who hadn't worked with me initially, but who I got to know and observe over time. She was headed for the top. Many years after *Prime Suspect* she got there. And she's still there today. Tough it most certainly was, but she did it.

Moreover, I was never against Jane being flawed, or even having a drink problem. What I objected to was that being a main focus. What I was being asked to write, I didn't want to deliver. For me, it was too much of a compromise.

Although my involvement with *Prime Suspect* stopped, I was exceptionally pleased that Helen went on win many more BAFTAs and Emmys. In every interview I've read, Helen has always thanked me for *Prime Suspect*. Zoë Wanamaker and John Bowe too have also been so appreciative of how it launched their careers. In 2021, we celebrated the thirtieth anniversary of *Prime Suspect* at a special event held at the British Film Institute. Zoë and John sat alongside me as we reminisced about that debut series. It was a wonderful, insightful event.

But as I write, a toxic culture of institutional racism, misogyny and homophobia remains a cancer at the heart of the Met Police, alongside other forces and institutions such as the Fire Service. That the themes I highlighted in *Prime Suspect* still resonate today makes me incredibly sad. When asked at the time what I wanted to come of writing *Prime Suspect*, I said that I wanted anyone who'd experienced tragedy in their family – be it murder, rape, or robbery – to accept a female officer if they stepped into their home to head up an investigation. I do feel that public acceptance of women in the force has changed. Somehow, though, I knew the internal battle against discrimination would take far longer to overcome.

Chapter 13
Entwined

Jeanne F. Bernkopf was a brusque New Yorker, and a woman who became my mainstay for a short while in the novel-writing world. There's a handful of people whose professional care and friendship I have cherished, and Jeanne is one of them. Like Verity Lambert had been with my TV scripts, Jeanne guided my novel writing with a firm but gentle hand and I will always be thankful for the contribution she made to my career.

The funny thing was, I hadn't actually chosen Jeanne. After the debacle with Michael Korda over my first novel, *The Legacy*, I was told by the dukkerin – the gypsy fortune-teller – that one day I was going to meet a woman wearing purple who'd become very important to me. By the early 1990s I was being represented by the literary agent Gill Coleridge and had moved to the publisher Simon & Schuster in the UK under commissioner Suzanne Baboneau, who I'd first met at Pan Macmillan. Simon & Schuster's sister company took care of the American publishing arm. And, when I walked into Jeanne's office in New York, there she was. Early-sixties. Purple dress. Mauve headscarf. I had no interest in meeting anyone else. Fortunately, Jeanne also turned out to be a giant among editors.

I hadn't written a novel since *Bella Mafia*. I'd put so much energy into *Prime Suspect*, *Framed* and *Comics*, and although I had some ideas swilling around, there was no biggie I'd been working on. Jeanne had an idea, though.

'I'm going to take you somewhere,' she told me when I was next in the city. 'I think it should be your next book.'

Jeanne was Jewish, and very connected to the Jewish community in New York. She'd heard of an extraordinary gathering that was to take place in a downtown hotel. As I recall, it had been arranged by a foundation whose work it was to reunite Holocaust survivors and to keep alive the memory of Jews who had suffered so much during internment in the Nazi war camps during the Second World War.

This meeting was to be one of the most emotional experiences of my life. More than that, it woke me up to a history I had very little knowledge of. Between 1943 and 1945 as many as 3,000 twins had been transported to Auschwitz-Birkenau in cattle cars and made the subject of the most disturbing and inhumane experiments, carried out at the hands of the so-called Angel of Death, Dr Mengele – SS officer and physician to Hitler. Some twins had been transported aged as young as three years old.

Identical twins were of particular interest to the German biomedical researchers who supported the Nazi ideology of racial science – the supposed superiority of the Ayrian 'race'. As well as being interested in genetics, Mengele wanted to understand whether twins were telepathic. They were subjected to blood transfusions, injected with diseases, their limbs got amputated, one was starved while the other overfed. They were also murdered. If one twin died, the other would be killed so Mengele could compare their organs. Appalling cruelty beyond belief.

When the camps were liberated by the Soviet Red Army in 1945, many twins were separated, each one unaware of whether their brother or sister had survived or where they'd been taken to. This foundation had worked to bring together twins, siblings and other survivors more than forty years later.

I don't recall names or faces, but if I close my eyes I can still feel overwhelmed at the memory of walking into the hotel's cavernous function room. It was a maelstrom of emotion – excitement, tears, laughter – an intensity like no other. Some adults were standing with cards hanging around their necks. The messages were incredible: *I was number such-and-such in the fourth bunk at a certain barracks. Do you remember me?* Lives filled with loss and longing, devastation and hope. I found it impossible to put myself in these people's shoes.

I stood quietly alongside Jeanne as she said her hellos to the people she knew. Then, the speeches began. One set of twins had been separated and had only recently been reunited. One had been found in Australia and the other taken to Israel. When they were found, they were wearing the same dress. Imagine that. More than a coincidence, surely?

'What do you think?' Jeanne turned to me. 'Do you think you could write about this?'

Honestly, I wasn't sure.

The enormity of these people's experiences had shaken me. When we came away from the venue I could barely speak.

'I don't know, Jeanne. I'm not sure I can,' I confessed.

'Think about it. I believe you can do it,' she told me firmly.

Jeanne's faith in me was far greater than any faith I had in myself.

My main hesitancy was that I didn't feel that this story belonged to me. As a writer, I always felt I had licence to explore worlds alien to my own, but this felt different. I wasn't Jewish. I didn't have family who'd suffered at the hands of the Nazi regime. What if I got it wrong? What if I offended someone who'd been there or whose life had been touched by such darkness? What if I cheapened it?

To do any story justice I needed to devote time and care to it, and this one even more so. It felt overwhelming.

'Let me think about it,' I promised Jeanne.

When I got back to the UK, I began some initial research. The British Museum had an extensive collection of Holocaust archives and I started my work there. Within days I was on first-name terms with the museum staff. They would be seeing a lot of me in the months to come.

I also began to contact organisations through which I could meet more Holocaust survivors face-to-face. Twins were almost impossible to find – so few were left – but I was very grateful for any first-hand interaction with people who had endured the camps. Whatever story I built, its backbone had to be based on truth. Nothing less would do.

As I started reading about survivors – some of whom were twins, others of whom were siblings – the same stories kept recurring. Relatives had not seen each other since the camps, yet when they were found or reunited they might be wearing identical glasses or own the same item of clothing.

As well as that remarkable aspect, I also became fascinated by what happened psychologically to the victims. Given my research into PTSD for *Civvies*, I understood that extreme levels of trauma could change the course of people's lives forever.

Admittedly, the horror of what these people went through, and continued to go through, was devastating. Many had never been able to live their lives without psychological help. They had suffered severe mental breakdowns. Survivors got routinely institutionalised, unable to break free from the torment. Many suffered ongoing physical problems.

I rang Jeanne. 'I've started, but it's a lot to take on. I don't think I can,' I repeated to her.

Jeanne was incredibly insistent. 'Yes, you can, Lynda. It's an important story. If your story is about twins, it's not been told and I want you to tell it.'

I took a deep breath and got back to work.

Becoming so invested in a book can be both a curse and a blessing. It gives your writing depth and authenticity but your mind can also get scattered in different directions. When I wrote *The Legacy*, it was my passion combined with inexperience that sent me to the far corners of the country. In truth, I was having such a good time researching. This time around it was deep emotion mixed with avoidance and fear.

I sketched out an initial idea. Mengele's twins would be at this story's heart. One – Ruda Kellerman – would never have recovered from the horrors of the camp. She would be psychologically marked – a child sex worker turned lion-trainer: criminal and dangerous. The other twin, Baroness Vebekka Maréchal, was to have led a very different life. One of privilege. On liberation, she would be taken and raised in Philadelphia, equally as scarred – a schizophrenic – but able to seek help. The Berlin Wall had not yet fallen when I began working on *Entwined* and that's where the twins would reunite with devastating consequences at the story's climax.

I booked a flight to Berlin and walked around the city, making notes. The stark concrete separating East from West; the checkpoints; the uniform greyness of the East compared with the Technicolor of the West; the image of two sides of the same city looking at one another, with no perfect symmetry, all swirled around in my mind.

Back in the UK at the British Museum, I became such a regular that archivists allowed me to watch film footage not for public consumption. Gruesome images of the concentration camps upon liberation. Bodies moving but barely alive, skin as thin as tissue paper. One film I watched was of the army searching an SS officer's villa during liberation. As the dining room door opened a whole family were sat eerily upright, dead in their chairs: familial suicide through strychnine poisoning. And then there were the documents of the experiments on prisoners themselves: savage in their depravity and dehumanisation. I found a lot of it almost unbearable to plough through.

Believe it or not, it is the one and only reason in *Entwined* that Ruda Kellerman is a lion trainer in a travelling circus. As I continued, I desperately needed a joyful distraction, another strand to the narrative to keep me going. Big cats, horses and monkeys all became my safety net. There was only so much of Auschwitz I could expose myself to.

Jeanne would check in now and again to see how I was doing. I suspect also to persuade me otherwise if she caught wind of any change of heart. At first, Jeanne's calls spurred me on.

'How's it going, Lynda?'

'Still researching.'

'OK, anything you need, let me know.'

'Sure. And thank you, Jeanne.'

The famous Barnum & Bailey Circus – billed the *Greatest Show on Earth* – had its base in Florida but travelled the length and breadth of the United States. I combined a meeting with Jeanne in New York with a visit to its big top. Gunther Gebel-Williams had been its most famous trainer there, now in a state of semi-retirement. Straw-blond hair, bulging muscles: that man oozed charisma. Yet when Gunther hopped off his chair to greet me, we were exactly the same height. The man was tiny!

'So, Lynda, what do want to know?'

'Well . . .'

Typical La Plante, so many questions.

Exactly how many days I spent with the Barnum & Bailey Circus I'm not sure but Gunther and the whole shebang captivated me. He'd been born in Hitler's Germany and had emigrated to the States soon after his circus show was discovered by American show owner Irvin Feld. Dozens of elephants, tigers, horses, and parrots all travelled with him across the Atlantic. Perhaps I imagined his muddle of animals to be a far grander version of the menagerie I'd grown up with in Crosby. I've always had a preoccupation with creatures great and small.

Gunther was famed for casually draping a leopard or a black panther around his shoulders like a scarf during shows. These are almost untrainable animals, yet he had this superhuman power to soothe these giant beasts. One of his panthers had developed an infected jaw and when he died, Gunther had him stuffed. As we talked, I stroked its head.

Gunther's German accent had softened over the years. 'You know, Lynda, there are wildings – lions and elephants – that can never fully be trained. These animals, they don't play games with you.'

'Really? Tell me more . . .'

'They will turn on a trainer, attack them.'

For all Gunther's scratches it was extraordinary that he'd never had a life-threatening moment. Although, as he explained, scratches could be more dangerous. Sepsis was common. The only time he ever had snipers trained on his tigers was when he took a bow in the auditorium; he was most vulnerable with his back turned to them. In *Entwined*, Mamon became my wilding lion, using every characteristic Gunther described. He also showed me how the animals were thrown meat, where they slept, what their habits were and how their personalities were unique. He talked me through the props and plinths and pedestals the circus used. One trick Gunther was famed for was back-flipping onto an elephant. He could get tigers to dance and jump through hoops of fire. In the ring, he'd been able to unite natural enemies: tigers, elephants and horses who performed in one steel cage.

'The Russians. These people are the most incredible trainers,' he told me. One very famous trick first performed in Russia can only be described as a human–animal Catherine Wheel. The tigers would form a large circle. Every time the trainer yelled the command the circle would become tighter: '*Upo . . . upahh! Hup! Hup!*' Then the tigers would split into two groups and weave around each other. Tighter and tighter they spun, keeping the circle revolving while the trainer remained at the centre of the pack.

'There's an old film of Russian trainers doing this. But I've never seen it,' Gunther said.

Every night after I got back to my hotel room I made my notes.

Jeanne rang again. 'You're still here, Lynda?'

'Jeanne, yes, I'm in still in New York. I went to the circus to learn how to train big cats . . .'

'Train big cats?'

'Yes, cats . . .'

'Train big cats in a circus, Lynda? What's that got to do with Mengele's twins? That's a helluva plot twist!'

'Well, it's just something I've been thinking about.'

'No, you're deviating, Lynda. You're deviating.'

'Yes, but there's this wilding lion . . .'

'No, you're deviating.'

I could never admit to Jeanne that the circus was my only form of escape from Mengele's twins.

'Well, OK, Lynda, but get back to Berlin and the twins soon, you hear me?'

Whenever I was in New York I would take Jeanne snippets of chapters I'd written and she would run through them line by line. Jeanne gave superb notes. She pointed out something about my writing that has always stayed with me. 'You're afraid of the perfect line,' she said. 'You write diamond lines, but then you cloud them with marcasite.' She was absolutely right; I didn't yet have full confidence in my novel writing. Her scored-out words and marks and mentorship taught me so much.

Back in the UK, I continued researching at the British Library. Then I stumbled on a poster for Chipperfield's Circus in Ham, near Richmond. Actually, I'd already found out everything I ever needed to know about big tops, big cats, big everything. But I didn't want to get back to the twins. In my story they'd both arrived in Berlin – Ruda with her travelling circus and Vebekka to seek treatment. Their pasts were yet to be revealed and they still had not met. I debated whether to include more gruesome descriptions of the experiments they'd both undergone, and the enormity of their physical and mental injuries – a hard call for any writer. I had to, I concluded. *It was real. It happened. Write what you see,* I told myself.

In the final draft, I included so much graphic imagery – I didn't want the story to be taken lightly – but even those details I tempered. There's a fine line between truth and knowing what an audience can take, knowing when to pull back. As I continued, I sought out more and more distraction.

In Ham, I poked my head around the tarpaulin to find a man with dyed black hair and a moustache, dressed in a safari suit. Two lions slept in the steel cage at the back of the tent.

'Excuse me, I'd like to find out more about your circus,' I said.

He smiled and agreed to talk. The lions were so old and arthritic. They could barely haul themselves up onto a plinth.

'I am waiting for them to die,' he said rather sadly. 'But you can never think a lion's life is over.'

Then, he told me a story. Not long ago, one of the circus hands had been placing rows of chairs in the tent when one row collapsed and ricocheted down. One of the lions had charged at him. Within seconds the animal was on the circus hand's back, mauling him to death. The young man had been saved only by the speedy reaction of those around him, who had rushed over and prised the beast from his body.

'I have footage of when these two were younger. Amazing creatures. Would you like to see it?' the man asked.

'Yes, please!'

His trailer sat at the back of the circus park. By God, it stank. Chimps were also part of his act and he let them roam free. I perched on a cheap foam mattress sofa and waited patiently while he rummaged around his stack of VHS tapes. As he did, a baby chimp that had been sitting at the sofa's edge crept closer and closer. Its hand grabbed my leg. I gently pushed it back. The man kept on searching. This chimp wasn't taking no for an answer. It jumped and began to grope my waist.

'Stop it!' I muttered under my breath.

Eventually, the tape of the lions appeared and the man knelt on his hands and knees adjusting the TV set.

With lightning speed, the chimp now had my left breast in its clutches.

'Get off!' I hissed, pulling its fingers from my T-shirt.

'Look, they were so young then.' The man looked dreamily at the screen.

When he turned, I was clobbering his chimp half to death. 'I'm so sorry!' I said.

The chimp now restrained, we talked on. I happened to mention Gunther and his story about the Catherine Wheel of tigers. And how the Russians were renowned for training those animals.

The guy stopped dead in his tracks.

'My family are Russian,' he said. 'My grandfather had tigers in a spinning wheel. Look, here.'

He rummaged around for another tape – this time an old Cine Tape, which he slotted into an ancient-looking projector. Absolutely remarkable. Old black-and-white footage of a trainer surrounded by tigers spinning.

'That's worth something,' I told him. It was simply marvellous and I have always wondered whatever happened to that footage and that man.

Jeanne checked in with me once again. Her phone calls were becoming more frequent and intense. In all honesty, I was starting to resent the extreme pressure she was putting me under.

'A chimp, Lynda? I don't want to hear about the goddamn chimp. What's happening with the twins? Have they met in Berlin yet?'

I couldn't confess to Jeanne that I'd reached another impasse. I was struggling to write a single word.

'Yes! They've met!' I lied.

Then one day, I simply broke down. *I can't write this book*, I thought. It's what I'd known from the start. This time I felt duty-bound to tell Jeanne.

'Jeanne, I'm so sorry. I can't go on. My book is an insult to these victims. It's about the Holocaust. It's about Mengele. What I am doing is not good enough,' I said.

There was a long, cold silence on the end of the line.

'Lynda, if only one person reads this book and it means something to them, then you've succeeded. That's all you want. One person. Now for Christ's sake finish it!'

Entwined limped on to the finish line.

After that conversation I got a phone call from Jeanne most Sundays. I sensed a desperation in her voice that I couldn't fathom. She pressed me so, so hard.

'I'm on the last chapter, Jeanne, but I can't finish it.'

'This has to stop now, Lynda. Finish it. Finish it. Finish it.'

I considered blocking Jeanne's calls, but I had far too much respect for her and I didn't want to let her down.

On the weekend I finally completed the manuscript I called her.

'Jeanne. I'm done. I'm finished. I'm putting a copy in the post.'

'Hallelujah, Lynda. I'm reading it the minute it arrives.'

Seriously, I *was* done. *Entwined* had drained me of all my spirit. There and then, I decided I didn't want to go back to novel-writing for some time. I'd also never been so anxious waiting for an editor's response. But Jeanne never called. Not that week. Nor the week after. Unfathomable for a woman who had been so unrelenting.

One evening the phone rang. Richard was at home and he answered it.

'Lynda!' he shouted. 'There's a call for you.'

'Who is it?'

'Someone called Mike Bernkopf.' He shrugged.

My stomach hit the floor. *Christ. Jeanne hates it and doesn't want to publish. She's got her bloody husband to tell me! I knew it. I should've listened to my gut,* I thought.

'I don't want to talk to him,' I mouthed to Richard.

'I think you should, he sounds kind of strange,' he whispered.

I'd never met Jeanne's husband, although she'd talked about him often.

'OK,' I conceded.

Richard was right. Mike did sound strange. Muffled, quiet, but calm.

'Hi Mike. Everything OK?'

'I'm going to make this very brief, Lynda. Jeanne died suddenly. I just wanted you to know that.'

My body started to crumple.

'I'm so sorry . . .'

'I also want you to know that she had your manuscript with her. She'd finished it. She loved it. It's her story, Lynda. The Holocaust is her story.'

My legs almost gave way under me.

It was only then I learned that many of Jeanne's family had perished in the camps. In the whole time I'd been working with her, she'd never mentioned it once.

To this day whenever I embark on a book tour, there's always someone in the audience who will ask me about *Entwined*. I still find it so emotional to talk about the book without feeling deeply affected by its subject matter or hearing Jeanne's voice: 'If only one person reads this book and it means something to them, then you've succeeded. That's all you want. One person.' I dedicated *Entwined* to Jeanne.

* * *

Entwined was published in 1992 – the same year that Jeanne died. But it was while promoting the book that I encountered another very curious episode. This time, I'd embarked on a worldwide speaking tour that took me to far-flung places like New Zealand, and it was there that past and present were to mysteriously collide.

Months before I'd finished writing *Entwined*, Richard's mother, The General, had been visiting my home. Upstairs in the guest bedroom, I kept a shelf of books. My old publishers, Pan Macmillan, had been getting rid of old or damaged novels and, instead of them being pulped, I'd brought a bin liner home. Prison libraries were always desperate for books and these could be put to good use. I picked out a selection to send to a male prison, setting aside a series of novels about a Victorian female detective. *Men probably won't read those,* I reckoned. I'd completely forgotten about them until The General appeared one morning.

'Lynda, I love these books. They're so exciting!' she said as she continued to glue her face to one at the breakfast table.

The books were written by a crime author called Anne Perry. When I took a closer look, I had an idea. *These could make a great TV series,* I thought. In my mind a classic BBC period drama. A female *Sherlock Holmes;* Sherlock with bosoms! That could be interesting ... When I contacted the publisher, Anne agreed to meet with me. Before that, I hadn't the faintest clue who Anne Perry was, only that she'd travelled to London for the meeting from a remote fishing village in Scotland where she lived. Admittedly, I didn't exactly warm to her. She was in her fifties, a quietly spoken lady, rather reserved and mistrustful, you might say. Her shoulders were wrapped in a plaid cashmere shawl and her tawny red hair looked cemented on.

'I'd really like to buy the rights to these,' I told her.

My proposal was to acquire rights to write one pilot episode which could then be pitched to network commissioners. After that we met a couple more times when I'd read more of her work. One story we discussed was of concern to me as I felt it wouldn't work on-screen. The murder was rather inconceivable as a wire cheese-cutter had been used. Why? And how?

'I'm just not sure about this,' I confessed.

Anne leaned in and said rather menacingly, 'Believe me. It will work.'

On around our third meeting Anne brought with her a stern-looking lady, apparently from Granada TV, who sat and took notes throughout. To establish the character of her detective, the pilot needed a bold opening, I explained. In the books her detective was a little tame. But all our discussions felt discordant from the outset. Anne conceded nothing, but increasingly deferred to her butch chaperone.

Any potential work with Anne remained on hold while I promoted *Entwined* abroad. Book tours can be exhausting and New

Zealand felt like another world away. One nice thing happened, though. Before I left, I'd received a message from an actor, Rea, now living in Auckland. She and I went way back. She'd performed alongside me in Aristophane's *Lysistrata* all those years ago at the Oxford Playhouse. She'd seen my name on a poster and asked if I'd join her for a coffee while I was in the city. We hadn't been close, but it would be lovely to meet.

In the intervening years, Rea had continued acting but she was also writing and producing theatre. Her latest play was a twisted tale of two schoolgirls who had bludgeoned to death one of the girls' mothers. The backstory was remarkable and had been based on a real case dating back to 1954. Two girls, Juliet Hulme and Pauline Parker, had had an obsessive, probably lesbian teenage relationship. When Parker's mother stopped them from being together they killed her. Hulme had agreed to help her friend commit the murder by wielding a brick in a sock. Both served time for the killing, but had been freed, handed new identities, and moved abroad.

'We've tried to get in touch with them to find out more, but it's impossible,' Rea said. 'We've researched it by pulling out all the press clippings we can find to piece together the story. Apparently, one girl went to America and joined a Mormon church. We believe she's dead now.'

The story captivated me from the outset.

'Can I look through your work?' I asked.

'Sure, we'd love you to.'

A couple of days later, Rea invited me to the little theatre where she and her husband had been rehearsing the play. In a back room they brought out all the clippings they'd amassed so I could sift through.

'Here, these are pictures taken at the time of the trial,' she said. 'This is the girl we now believe is dead.'

I glanced down at the inky black-and-white shot. I looked again, peering into the picture.

'I don't think she is dead,' I said, startled. I could barely believe it.

'I beg your pardon?'

'That girl. She's not dead. I'm sure of it. Her name is Anne Perry and I'm working with her,' I said.

The girl had the exact same stuck-on hair, the same eyes and the same roundish face. *Unmistakable,* I thought.

'This can't be true!'

'Believe it. I'm 99.9 per cent sure,' I concluded.

That afternoon, my promotional schedule kicked in with a radio interview with the main broadcaster in Auckland. *Entwined* was all about coincidence: two girls with a shared past brought together by chance. The host wanted to explore that further.

'I don't believe in coincidences,' I replied.

'You don't?'

'No, life happens but coincidences exist outside of fact. They don't just happen,' I said.

The interviewer kept pressing me on the subject, all of which got me rather irritated.

'Look, I'll tell you about a coincidence,' I said. 'There's a theatre production on in this very city and the producer of that show believed one of the girls portrayed in it was dead. But she's not dead. She's called Anne Perry and I'm working with her.'

At the time, I didn't think too much about blurting Anne's name out. I was still so shocked at the bizarreness of it all. But that evening, back in my hotel room, my phone rang.

'It's reception. Can we put a call through to you, Mrs La Plante?'

'Of course, sure.'

I still have no inkling who was on the other end of the line, but the voice was female, gruff and very threatening.

'We heard you on the radio. We're warning you. Don't ever mention Anne Perry again. We protect her privacy and we don't like it.'

At that, the line clicked off and I sat on the edge of the bed, feeling shaken. I didn't mention Anne Perry again, not in New Zealand and not when I returned home to the UK. I had one more meeting with Anne, but she was incredibly hostile. The offer of me buying the rights to her novels was suddenly removed from the table.

'We don't want to pursue this project. Granada TV will do it,' I was told.

The whole episode completely disappeared from my thoughts until a couple of years later when I opened up a newspaper. There was Anne staring out at me once more. *Extraordinary!* Same eyes, same face. A film was due to be released about the Parker-Hulme trial called *Heavenly Creatures,* directed by Peter Jackson and starring Kate Winslet. A journalist had tracked Anne down to her village in Scotland. She was still a Mormon and a prominent figure in the church there. In the feature she admitted to being the real Juliet Hulme, a murderer who had served her sentence but who'd been trying to live a normal life thousands of miles from the scene of her crime. Part of me felt vindicated. The revelation also went some way to explaining Anne's coldness. Is it ever possible to shake off such a past? And what a strange fate that brought her and I together . . .

Chapter 14
Civvies – The Return

Writers for TV rarely experience hits. Two hits are even rarer. In my view TV doesn't nurture talent like it should. All too often it moves on to the next hot new writer and discards whoever it perceives as a failure. Failure, by the way, is hardly ever the sole responsibility of any writer. Doubtless, some scripts are beyond salvation but successful programmes also get shoved into graveyard slots with no explanation, actors get wrongly cast, budgets get squeezed and production values get compromised – a complicated array of factors I had been grappling with from the beginning. Yet with the double hit of *Widows* and *Prime Suspect*, my phone was red-hot for the first time in my career.

One call was from my then TV and film agent Duncan Heath's office. A message had come through my agent's wife, Hilary, that Mick Jagger and David Bowie wanted to meet with me to discuss an upcoming movie project – a crime thriller, apparently.

A date was duly arranged and I trotted off to meet them in a central London hotel where they'd booked a suite for the day. I'd not met either before and when I did, I wasn't quite sure what to make of them. Both looked rather pallid and they were clearly hungover.

'OK, well, let's kick off. What kind of story are you looking for?' I asked, sipping a morning coffee.

'Well, we thought of . . . a murder mystery . . .' Jagger piped up.

'OK . . . a murder mystery . . . on the road?' I enquired.

'Yeah . . . on the road . . .' he said, before turning to Bowie to double-check.

'What do you mean "on the road"?' Bowie asked.

'Well, as in a murder on the road – while a rock band is touring?' I replied.

'Oh no, no, no,' Bowie shook his head. 'We didn't want that. We wanted a murder on the Orient Express . . .'

Suddenly, I could see Jagger frowning.

'No, David . . . we decided against the Orient Express . . .' he said under his breath to Bowie.

'Well, we thought it would make a great movie. Agatha Christie's done it, hasn't she?' Bowie continued as if he hadn't heard.

I sat and smiled politely, but the truth was I could barely believe that this was their big idea.

'So, you want a murder on the Orient Express? Are you going to be rock stars travelling on it?' I probed a little further.

'Oh no, no, no,' Jagger frowned again. 'We don't want to play ourselves. We want to be characters . . .'

'Right,' I said. After that, I sat for a good fifteen minutes while Jagger and Bowie batted back and forth, trying to recall whatever plot they had discussed the previous evening under the influence of God knows what.

'I could be the assassin!' shouted Jagger at one point.

'No, I wanted to be the assassin,' Bowie replied.

'OK, but if you're the killer, who am I?' Jagger shot back.

In the end, I lost patience. It seemed pointless me even being there.

'Look, you two. When you have an idea, call me. I'll come back and talk then,' I said.

Needless to say, I never heard from either Jagger or Bowie again.

Another one of those random calls was from Peter Cregeen, head of series at the BBC. Suddenly, the broadcaster wanted to resuscitate *Civvies* long after it had died. Lynda La Plante was now a saleable, promotable 'name'. My reply?

'Big problem, Peter. Big, big problem.'

My original script had told the upbeat story of a group of ex-paratroopers, rejected from mainstream employment after they'd returned home traumatised by war. They'd launched their own security business and made a success of it. Initially Peter thought I could simply dust off the script for *Civvies*, but I couldn't.

'OK, so what's the problem, Lynda?'

'Well, the business didn't work out. It failed. They destroyed everything.'

And that's exactly what had happened. Back in 1987 when I'd started writing *Civvies* my £30,000 bank loan had got the company up and running. The Sentinels were a taxi firm going places, but it didn't take long for the wheels to come off. Months in, Barclays Bank had contacted me. The initial repayment hadn't been made and I was in danger of defaulting on the loan. When I rang the office, the line was dead. When I swung by, it sat empty. No cars, no van, no trace of the men whatsoever. And no word from the ex-paratrooper Jim, who I'd spent so long with meticulously recording his story, and those of the other men struggling to survive.

Peter was all ears. 'So, what happened to the men?'

'Well, the majority are in prison. Some for nasty offences, too.'

In fact, it had taken me a while to find out what did happen. My money had gone, I'd accepted that. But when I dug around my contacts I found out that one man had committed suicide. The rest were in prison, either on remand or serving a sentence. One had committed rape. There was theft and violence. As far as the business was concerned, the cars had been trashed and the van used in a bank robbery.

'I'm sorry, Peter, the uplifting finale doesn't wash any more. The story ended on a rather bad note, I'm afraid.'

Peter mulled it over. 'That *could* be more interesting. Might you be willing to rework it?'

Emotionally, I felt pulled in all directions.

'Let me think about it,' I said.

Initially, I kept asking myself: do I *really* want to revisit this story? I was still furious with those men, betrayed by them. On the other hand, perhaps Peter was right. My original script had been a hard-hitting but a sympathetic portrayal of men offered no support. They were all suffering from PTSD. Whatever they'd done, didn't their current situation reinforce that need for help? The first Gulf War had been over for just four years and British troops were still stationed in Northern Ireland. To this day there isn't adequate help for men who have returned from war. *Civvies* was an angry plea to the government to recognise the condition and do something. *Do it and be dammed*, I thought. Damned I most certainly was . . .

Revisiting *Civvies* would involve tracking the men down to whichever prison they were incarcerated in and re-interviewing them. That didn't fill me with much joy. *Civvies* had been tough to research and write. However, with my network of prison contacts it didn't take me too long to find them. Jim agreed to talk and, when I arrived one afternoon at the prison he was housed at, he looked beat.

'What happened?' I asked.

'I don't know,' he told me. 'I couldn't get anything right. We couldn't get anything right. We lost control of everything.'

In all the months I'd spent with Jim, I'd seen a proud military man but underneath all that machismo there was a lost child. Now it was ever more apparent that it was the lost child I was speaking to.

That day, a very strange thing occurred after I left the prison. As I got into my car, I was just about to turn the ignition key when I felt something clatter against my ankle. I looked down and stopped dead. Sellotaped to the end of a toothbrush was a sharp blade. *Who's been in my car?* I panicked. This homemade shiv – an improvised prison knife – was the most lethal weapon I'd ever seen. I racked my brain. I'd never transported a prisoner, and this was 100 per cent prison-made. I still have no clue how that knife found its way into my car or who hid it. Whoever it was was very, very dangerous.

I reworked *Civvies*. I wanted it to be an uncompromising watch but, just like the first version, a nuanced portrayal of these men and their families. I could not have predicted what a fraught journey it would be. My heart hit the floor when I found out which director had been assigned to the project. Karl Francis wasn't a person I knew to be across detail in the way that Ian Toynton or Christopher Menaul had been.

In fact, Francis went on to direct another of my scripts after *Civvies* – an episode of a production I simply had to wash my hands of. It was called *The Lifeboat*, set on a Welsh rescue boat. Francis was also one of the executive producers, and Irish actor Brendan Gleeson had been cast as the lead coxswain.

'He's *Irish*. It's a drama set in Wales, with a Welsh coxswain,' I argued.

'Ach, it doesn't matter. No one will notice,' Francis had tried to mollify me, as if I shouldn't worry my pretty little head about such a glaring oversight.

While Brendan Gleeson was, and is, a fine actor, it *did* matter.

When Ruth Caleb, also an executive producer, brought me a tape of the title music it felt like the kiss of doom. An operatic din.

'Are you serious?' I asked.

Eventually, when *The Lifeboat* aired in 1994, some people thought it was wonderful. In my mind, it sank without much of a trace.

As far as *Civvies* was concerned there were also major casting errors. Jason Isaacs was to play the lead role of Frank Dillon, the character I'd based on Jim. Talk about a bull in a china shop. Jason had an over-inflated ego from the off. Before he'd even walked onto set he was demanding fake chest hair, insisted on doing his own make-up and wanted to do fight scenes without a stuntman. Yet he was *so* inexperienced. Worse than that, I felt he simply didn't understand the complexity of the character.

In one read-through I remember coaching him over and over. It was a sequence where Frank was at home with his wife, struggling to readjust to domestic life: a rare moment of intimacy between the couple and where Frank's vulnerability was laid bare. What was Jason Isaacs doing? Stomping around, chucking his cigarette butt on the floor, growling like a grizzly bear.

'Why are you turning this character into an animal?' I asked him. 'He's at home with his wife and family, for God's sake.'

But he wouldn't listen and turned the volume up to full blast at every turn.

In the end, I found Jason Isaac's performance loathsome. Some years later he was mooted for a brief role in the series I made called *Trial and Retribution*. I wasn't keen but I agreed to give him a shot. He didn't even bother turning up to the audition. *Fuck you*, I thought and I never asked again.

That said, I do believe there were outstanding performances in *Civvies*. Peter Howitt – who played Steve Harris, the ex-paratrooper with the throat injury – did so wonderfully. He had originally read for the lead role, but he didn't have quite the right physical presence. And Lennie James – a complete unknown – gave a superb performance as paratrooper Cliff Morgan. I loved Lennie from the off. He turned out to be such a versatile actor with a great range and emotional directness. After *Civvies* I used him again. I have always championed Lennie. What's more, he's a delightful man to boot.

Unbeknown to me, Lennie could also sing. He ended up recording the theme tune to *Civvies:* a track called 'Go and Be Brave'. Originally, I had been lucky enough to secure the Dire Straits song 'Brothers in Arms' – a haunting tune inspired by the Falklands War. Moreover, the band had very generously offered it to me free of charge. One of its members had known Eva Mottley, who'd so tragically taken her own life during the making of *Widows* series two. 'Please use it. This is for Eva,' was the message I received from Mark Knopfler and Co. We did use it, but not as the title track. Instead, the series producer Ruth Caleb had commissioned a song from the composer Michael Storey and asked Lennie to sing it.

'Tell us what you think,' she said to me.

Frankly, I was rather resistant at first. 'Sure, but I don't think anything can top "Brothers in Arms",' I told her.

Yet when I listened to it, it was such a strong and rousing ballad.

'My God. He's done it. It's so powerful.'

Lovely, too, that Michael Storey who wrote it went on to win the Ivor Novello Award the following year for Best TV Theme Tune. To this day, I receive requests for that song from people searching online.

Still, other more serious problems beset *Civvies*. As it was filmed in Wales, it meant spending time on location throughout its production. Experts were on hand to check all the details – real paratroopers giving advice on how actors should wear their uniform, hold their rifles and so on. But shoots can be unwieldy, especially headed by a poor director. An actor may have his beret positioned correctly for one scene, break for lunch, and tilt it the wrong way when the action resumes. Very experienced actors will understand continuity down to the nth degree; the cast of *Civvies* were not long out of drama school.

When it finally aired in September 1992, the series got the most savage reception I had ever experienced. Of course, I'd wanted its subject matter to cause a stir. I wrote *Civvies* not to glorify violence but to highlight the loss of young ex-combatants to prison, to the streets. That the critics panned it was hard for me to swallow. I was mauled, but it did bring out the tigress in me who needed to defend my story. Disappointingly, the BBC were not going to help me out on that score. Mostly, though, it was the outright denial by the armed forces that PTSD was ever an issue that I found the most disgusting.

On one television debate I went head-to-head with the Parachute Regiment's Colonel Commandant Lieutenant General Sir Michael Gray. He'd already submitted a list of inaccuracies to the BBC, forgetting that *Civvies* was a drama, not a documentary, and certainly not a public relations film for the armed forces. For me, the worst falsehood was when he point-blank refused to acknowledge that any paratroopers were rotting inside Britain's jails.

'What a revolting lie. There's not a single ex-paratrooper in prison. Your film is preposterous,' he said.

'It's not a lie and I have photographs and testimonies to prove it,' I told him.

Gray harrumphed, I seethed quietly, and the interview chugged on.

During that time and for years to follow, it felt as though I was existing in some alternate universe. On the one hand, I was reading what the army and others had to say about *Civvies* – less than complimentary – and I received vile hate mail, death threats too. On the other, I was opening sackfuls of letters from wives, girlfriends, parents, siblings and friends. All those letters thanked me: 'That's my brother'; 'That's my uncle'; 'Thank you. We've been living with this trauma since my son returned from the Falklands.' Even now, more than thirty years later, I *still* get the occasional letter about *Civvies*. Unbelievable how the military could simply dismiss the extent of a mental health crisis that remains ongoing today.

To say that *Civvies* left me wounded would be an understatement. I had to move on and not let the wound fester, but it was an isolating experience. My work had been rubbished, even those elements I had no control over. Yet worse was still to come. Just when I thought I'd seen the last of *Civvies,* its ghost revisited me like a horror movie. Jim had kept in touch. Occasionally, I received a letter from him in prison and I sent books to him. He loved *Bella Mafia*. He told me, 'If I lie on my bed, I can actually picture the villa and the characters.' I even entertained his wife and kids while he was inside. 'They haven't stopped talking about it on every visit,' he wrote.

Yet when Jim was finally released, he tried to sue me for defamation of character. I was gobsmacked. At first I couldn't fathom why, but then the realisation hit me. What he would get was publicity. The audacity of this man was astonishing, and I'd underestimated his duplicity. He wanted people to know that he was Frank Dillon in *Civvies* – he was desperate for that fame. He wanted to say, 'That's me: the amazing paratrooper.'

I was all ready to take the matter to court, but soon after I took legal advice. Eventually I came to the conclusion that it would be less damaging to myself if I paid Jim off, which I did to the tune of around £30,000. After everything that had happened I wanted to forget the whole episode, have nothing to do with him. That was wishful thinking.

Not long after I settled with Jim I received a call. I couldn't believe the voice on the other end.

'Hello, Lynda. It's Jim. Can I come and see you?'

What the hell does he want? I thought. I was shocked, but also rather intrigued about what he could possibly have to say.

'I'm not sure about that, Jim. I don't think there's anything to discuss.'

'I've got things to tell you,' he continued.

'OK, you can come to the house. I'll listen,' I agreed.

On that day, I would have been alone if it hadn't been for my wonderful driver, Lol. I asked him if he could keep a watchful eye on me, but not make his presence known. When Jim arrived, I directed him in through the back gate, so that Lol could watch from the window in the music room. Would Jim attack me? Hurt me? Or just talk to me? I had no clue.

I watched from the kitchen as he strode up the path.

'Hiya, Lynda! How are you doing?'

Jim's disposition was incredible. He danced through the garden smiling, filled with the joys of spring.

'What is it you want, Jim?' I asked flatly.

'I've got stories. Stories like you wouldn't believe. Stories about paratroopers . . .'

'Oh really?'

'Stuff that will make your hair stand on end!'

'You've come to sell me stories?'

After everything that man put me through, *this* was his offer?

'I think you'd better leave. Just go,' I said firmly. I was terrified. At that moment I realised just how damaged Jim truly was.

* * *

Creatively, *Civvies* was the last straw for me. I lacked so much control over my own work and I hadn't felt supported. I also distanced myself from other scripts in process, such as *The Lifeboats*. *Seconds Out,* a one-off drama I'd written about a down-on-his-luck boxer aired at around the same time as *Civvies*. That, too, almost destroyed me. The actor Tom Bell, who'd starred in *Prime Suspect*, had a lead role but spent most of filming paralytically drunk. No one on set could handle him, and then a Swedish woman got cast as the lead East End gangster's wife. Ridiculous! Another drama eviscerated by the BBC. Rather hilariously, someone had made a promotional poster prior to *Seconds Out*'s screening. It mirrored a billboard advert for an upcoming boxing bout and featured all the names of the main cast and crew. *Lovely*, I thought, when the director unrolled it. But when I looked closer, no one had remembered to include the writer, without whom they wouldn't be there.

'Where's my name?' I asked.

'Oh, sorry, Lynda!'

The disrespect was mind-blowing.

I felt that I'd relinquished so much control over the years that it had now become unbearable. I wanted command over my own work, so that year I set up my own production company, La Plante Productions. Of course, a company is just a piece of paper. The hard work was about to begin.

For my office, I began by renting a tiny cubbyhole off a corridor in my then TV and film agent Duncan Heath's office. A couple of staff came on board initially, and mainly by chance. A year or so before, I'd written a two-part mini-series produced by Sarah Lawson called *Seekers*, which ended up starring Josette Simon and Brenda Fricker. Sarah, who'd been married to then chief executive of Channel 4 Michael Grade, was remarrying and leaving to live in Ireland. She rang me one day in a panic.

'Lynda, I've got an assistant who I can't use any more. Might you have a position for her?'

The assistant was a young girl called Betina.

'She really is very good,' Sarah continued.

I met Betina at Sarah's mews house in Curzon Street in Mayfair. Immediately I liked her, but she did have the most extraordinary face: elongated as if it had been caught between elevator doors and never fully recovered. Partly, I felt rather sorry for her.

'Sure, come and work for me,' I said.

In fact, Betina turned out to be as good as Sarah had promised. At first she took care of the paperwork for ongoing projects and established the groundwork for our fledgling productions. Betina was later to combine work as my PA alongside some script editing.

Then, I hired a woman called Liz Thorburn. Liz was very plummy, rather like employing a maiden aunt, but she did turn out to be a force of nature. The actor Robin Sachs, who was married to my friend Sîan Phillips, had met her in LA and told me Liz was in a bit of a pickle. For years she'd worked for Elizabeth Taylor, first as her chef and eventually as some kind of carer for the star who was, by then, drugged up to the eyeballs on Quaaludes. Apparently, Liz was sacked on a whim and she needed work. I couldn't promise her the perks of that job, but when I offered her an administrative role she was practically on the next flight back to England. Liz did turn out to be the hostess with the mostest: a whizz at ordering flowers and wonderful at making actors feel comfortable. Liz got things done.

One of the first trips she and I went on was to Moscow. We travelled there via Poland by car on a fact-finding mission for a potential project I had been researching for Sean Connery's film company – financed by a wealthy Russian arms dealer. What a wild goose chase that turned out to be! The premise for the film was whether Red Mercury, a supposed substance pedalled as a valuable nuclear material and smuggled from behind the Iron Curtain, was an elaborate hoax or real. On that kind of mission, travelling light and alone may have been better. Liz brought with her a massive trunk and insisted on having all her clothes dry-cleaned. I also heard her outside my hotel room complaining that she'd had to sleep in a single bed.

The least of our worries, I thought. More pressing was the Geiger-counter still being used to test for contaminated food in the markets several years after the Chernobyl reactor disaster. 'Don't eat anywhere but the hotel,' had been the instruction given to me.

Besides, my itinerary involved meeting with undercover agents, arms dealers, police officers, all introduced to me by both the film's financier and a journalist I'd been put in touch with in Moscow. Plus, I had a checklist of places to go – a diversion from Red Mercury but what the hell. One was the city mortuary. That day, I left Liz behind and took with me an interpreter with almost flawless English, even though she'd never stepped a foot outside of Russia. But I lost her soon after we arrived. I did feel rather sorry for her in the end: the subject matter was grim.

'Snowdrops. That's what they call them.' The rather hefty female pathologist in wellington boots and white overalls had asked her to translate from the Russian as she guided us round.

'Really? Why?' I wanted to know.

'The Moskva River. It freeze over in winter. When ice thaw in spring, the bodies they pop up like snowdrop,' she explained.

'Gosh.'

In one room, apparently a kind of reception, there was a large steel chute with water cascading down into a large tub. I couldn't for the life of me work it out. My interpreter had her back to the slide as she began to explain.

'So, the body it arrive on truck and come for examination. For autopsy.'

What she couldn't see was just at that moment a mass of blubber hurtled down and plopped into the collection point.

I stopped dead. Her eyes followed my eyes.

'So the body comes . . .'

Her words tailed off, and that was the last I heard of her translation. As her head turned, her jaw dropped and she keeled backwards.

'I'm sorry, I have to go home,' I heard her repeat as two men in white coats arrived to carry her out.

Now I was left with a pathologist who couldn't speak a bloody word of English. She led me through a set of large iron doors and into a cold storage unit where bodies hung by their feet like animal carcasses or were laid out on slabs. Each one had a number attached to it on a tag.

'Bang bang,' she shouted and pointed at one. Her fingers made the shape of the barrel of a revolver as she acted out her head being blown off.

'Bang bang.' She signalled at another who'd been shot in the chest.

'He, dead like this . . .' she pretended to garrotte herself with one hand while the other waved towards a man hanging up. A couple of women were being stored there, too. The fact that they had been murdered felt particularly shocking to me.

As with all of Moscow, so much took me by surprise. The amount of English villains there was incredible – all selling dodgy fax machines and coining it in. There was poverty beyond belief. Beggars with one shoe on and holding up the other as a container for spare change. As for Red Mercury, I learned very little and came to the conclusion that it was a load of old tosh. Certainly, I didn't have enough research to put a script together. I came home empty-handed and got on with La Plante Productions' first venture.

It was a production we would work jointly on with Verity. In the intervening years Verity had kept her company, Cinema Verity, ticking over but also worked freelance as a producer, including at the BBC. She'd presided over the ill-fated soap *Eldorado* set in Spain in an ex-pat community. It had been one of the BBC's most expensive productions. When it failed abysmally, Verity was judged incredibly harshly, in my view. Forty years of outstanding programme-making, one bum note and she may as well have contracted the plague. That's the TV industry for you! Particularly galling because around fifteen years later the sitcom *Benidorm*, set in the Solana all-inclusive hotel in Spain, became such a roaring success. As ever, Verity was ahead of the curve. Towards the end of 1992, however, she was reeling from the aftermath and in need of a project.

Verity came to see me at home.

'Would you consider doing another *Widows*?' she asked.

Not really, I thought. I'd resisted previous calls to repeat *Widows*. Besides, would resurrecting a programme after almost eight years work?

'What would be the storyline?' I asked her. 'I mean, Dolly Rawlins would be getting out of prison for Harry's murder around now, but that's it,' I said.

'That's a good story, Lynda.' Verity's eyes lit up.

Verity left empty-handed. My heart didn't jump, but I did want to help her. Throughout my whole career I'd felt a fierce loyalty to Verity. Rather naughtily, I thought I'd be clever. Not to look as though I was letting her down, I'd devise a storyline that was so preposterous I knew she'd never agree. *Fuck it,* I thought. *What's the most expensive production I can think of?*

Even now, I can picture Verity standing by the fireplace in my dining room when she returned for my answer. She had her back to me.

'Will you do it, Lynda?'

'Yes. But only if Dolly Rawlins is released from prison and becomes the mastermind behind a train robbery. I want an almighty train smash.'

'OK.'

Christ almighty! Verity didn't even sound surprised.

'Oh, and I want the stolen money transported by women on horseback.'

'You have it, Lynda.'

'I do? *Fucking Ada* . . .'

And that's how the sequel to Widows – She's Out – was born. Thankfully, Ann Mitchell agreed to play the lead of Dolly once more. And when I'd finished the script, casting began. Alongside Ann there would be six other women needed for its lead roles. They'd know Dolly from prison and, on release, conspire with her to plan the most audacious heist. One part we had trouble casting was for Gloria Radford, a former arms dealer and criminal fence. Lots of female actors had come through the door, but no one rough-and-ready enough to take on straight-talking Gloria.

One day, Verity and I were in her office almost at the end of our tether. Hot sunshine was streaming in through the open windows. Suddenly, we heard a car engine turning over and a voice yelling from the roadside below.

'Aaawwww much?'

Verity and I peered out to see the last woman to audition that day harassing a poor cabbie through his wound-down window.

'You're chargin' me aaawwww much? You faaaackin' dirty baaastard!'

'Well, I think we've found our Gloria.' Verity smiled.

The actress turned out to be Maureen Sweeney, and she really was a hoot. When she greeted us moments later she tried to put on so many airs and graces: 'So lovely to meet you.' I'm not sure she'd done much acting previously, a couple of adverts perhaps. And when filming started, she had everyone in fits.

Ian Toynton, who came back as director, had some great stories about Maureen. One afternoon he'd had to stop her. 'I'm sorry, Maureen, you're not quite hitting your mark.'

It was during a scene where Maureen had to Hoover the cottage where the women were hiding out before the raid.

Maureen looked like she was going to swing for him. 'I fucking did! I hit it spot-on! That Hoover's cleaned every speck of dust on every take. It's you, you keep fucking stopping me!'

'No, no, Maureen, it's not the dust. It's your mark. You're not quite hitting it.'

'Well, why didn't you fucking tell me that then?'

Back in 1992, however, filming for *She's Out* was some way off. First I had to write it. Over that entire period, my output had been continuous and remained so. Even Richard noticed how exhausted I was. 'You're working yourself into an early grave, Lynda,' he told me.

Partly, I did so because I loved working. I never wanted to fail at hitting the high standards I'd set myself. Admittedly, I may also have buried myself in work to push through the emotions of not having children. Despite years of trying, it never did happen for me. Richard and I had given up on conceiving so writing became my stability, a way to keep moving on. Instead, we'd placed our names on adoption lists mainly in the States. There, the process is easier than in the UK. Given Richard's American citizenship, and the fact both of us were travelling there often, it also made sense.

That winter, however, we decided to relocate to The Hamptons for a few weeks. The music producer Chris Stamp, a friend of Richard's, lived there and we stayed with him and his wife. Yet what started as time out to relax and write became a rather different proposition in Richard's mind. Suddenly I was being introduced to real estate agents.

'It's a place of such wonderful calm,' Richard said.

He was right. There were winters in the States that I loved: frosty, snowy and sunny – an idyllic combination. But we couldn't buy a home there.

'I've just started my company. We don't have any income at the moment,' I reminded him.

'Oh, don't worry. We'll sort something.'

Of course, when Richard said, 'We'll sort something,' it meant I'd sort something. Then, on Boxing Day, this little old hunchbacked lady appeared with glasses perched on the end of her nose.

'I have a property you're just going to love. Trust me,' she said.

I half-thought it was a home we would rent. I remember it being a long drive, almost to the end of the limb of islands that make up The Hamptons. We turned into a long driveway, pulled up and stepped out of the car.

'This is it,' Richard said.

'This is what?' I asked.

'This is the house we have to buy.'

'Buy? How much is it?'

'I don't know, but this is it.'

In truth, it was the one thing that Richard turned out to be right about, although I didn't think so at the time. The house overlooked Accabonac Harbor. The view of the ocean; the stillness of it; the beauty. It was all there. The house itself was odd and misshapen: a fairytale property, but nothing conventional about it. It also had a pool, rare in The Hamptons so close to the ocean. We bought it on a whim. What can I say? I'm a risk-taker. And I didn't need much encouragement. In years to come, it was to become my summer retreat and a location I was to fall in love with. Back then, however, it wasn't quite the relaxing place Richard had promised. Instead, I ploughed myself into more work to pay for it. Over the years, I built crazy extensions without much thought. No one stopped me or told me it was insane. But when I sold it around five years ago it more than paid for the investment. The upkeep was becoming too difficult and expensive. But it felt like such a wrench. My love of The Hamptons and the wonderful people I met there grew over the years – so many happy, happy memories.

Chapter 15

Bars, Brothels and Broads

My home in The Hamptons was taking shape, and I loved jetting back and forth between LA, New York and the UK. Since *Prime Suspect*, the US had begun to open up to me although dealing with the large production houses there could feel bruising. In Hollywood, you're either in or you're out. It became another steep learning curve.

I did have some luck, though. On one trip I'd been travelling in an aisle seat on a Concorde flight to New York when an alarmingly obese gentleman tapped me on the shoulder.

'Excuse me, ma'am. Would you mind moving to the window seat so I can stretch out?' he asked.

'Sure,' I agreed.

When the food trolley arrived I looked on with incredulity as he balanced his tray on his distended stomach and stabbed at his full English breakfast with his fork. Suddenly, a sausage somersaulted into the air and almost took out the eye of a woman relaxing in the aisle opposite. He very politely leaned over.

'Excuse me, ma'am, I believe you have my sausage,' he said, reaching in to scoop it from her blouse with no hint of embarrassment. Later, I found him stashing the airline freebies, like the leather passport holder and headphones stamped with the Concorde insignia, into his bag.

I'm going to have fun with you, I thought. We started chatting. He turned out to be terrifically entertaining and occupied me for the entire journey. On landing he opened his wallet and brought out his business card.

'If you ever need to fly Concorde again, just call me,' he said.

What were the chances? I'd been sat next to one of the airline's top brass! From then on I *always* flew Concorde whenever I could and until it ceased flying. Super-fast three-hour flights at heavily discounted prices meant moving between London and the States became so much easier.

One of my favourite moments was bumping into Jill Gascoine, who I'd acted with all those years ago in *The Gentle Touch*. She was a dreadful flyer and always knocked herself out with pills.

'Try it, Lynda, they're great!' she told me.

The next time I looked up, Jill was face-planted in her airline dinner and a hostess was gingerly attempting to shake her awake.

The whole experience did feel like being on top of the world. For the first time, I started to enjoy my success. But while *Prime Suspect* had given me a foothold in the States like no other, some of it did feel overwhelming. One time I'd been at home in London when I received a call.

'Hi, is that Lynda?' I thought I recognised the voice immediately. An actor friend of mine, Barbara Thorn, was always ringing me up with a fake American accent: 'How ya doin', kid?'

'Hi Barbara!' I replied.

But it was a little difficult to make out what Barbara was saying. In the background I could hear a strange rhythmic pounding. *Are you on a treadmill?* I wondered.

'So, Lynda, *Prime Suspect*. I need to know why George Marlow says he's not guilty in the final scene.'

It was a bizarre question and so early in the morning, too.

'Well, he's a psychopath!' *Stupid woman,* I thought. And why the hell is she ringing to talk to me about *Prime Suspect*?

'OK, Lynda, I need to know. It's just that when I directed *The Prince of Tides* and starred in it . . .'

The Prince of Tides? Holy shit. It was Barbra bloody Streisand calling me from her morning workout. I dissolved into an incoherent wreck.

'Barbra, I have all your albums.' Sick-making when I look back now.

Barbra had wanted to buy the rights to *Prime Suspect*, but sadly, they weren't available. In the UK, Granada owned them, and they'd been sold in the US to public broadcaster PBS. In fact, *Prime Suspect* sold in 179 territories across the world, yet I didn't own a single character on TV – the perils of signing a paper-thin contract, unaware that I would be tied to it in perpetuity.

'I'm sorry, they're gone,' I broke it to her.

In the States I'd also been working on a TV film called *The Prosecutors* with the wonderful Tom Fontana, the writer behind groundbreaking series like *Homicide: Life on the Street* and, later, the prison drama *Oz*. Tom was frightfully mischievous, which is why I adored him. He and I once pitched a whole series we'd named *Murder.com* to executives at Universal, only when it came to the time of the pitch we'd not yet come up with a coherent storyline.

'I'll tell you what,' Tom suggested as we waited for our slot. 'When they ask for the pitch I'll start, and when I slap your leg, you take over.'

Tom was so highly regarded that when we entered, I thought I could probably leave it to him to do most of the talking.

'Well, it's a fantastic series about a detective and his wife ...' Tom announced to the semi-circle of po-faced executives before jabbing me hard in the leg. *Thanks, Tom.*

'... the wife's a psychiatrist, and they work well together because ...' I continued, before returning the favour with a hard jab back. We traded lines throughout, each one becoming more ridiculous than the last. By the end, the detective had had a nervous breakdown and his wife had bought a Great Dane. What was even more ridiculous was that Universal loved it! Though perhaps, unsurprisingly, *Murder.com* never made it onto any screen.

The Prosecutors, on the other hand, had been picked up by NBC. It featured a wheelchair-bound attorney forced to take over a court case. A ruthless legal mastermind, but who'd so often been discounted on account of her disability.

Casting for *The Prosecutors* had been infuriating. Of course, I would have *loved* it if an actual disabled actor had come forward to play the part. Not only did none audition but, unlike today, a disabled anyone – let alone a woman – wouldn't have been considered by the studios. Even the famous San Francisco cop Robert T. Ironside, also wheelchair-bound, was played by the able-bodied actor Raymond Burr. Instead, I wanted the phenomenal Irish actor Fiona Shaw to play the lead role of Ingrid Maynard. Even then the studio had problems: 'She's not pretty enough; she's too hard; she's too old; she's a lesbian.' All those prejudices thrown in the way of mind-blowing talent. Tom understood my frustration. When Stockard Channing, who'd made her name in the 1970s classic *Grease*, came to read for the part, Tom whispered to me beforehand, 'I'll take bets on how long it is before she asks about the wheelchair.'

Sure enough, around ten minutes in, Stockard chirped up, 'Sorry, can I just ask, does the character really have to be in a wheelchair for the whole film? I mean, when does she get out of it?'

She doesn't. That's the whole point of the character. She's disabled! I gritted my teeth.

Stockard did end up playing the lead role, and well enough. But the fact that women themselves were pandering to a wretched Hollywood ideal bothered me. *Do it! Be fearless!* I wanted to scream.

Now, if I'm ever being interviewed, I can guarantee someone will say, 'You champion strong women.'

'No,' I reply. 'I champion *real* women.'

And there's a difference. I've never buried the feminine, although I have written characters who would be deemed more traditionally macho than others. I've never shied away from complicated or flawed women, either. Even tough and determined Jane Tennison wasn't infallible. What I've hopefully shown is women fighting for agency over their lives.

Most of all I want women I can *believe* in, whatever their age or background. To me, it's no surprise that a programme like the BBC's crime drama *Happy Valley*, created by Sally Wainwright, enjoyed award-winning success and became such a hit with viewers, too. Sarah Lancashire, who played Sergeant Catherine Cawood in a rural police force, portrayed a *real* woman – middle-aged; carrying some weight; sexual; angry; caring: a gritty, no-nonsense officer taking pride in her job. You can't put a twenty-something into a role like that, and it feels preposterous to me these days when dramatic licence gets stretched beyond belief.

And sometimes *real* people do come into your life who are impossible to ignore. In the States in the mid-1990s the most incredible woman was to enter mine. Real she most certainly was – a magnificent wreck.

I'd been staying at the Hotel Bel-Air in Los Angeles, combining wrapping up *The Prosecutors* with picking up an Emmy for *Prime Suspect*, when I got a call from reception. The Bel-Air had luxury cottages in its grounds – extortionate to stay in, but amazing if someone else was footing the bill.

'There's a journalist here to see you,' the receptionist told me. How any journalist had found me at the Bel-Air was anyone's guess, but I had flown into the States via New York to be interviewed on morning TV. The presenter had asked where I get my stories from. 'I pay for them,' I replied. 'And if anyone wants to sell me one, get in touch.'

At the Bel-Air, I drifted out to reception. Standing to attention was a woman: stocky frame, pushing six foot and dressed in an ill-fitting white PVC jacket tied at the bottom. A most unflattering look.

'Hello,' I held out my hand. *This is no journalist,* I thought. Her dyed black hair obviously hadn't been brushed and immediately I noticed a scar running from her left eye down to the top of her cheekbone.

'I'm sorry, I didn't catch your name. What publication are you from?' I asked as I ushered her through the hotel.

The woman's voice was thick West Coast. Guttural, too. She revealed her name but I've never used it publicly, so I'll call her Lorraine.

'I'm here to sell you a story,' she said.

'I'm very busy,' I replied. It dawned on me that she might be a complete crank – always a risk when money is on the table. 'I'll tell you what. Pitch your story to me. Do you know what a pitch is?' I asked, gesturing for her to take a seat. She refused and remained standing.

'Sure,' she said, banging down her large scruffy holdall.

As she spoke, I noticed two of her side teeth were missing.

'I was a police lieutenant. Worked my way up. Had a husband, two kids. Had a work partner and I got into a difficult situation. I was drinking. He was drinking. We had an affair, he died and then I killed a kid. I got kicked out the LAPD. Cold-shouldered, it's what they call it,' she said.

'Whoa, that's quite a story! Your partner died and then you killed a kid?'

'Yeah, partner got shot. Died in my arms. I was a mess after that. Drinking. Then I got a call-out. Black kid in an alleyway. I thought he pulled a gun. Turned out to be his Sony Walkman in his pocket. I shot him. You want the story?'

I couldn't quite believe what I was hearing, but her story didn't end there. Because the victim was Black, publicity around the killing was easily hushed up. Within the LAPD, however, Lorraine was history. She fell further into alcoholism, then drug addiction. She'd worked as a prostitute to make ends meet. All she wanted to do was clean herself up and get visitation rights to her kids, access to whom she'd also lost.

'How long have you been living on the streets?' I asked.

'Round eight years.' She shrugged. 'One minute I was putting addicts and prostitutes behind bars, next I was living with them.'

We talked for a while before she delivered her next bombshell. 'You want the story? I have a guy out front with a contract.'

'You do?'

Just as she said, when Lorraine led me back through to reception there was a scrawny-looking guy loitering around the car park, brandishing a couple of sheaves of paper. Her lawyer, she claimed.

'I don't just pay people like that,' I told her. 'I'm going to have to find out much more about your life. Can you take me to the places you've described? Walk me through your story?'

'Sure, I'll take you anywhere you want to go, lady,' she said.

In the end Lorraine and I made an agreement. I would pay her a total of $10,000 but not in one go. She'd get an initial sum up-front and the rest in instalments. A wise move, it turned out. I had a funny feeling I was going to be in for one helluva ride.

Lorraine turned out to be the worst chaperone I'd ever worked with. On the first time we ventured out in a beat-up rented car, she left me in one of the dodgiest parts of LA and simply disappeared.

'Lorraine, the deal's off if you go AWOL or put me in any danger,' I warned.

'OK, OK, no problem. I'm fully armed,' she brushed me off.

'You're fully *what*?'

'Armed!' she said, pulling a gun from her handbag.

Christ, that's all I need, I thought. But my concern didn't stop Lorraine parachuting me into more knife-edge scenarios.

One location was a crack house in downtown LA. She'd lived there on and off and knew most people there. Its nondescript frontage hid the filth inside. Bodies lying around comatose, out of their heads on crack cocaine. I'll never forget the front room where a kid was crawling on the floor, among the roaches and tinfoil and needles, picking up discarded bullet shells.

One guy I got introduced to had been a college professor. He looked around fifty years old, though age was hard to pin down in his drug-ravaged state.

'I'm just going to grab a coffee. I'll be five minutes,' Lorraine announced as he and I sat chatting.

An hour later there was still no sign of Lorraine. It's hard to have a conversation with a junkie for that long. However, I was interested in how someone of his stature had gotten so low.

'What's crack to you?' I asked.

'Everything,' he replied.

'Hasn't there ever been anything in your life that's come close to how it makes you feel?'

'Nothing,' he said. 'It's the best feeling.'

Another guy sat next to him had been a nurse. When I asked him the same question he said he used to work with children and only one memory supplanted the feeling of crack.

'I looked after a girl who couldn't walk. I held her arms up and placed her feet on top of my feet and stepped with her down the corridor. She was so happy she thought she was walking,' he told me.

How sad, I thought. Time was also ticking on. *Where the fuck is Lorraine?* I began to panic. Back then, mobile phones weren't easily available. The longer I remained there, the more paranoid I became. Why were bullet shells strewn everywhere? What if I got caught in a police raid? Or a shoot-out between rival dealers?

When Lorraine did finally put in an appearance, it was like she'd never left.

'You can't leave me in these places. I don't want to have to pay for protection,' I reminded her.

'Yeah, sorry, Lynda,' she said, but Lorraine was obviously out of it. She was an ex-cop with a raging alcohol problem on top of a nasty heroin habit.

As our meetings progressed, I met a kaleidoscope of weird and wonderful characters: transexuals, pansexuals, hookers, johns, junkies. If I was back in London or The Hamptons, Lorraine and I weren't in touch, but every time I landed in LA I'd drop her a line at the only hostel I knew she stayed at regularly, and followed more of her story. Sometimes it would take her days or weeks to return my message and we'd meet.

Around the third time I saw her I noticed Lorraine had used some of the money I paid her to have veneers fitted on her broken teeth. She also had new clothes. For once she'd started to turn up looking respectable.

You were a good-looking woman once, I thought. Beforehand, I'd not been able to imagine her as a go-getting lieutenant – a woman who'd risen up from lowly uniform to such a high-rank and had the world at her feet.

Within time she introduced me to her ex-husband, a lawyer – a really decent man. She claimed initially she'd put him through law school with her earnings but when I asked him he denied it. I suspect it may have been true, but with Lorraine it was difficult to know what to believe.

'You cannot trust her. She's made so many promises to her daughters. She lies about everything,' her ex-husband warned me. And he was right about another thing. She stole with impunity. I learned never to leave valuables lying around if she visited. I knew she'd stolen from me. At times, I believe she felt it was her right – like her life had gotten so shitty that everyone owed her. My handbag was always zipped tight and clasped to my shoulder.

Lorraine could be nasty, too. Especially when she was on the cusp of an almighty bender. At those times, she became a twister of aggression and self-pity.

'You wanna cigarette?'

'No, I don't want one.'

'Go on, have a fuckin' cigarette. Have one!'

'No, thanks.'

'You don't want one? Well, fuck you, lady!'

Lorraine would light up, her hands often trembling. 'D'you know what it's like to be me? You know what I've been through? Let me fuckin' tell you what it's like . . .'

Then Lorraine would launch into some disgusting story about what punter she'd given a blow job to in a back alley, or fucked in a supermarket car park. She'd worked in and out of licensed brothels, too. So, aside from the doss-houses Lorraine moved around, I wanted to see where she'd been a prostitute.

'Sure, I'll take you there!' she offered the next time I met her in LA. Off we drove once more in our rent-a-wreck car, miles out of the city and into the sweltering desert. We turned off a highway into a ranch with a wooden frontage and a large car park out front.

'Here?' I asked. It all seemed faintly absurd.

'Here.' She nodded. Through the swing doors, Lorraine greeted everyone like they were best friends. In fact, in every place we turned up – bars, squats, brothels – everyone's face lit up when they saw Lorraine.

'Hey, baby! How ya doin'?'

In some ways, it was like being out with a celebrity.

'Hey, mind if I show her around?' she asked the girl behind the desk.

Past reception was a large window with closed slatted blinds. As we pushed through a side door eight or nine women were lounging around in skimpy dresses, or scantily clad in sequinned underwear or leopard-skinned leotards. Off that room, the building had been partitioned into separate cubicles where negotiations took place and the girls did their business.

'She's writin' about my life,' Lorraine introduced me. 'Tell her about how ya know me, when I was here.'

At that, there was some laughter. At times Lorraine had gotten so low that even the brothels refused to have her work there.

As I perched on the edge of the sofa the women began talking. They were open, friendly and funny.

'I'll be back in a few minutes.' Lorraine got up and moved to head out.

Oh Christ, I thought, shooting her a look. A few minutes? Or a few hours? The girls asked if I wanted a coffee from the portable trolley in the corner. I had a feeling I was in for the long haul. Suddenly, a red light flashed above the door. The slatted blinds glided to one side and a rather grubby punter stood on the other side of the glass, peering in.

The men never came into the room, the girls explained. Instead, they chose a hooker from through the window before being led through a side door to the cubicles behind.

Whereas beforehand everyone had been lolling around, filing nails, drinking coffee and chatting, now they were upright, silent, striking a pose, pouting their lips and flicking their hair. Puppy dog eyes on full show. The redhead in the sequinned underwear got the call and off she tottered.

Despite seething at Lorraine, I did find the whole set-up fascinating.

'Don't you feel like you're in a goldfish bowl?' I asked. Although I had on a dress and boots it still felt awkward to be sitting behind that glass.

'Nah, get used to it.' One girl shrugged.

'The funny thing is men coming in and out probably think I'm one of you,' I joked.

'You're fully dressed! Bit of a giveaway,' one of the Mexican girls laughed.

'You wanna be one of us? Take 'em off!' another shouted over.

The room shook with laughter.

'Oh no, I couldn't,' I said, regretting I'd ever mentioned it.

'Go on, lady, take 'em off!'

I don't know what possessed me, but talk about suffering for your art. After some more cajoling, I yanked my dress over my head and pulled my boots off. Being a gym freak and a tennis player, I had on the most unflattering sports bra and tennis knickers – white T-shirt fabric with a pocket for the ball, for Christ's sake!

'Happy now?' I said.

The girls erupted with laughter once more.

'Jesus, lady, your underwear!' one shouted. They couldn't quite believe how dreadful and drab it looked.

'And what the hell are the pockets for?'

'Well, for the balls . . .' I replied, at which the room almost exploded.

'. . . the tennis balls,' I quickly clarified.

Sitting in that room, air-conditioning whirring, was one of the most uncomfortable experiences of my life. Worse still, not a single punter who pulled up that afternoon picked me. *Thank Christ*, I thought. That would be beyond the call of duty! But I also felt an unexpected pang of rejection. Crazy, I know!

Where the hell is Lorraine? I kept wondering. By now she'd been gone more than a couple of hours. *Was she seriously going to leave me here?* When she finally did show up, not only did she look utterly dishevelled, but when she saw me, her eyes almost popped out of her head.

'What the hell are you doing in your underwear?' she shouted.

You're saying that to me? I thought. This woman really was something else.

Lorraine could be very, very funny. A couple of times I sat with her in the back of Alcoholics Anonymous meetings in rundown parts of the city, during the times when she'd got serious about cleaning herself up. She'd met her friend Rosie there – her tall, Black sidekick who was as hilarious as Lorraine.

'I'm the one with all the contacts,' she always told me when we met, tapping her nose and winking.

On other occasions I listened as Lorraine trotted out the unbelievable lies she'd told in AA just to pick men up. She'd also raid charity shops and act out different parts.

One afternoon I turned up to find her wearing a safari suit.

'That's very elegant!' I said, somewhat surprised.

'I know it's fuckin' elegant. It's a goddamn safari suit,' she cried.

God knows who she'd been trying to seduce wearing that.

She'd faked being married to a famous gynaecologist just for the hell of it. And pretended to be a receptionist in a luxury hotel to pull another guy.

'He was in his early fifties, real gent,' she told me.

'So what happened?'

'I fell over,' she laughed.

'You fell over?'

'Yeah, we were walking down the street. When he saw me fall, he said, "My God, lemme help you up!" He had no idea how many times I've been found in the gutter.' She roared with laughter.

Lines like that made me warm to Lorraine even though she was often hard to like. The saddest thing was, she was exceedingly clever. Sharp as a tack. She gave me the idea for the plot of my first book using her character. We'd been at an open coffee bar on Rodeo Drive when she had been explaining how prostitutes stop men in their cars in the street.

'Hey, I've got the perfect crime for you!' Her eyes lit up. 'I'm giving the guy a blow job in the car. I feel his hand going for something in the glove compartment. It's a claw hammer. He tries to kill me!'

Perfect, I thought. Lorraine, a down-on-her-luck ex-cop, on the trail of a serial killer comes face-to-face with the killer herself. Having been cold-shouldered from the force, she sets up her own detective agency to solve a string of murders. My first book would be called *Cold Shoulder*. As for the information I needed to understand the State's police force, I had to go to places like Orange County, far from the reach of the LAPD. Lorraine's name was dirt there, and it had been hard to get anyone to talk to me.

Lorraine's life had all the highs and lows of a fairground big dipper. During the year or so I kept in contact with her she was in and out of rehab. She won visitation rights for her kids, but quickly lost them. She looked clean and together, then the next time she was back on Skid Row. In the end, after one book, I had to cut Lorraine loose. She was becoming a liability and simply too dangerous to know. I felt so guilty, but when I told her that I couldn't see her any more, she shrugged.

'You're just like everybody else,' she said.

At that point I felt I was probably doing the right thing.

I would go on to write two more books using Lorraine's character, but eventually I had to kill her off. That's such a tough thing for a writer to do. She'd been so alive in my mind and on the page for weeks, months, years, but I couldn't have her in my life. In my heart, I'd wanted her to get clean and stay clean. But that was wishful thinking, I realised.

The Lorraine Page trilogy – *Cold Shoulder*, *Cold Blood* and *Cold Heart* – was published between 1994 and 1998, but it wasn't until after that last book had been released that it was mooted for TV. The producer Gail Berman had visited me in The Hamptons also wanting the rights to *Prime Suspect*, which still hadn't been made in the States.

Gail and I are still in touch to this day. I have tremendous respect for her, and her company, The Jackal Group, has gone on to make some outstanding films, such as Baz Luhrmann's *Elvis*.

As for the rights to *Prime Suspect*, she was as out of luck as Barbra Streisand.

'Sorry, they sold ages ago.'

'Have you got anything else?' she asked.

'Not sure I do . . .'

'What's this?' she said, pointing to a folder sitting on my shelf with the words *Cold Shoulder* written on the spine.

'Sure, take a look.'

Gail did end up buying the rights to *Cold Shoulder* and, by God, that woman moves fast. Within weeks she had a TV pilot set up, for which I wrote the script. Unfortunately, she also brought on board the director Charles Haid, though none of us could have predicted what a lunatic that man would turn out to be. Charles had played Officer Andy Renko in the long-running US cop show *Hill Street*

Blues in the 1980s but had since moved into producing and directing. And if ever there was a director who epitomised everything that was wrong with the way US studios viewed female characters it was him. Never in my life had I seen such a procession of drop-dead-gorgeous twenty-somethings lined up for that role.

'Charles, Lorraine is in her late thirties, early forties. She's an alcoholic and a junkie.'

I tried to drum that into him over and over.

'But she gets cleaned up,' he argued.

'Yeah, but not right away. She's not pretty from the start. She's beat.'

'We'll lose viewers. We can't have her strung out,' he said.

Viewers aren't that stupid, I thought.

I was almost at breaking point on the day we auditioned Lorraine after Lorraine after Lorraine. Not one of them was right. Then, I happened to walk out of the casting room when I saw a woman hunched up on a chair in the corridor. She'd come to audition but she was some way down the line. I had no clue who she was, but in that moment I needed to do a double take.

Christ Almighty! It's her!

She could have been the spit of Lorraine Page.

'Excuse me, are you here for *Cold Shoulder*?' I asked.

The woman looked up. She looked clean but she looked beat, like she'd been put through the wringer. She was shaking, too. Unbelievably nervous!

'What's your name?' I asked.

'Kelly . . . Kelly McGillis.'

Holy fucking Christ! Now I was freaking out of my head. *Kelly McGillis?*

There was only one story I knew about Kelly McGillis, other than she'd made her name in *Top Gun* alongside Tom Cruise.

A director friend of mine, Jonathan Kaplan, had been casting for the film *The Accused* back in the mid-1980s. He'd received a phone call to say Kelly McGillis was interested in a role. The film, depicting the story of the gang rape of a woman and her subsequent struggle for justice, had been controversial at the time and Kelly wanted to come over and discuss it with Jonathan. His apartment was a mess, he told me, so he rang his cleaning agency.

'Can you send someone over? I've a meeting and I need my apartment spotless,' he asked.

A cleaner was arranged and when the doorbell rang, he opened up to find a rather scruffy-looking woman outside.

'I'll take you through to the kitchen, there's a mop and bucket and the vacuum cleaner's there too,' he said, ushering her through.

'Sorry? I'm Kelly McGillis, I'm here for the part . . .' she replied.

During the meeting she sat and drank a whole bottle of Bourbon.

In the years after *Top Gun*, Kelly had been abusing drugs and alcohol. And when I saw her in the corridor I thought, *That's it. You're it. You're the real deal.* What I hadn't known, and what she told me that afternoon, was that she had been raped at knifepoint alongside a roommate by two men in her New York apartment. It happened before she'd even made *Top Gun* and her spiral of self-abuse began right there. Truly, my heart went out to her.

That afternoon, I spent a lot of time with Kelly talking her through Lorraine's character detail by detail before she read for Charles and me. Since *Top Gun* she'd continued acting on and off but hadn't starred in anything notable, and never in a high-profile TV series. She confessed how terrified she was.

'Be confident. You're perfect,' I told her.

When I stepped back into the room I laid it out straight to Charles.

'Lorraine Page is out in that corridor and that's the actor we're having. Forget the twenty-something blondes. I want Kelly McGillis or nothing.'

Without doubt Kelly put in one helluva performance. Absolute perfection. She had every single nuance of a drunk and an addict down to a tee. I had to fight for her, but in the end I got her for the pilot. Yet even then I had to battle Charles Haid throughout its entire filming.

'She's looking kinda bad,' he kept telling me in the initial sequences.

'That's the point! Give it time before you clean her up. Don't give her new teeth yet. Leave her alone until the time is right!'

That pilot seriously kicked butt, and I felt sure it would have been the break Kelly needed to revive her career. And to have a brilliant Black female lead – the wonderful Loretta Devine – as her sidekick, Rosie, was also rare on US TV at that time. Everything felt so fresh and right.

It is still one of my biggest regrets that *Cold Shoulder* never got made. When we took the pilot to CBS, there was stiff competition and they opted for *CSI: Miami* instead, simply a far bigger show. You win some, you lose some, I guess. And I do often wonder whatever happened to the real Lorraine Page. My sincere hope is that she did clean herself up, get to see her kids, and is living happily somewhere in LA.

Chapter 16

The Governor

La Plante Productions was up and rolling. With *She's Out* beginning production, I combined that with work on our first major solo project, *The Governor*.

The idea had come to me a couple of years before. My prison work had been ongoing – mainly lectures and writing workshops under the auspices of several charities. Wherever I visited a prison, lateness was never tolerated. Moving inmates from their cells to a lecture hall or a classroom needed to run like clockwork, plus I was required to get through all the entry checks. One day, heavy traffic meant I almost didn't make it.

'So sorry I'm late.' I arrived out-of-breath to the front gate of the prison.

The governor had wanted to greet me before my talk, but there wasn't time.

'I'll do the lecture, then I'm afraid I'll have to go,' I explained to the welcoming officer, knowing the drive I had to get back to London.

Afterwards as I was rushing out, the same officer stopped me. 'Got a moment for a quick word with the governor?'

'Well, sorry. Actually, I am a bit strapped for time . . .'

'The governor would like a word, Mrs La Plante.'

'Right, OK.'

I was led into a small office, where there was a woman sat behind a desk.

'Do I wait here for the governor?' I enquired.

She shot me a rather disparaging look. 'I am the governor.'

'I'm so terribly sorry.'

'And you're Lynda la Plante, I presume?'

'Yes,' I replied sheepishly.

The woman was in her mid-thirties, smartly dressed and holding a cup and saucer with delicate precision. 'I always bring my own china.' She smiled. 'Do take a seat.'

We chatted briefly. I was filled with admiration for where she'd got to in her career – there were fewer women prison governors than female DCIs – but I did find her exceedingly aloof.

'I am the youngest female governor in England,' she announced before explaining that prisoner rehabilitation was at the heart of her approach.

'I believe prisoners must be given more freedom. It's the only way for them to develop purpose and that will limit reoffending,' she told me. She was very confident in her ability to shake up the prison service.

It must have been a year or so later when I was invited to a prisoners' welfare function organised by the prison authorities. At the end of the evening I glanced over to see a woman sitting on her own. I had to look twice. It was the same governor. Still smartly dressed, tall and rangy, but with none of her poise. She cowered like a husk of the person I'd met.

'Hello.' I made a beeline straight for her.

Immediately, I sensed that she didn't want to talk to me. Later, I found out that her rehabilitation programme had failed. Two inmates had escaped over the wall and committed rape. She'd been demoted. As a writer, I saw the potential immediately.

What a fascinating tension, I thought. A prison for male inmates headed by a woman and a failed approach. Rehabilitation was all well and good in theory, but I also knew that the prison service wasn't properly funded, properly staffed, and prisons themselves were in desperate need of an overhaul. The situation is even more at breaking point today. Fertile ground for a TV drama.

Fortunately, the wonderful Nick Elliott at ITV thought so too. Nick was a guy who could make a decision with a snap of his fingers: 'Go for it!' he said. Those were the days when passion ruled and chances got taken. Now commissioners can't fart without twenty mainly inexperienced people chipping in, but don't get me started on programming by committee!

Having that commission was critical because without it I couldn't have raised the finance for *The Governor*. For such an ambitious project, Barclays had to agree to upwards of ten million pounds. That finally secured, I needed the best directors, producers, camera crew and location crews I could find. When executive producer Steve Lanning came on board he became the production's engine, firing the whole thing up.

From the outset there would be difficulties, we discovered. A Home Office ban prohibited us from filming inside or outside any UK prison. We would need to relocate to Ireland. There, we could take over a disused brick factory near Dublin's Point Theatre, and rebuild a prison set within it. We could also film some scenes in Wheatfield Prison in the south-west of the city.

My fictional high-security Barfield Prison would be run by Governor Helen Hewitt, brought in after a prison riot. Of course, I'd been in many top-security prisons before but this time around I needed to understand its layout, from the recreation yard to the cells to what is known as The Block – a prison within a prison, holding terrorists, mafioso, the worst offenders. Exceedingly dangerous men. Our replica across the Irish Sea had to be spot-on, right down to the prison library and the posters on prisoners' cell walls. Those governors who allowed us access to prisons in the UK to research were simply marvellous. So many got behind the production 100 per cent.

Again, the pressure was on me to produce a compelling script. There's no way my conscience would have let me spend two hours with a prisoner only to trot out a hatchet job. That would have been disgusting. Yet to nail it, I needed access to inmates – all kinds of inmates – including some of Britain's most serious offenders. Let's just say there was a lot of to-ing and fro-ing with authorities on those requests.

Enter Charles Bronson – one of Britain's most notorious prisoners – who became a regular contact. He'd been inside since 1974 for armed robbery but recurrent attacks on prison officers and hostage-taking has meant he remains inside to this day, despite his pleas for parole.

Bronson was always polite, never failed to call me Mrs La Plante, though if he ever wrote to me the spelling of 'Plant' got reduced to mere shrubbery. I still have a stack of Bronson's letters, drawings and poems, and I always paid him in artist's materials for his time. However, which Bronson you visited became a lottery. On some days he'd grown his beard like Rasputin and greeted me behind little round sunglasses. On others he was clean-shaven but for a waxed handle-bar moustache. God knows who sent him hair dye because I'd often turn up to find him with bright purple hair.

As for Bronson's reputation for extreme violence, I never saw a flicker. But unbeknown to him, I did speak at length with deputy governor Adrian Wallace, whom Bronson had held hostage in 1994, leaving him in fear of his life. Bronson broke that man, left him with serious psychological difficulties and unable to work. Preposterous, in my view, that he should ever be considered for release.

Eventually I had to cut contact with Bronson when he upset the girls in my office with lewd phone calls – the man was obsessed with crotchless knickers. And the last letter he wrote to me was in 2018, asking me to fund a headstone for Ruth Ellis, the last woman to be hanged in Britain in 1955. I didn't reply.

I'm still sworn to secrecy as to where or how I had a ten-minute audience with the Yorkshire Ripper, Peter Sutcliffe. He was vacant, monotone, a man of few words and obviously heavily medicated. His physicality was bizarre: a very large head on a short and rather spindly body, and someone who never looked you directly in the eye.

I met the serial killer Dennis Nilsen when I was being shown around Full Sutton Prison. One officer told me that of all the head-shots of prisoners pinned up in the main office it was Nilsen's that got repeatedly stolen, like some kind of trophy. When I passed his cell and looked through the open door there were teddy bears and little toys all lined up. VHS tapes were also stacked neatly against the wall. As we filed through, he was playing table tennis in the recreation area. I always imagined Nilsen to be a slight man but he was surprisingly tall. Later, when I did chat to him, he was bland to the point of being beige and expressionless – quite chilling really.

These encounters were too brief to glean any valuable information from these killers, but sitting in front of them gave me a sense of their presence and mannerisms, so important when applying the brush strokes in casting; a sense of how the surface can never reflect the monsters they truly are.

All the characters in *The Governor* were based on aspects of them, alongside other inmates and prison guards. But I wrestled with my conscience on a daily basis. Bronson especially bothered me. Of all the high-security inmates, I had the most access to him. He knew that I was basing a character on him – the prisoner

Victor Braithwaite who in the series changes his name by deed poll to Tarzan. While I had to protect Bronson as my source, I also had no desire to laud his violence or feed his insatiable appetite for fame. In my eyes, he wasn't the hero everyone thought him to be. Unbelievable to me that a film was released about him in 2008, doing just that I fear.

Instead, I set out to understand the complexity of housing a prisoner like him. I recreated a hostage situation, but thought hard about using Bronson's character to tell that story. In the end I decided not to. It felt like the right decision. After the series ended, Bronson even wrote to me to ask if the actor Terry O'Neill who played Tarzan would visit him, and got rather upset when he didn't.

'Who does he think he is, Omar Fucking Shariff [sic] or Elvis? I'm the world champion now. I done 1,790 mediocre sit-ups in one hour non-stop. You tell Tarzan to try it,' he wrote to me from Belmarsh Prison. Hot on the heels of that letter, he wrote requesting that Terry come to the prison and act the part of Bronson in a play he'd written about himself. Bronson was clever, creative but an incredibly narcissistic and tormented soul.

Casting for *The Governor* became a colossal task. Including extras, there were around 200 people on the cast. The lead of Helen Hewitt was to be one of the most challenging. Any female governor needed to be taller than most men in there. If there was a showdown with a prisoner or a subordinate officer, they could hardly come up to the man's waist. It would look ludicrous! Janet McTeer became the only actor in the frame. Being almost six foot she was both tall and tough. She'd excelled in a handful of TV roles but was relatively unknown. That said, I do recall finding any love interest for Helen Hewitt rather difficult. Janet seemed to have dated half the male members of Equity!

'Oh God, not him!' she said as we flicked through headshot after headshot.

Yet there's always that moment during filming when you know that any risk has paid off. Janet was quite simply brilliant, and it was her attention to detail that impressed me the most.

One day during filming I watched her on the monitor from the edit suite. Cameras were still rolling even though filming had halted for lunch. Over and over again she was opening and shutting, locking and unlocking the prison door. *What the hell is she doing?* I thought.

Later, I asked her, 'Janet, is there a problem with the door on the set?'

'No,' she laughed. 'But I'm the governor, and it's going to look bloody ridiculous if I don't know which keys I'm supposed to be using.'

Admittedly, I also made mistakes in casting. I should have listened to my gut when I hired John Forgeham as Governor Wrexham in *The Governor's* second series. Why I didn't, I have no idea. He'd been the grade-A arsehole who'd played DCI Shefford in *Prime Suspect*. In the intervening years, he'd graduated to weapons-grade. One fabulous actor complained, 'John Forgeham told me I'm crap because I haven't been to drama school.' *I went to RADA and it was crap*, I thought. After two episodes I fired my first employee. I couldn't have John rubbing talented actors up the wrong way.

One absolute wild card was Terry O'Neill. The man had barely acted a day in his life! He practiced karate with Richard so was often at the house working out in the gym. Terry lived like a samurai, had an adoring wife called Bernie and near God-like status in the martial arts world. Back in the 1980s he'd even taught Arnold Schwarzenegger karate kicks for the film *Commando*. Terry did have a bit of a reputation. Rumour had it he'd been a tough guy in his hometown of Liverpool, but it was impossible to ignore his powerful magnetic aura. At my request, he'd featured very briefly in an episode of *Civvies* and also in *Comics* but had never taken on a major role like Victor Braithwaite.

'Give me a go at playing Tarzan,' he asked one day.

I didn't hesitate. It was one of the best decisions I made. Terry was wonderful.

What I found so sad about Terry is that a few years after *The Governor* aired, I met him at an event up North. I was shocked to see he'd become a shell of his former self. His marriage had failed. He appeared withdrawn and washed up. The one person who seemed to keep him going was his beautiful teenage daughter. Sometimes now when I think about Terry I almost see aspects of Bronson. A very bright man, talented but ultimately self-destructive.

The Governor also starred Idris Elba in one of his first meaty TV roles – not that he's ever credited me for it! Idris was always hanging around my office saying, 'Giz a job.' So I did. As an actor, I considered him heavy on charisma rather than technical range, but I was happy to try him out. And while Black actors at that time were still mainly consigned to playing thieves on *Crimewatch* or drug dealers on *The Bill*, I set out to write more into positions of power – Idris played the prison officer Chiswick.

Another big chance I took was when I hired the director Aisling Walsh for a few episodes. In my mind Aisling has gone on to become one of Britain's finest TV directors, but back then she was very green. Verity, of all people, had warned me against hiring her on account of her lack of editing experience. But that was one decision Verity and I disagreed on.

I had no clue how to edit until I sat and watched during Widows, I thought. So, I suggested that Aisling come in and learn that way. She cut her teeth on *The Governor* and truly blossomed. But it was her ability to extract the best performance out of actors that was simply knockout. The Actor Whisperer, I called her. She did it with Terry O'Neill: so calm and so encouraging. She built up rising stars. And, by God, it worked!

Yet as casting continued, the production hit against some serious obstacles. I wasn't exactly thinking small when I wrote a prison break-out scene using a helicopter. Not such a ludicrous scenario, however. Less than a decade before, two prisoners had escaped from HMP Gartree in Leicestershire after a helicopter hijacked by an ex-prisoner landed in the yard and picked up two inmates: three men on the run in one of Britain's most audacious prison getaways.

I visited Gartree to find out more. Some conversations were hilarious! The bravado of inmates claiming to have masterminded the whole break-out left me in stitches. There were others who boasted about being linchpins in the operation's final execution. In reality, it was a number of lifers who'd assisted, knowing they had little chance of parole.

'I got the bats!' I remember one man bragging.

'Bats? What on earth do you mean?'

The guy looked at me as if I was an imbecile. 'You know, from the dayroom!'

'Yes, but what bats?'

'The tennis table bats. Been hiding 'em for a while.'

'Yes, but why?'

'To bring the helicopter in!'

Honestly, I couldn't have made that one up.

Another claimed to have been stood next to one of the escapees when the sound of rotor blades reached deafening levels and the helicopter rose like a giant insect over the prison wall.

'I thought, fuck me!' he said, before describing how the bloke next to him turned on his heels and legged it in the helicopter's direction, jumping in as soon as it landed.

'He still had his mug of coffee in his hand,' he laughed.

A throwaway comment, but the kind of comical detail that I'd only ever be able to pick up face-to-face. I used it in the final cut.

The stunt itself was to be filmed at Wheatfield Prison in Dublin. Technically we had permission, but it was only granted because it was patently obvious the governor didn't think we had the faintest hope of landing the thing.

'A helicopter?' His voice raised several octaves as we sat in his office.

'Yes, that's right. Over the wall.'

'Oh, lady wants a helicopter, does she?' The governor cocked his head in my direction, and winked to everyone else in the room. All male, of course. 'Been on the black stuff, have you? That'll be more of a miracle than the immaculate conception!'

That was a red rag to a bull.

'No, we'll do it,' I said, biting my lip.

Actually, I did not have a clue how we could. The prison yard was very, very small and there was only a narrow gap for a pilot to land in.

'I'll tell you what. If you can bring a helicopter into my yard then I'll allow it. Go on, I dare you!' he said, grinning.

'Right. Fine.' I left the room to a cacophony of guards falling about themselves laughing.

Thankfully, it was Steve Lanning's team who eventually brought in a pilot crazy enough to attempt it. Christ knows where they found this guy, but he'd flown helicopters during the Vietnam War and was only too keen. He seemed very calm when I flew over to Dublin to meet him.

'Ma'am, I've had a good look at the prison yard.'

'Yes, not terribly big, is it? What do you think?'

He smoothed his hair back and nodded. 'Reckon I could bring two in, ma'am.'

'Two? Christ Alive! Well, OK, if you're sure!'

We needed a practice run. On the day, the governor was still grinning wildly. And I'll always remember the prison's real inmates hoisted up on their bunks, peering through the window bars, desperate for a front-row seat. We all stood in disbelief as the pilot skilfully landed this behemoth in the yard to the sound of jeering and toilet rolls being thrown from cell windows. When the real event was filmed we requested that no inmates were present.

Filming in a real prison also brought other challenges. Often, we'd have to file through its communal areas to get to a certain wing.

'Do not fraternise with any of the inmates,' I warned the team, but so many ignored my orders. One day I found the actor Craig Charles, not long out of prison himself, bringing in cigarettes to prisoners and handing them out like he was some kind of tuckshop.

'You can't do that!' I reminded him.

And I had to reprimand assistants, including my own PA Betina, who turned up to prison fact-finding missions in tops and blouses so low-cut you could practically see what she had for dinner.

'It's a Category A male prison!' I shouted. 'Cover up your cleavages, for goodness' sakes!' What were they thinking? Unbelievable!

Filming in Dublin also added another layer of complexity. Actors had to be shipped or flown in and put up in hotels at considerable cost. The edit suite was also housed on-site, meaning I was pulled in all directions: juggling script writing at home in London, then flying to Dublin to run through edits. I also needed to drop everything whenever problems arose.

While Steve Lanning created a marvellous set, he was incredibly adept at passing responsibility to me if anything went wrong.

One day, Steve rang me. 'Do you want the good news or the bad news?'

'Just break it to me, Steve . . .'

'Well, you know the actor playing the violent paranoid schizophrenic prisoner?'

'Yes . . .'

'He's a really good actor . . .'

'OK, so what's the problem?'

'Well, you know the scene where he gets put into the straightjacket?'

'Yes . . .'

'Well, we got him in the straightjacket, but he won't be getting out of it. He's been carted off. He's been sectioned, Lynda!'

'Ah . . .'

Cue a mad scramble to find a replacement for the part of Norman Jones – a terrifying inmate who in one episode carries a razor blade in his mouth. Not an easy part to fill, but I had around twenty-four hours to find another chap, who ended up being Anthony Higgins. Anthony learned fast and played the part superbly.

Another call was far more horrifying. In order to film in Ireland, I needed to agree to a percentage of the crew being Irish. I contracted out the special effects team to a homegrown company whose role from the outset was crucial. The opening feature-length episode would begin with a prison riot and the death of a man in his cell. Windows and doors needed to be blown off in A and B wings as fire ripped through the upper floors. But the pyrotechnics team got a little over-zealous.

Steve Lanning was on the phone again, sounding very panicked. 'Lynda, you need to get here immediately.'

'Whatever's the matter?'

'The explosion . . . it over-exploded. A fireball's torn down the stairs.'

Jesus fucking Christ.

'I'm on the next flight.'

Indeed, a fireball had leapt down the stairs, leaving a massive crater on the lower floor of the reconstructed prison. Damage to the set was fixable; damage to the crew was not so easily patched up. Several people had suffered burns. Some quite severe, in fact, and had to be rushed to hospital. Thank God no one died, but it was a close shave. I had many sleepless nights turning over what could have been. After that disaster I needed to remain in Dublin until the insurance company could assess the damage. As the surveyor wandered around with a camera glued to his face, I balanced in stilettos on the edge of the crater, trying to shield him from tumbling in.

Fortunately, those who were hurt accepted an offer of compensation. Very graciously, I might add. Not only could we have been sued, but it would almost certainly have been the end of *The Governor*, and quite possibly of La Plante Productions. I was learning that no matter what contingency plans I'd put in place, a gargantuan curveball could strike at any moment.

And on a personal note, it did. In full, glorious Technicolor. As well as churning out scripts for *The Governor*, I also got called onto the set of *She's Out* if there were any problems, although that happened rarely. In truth, I avoided going on set on most productions. I remembered back to my time as an actor. The words, 'The Suits are in' became synonymous with an executive turning up to fire someone. Now I was 'The Suit'. However, when crisis struck, I had to go. *She's Out* was being filmed in Buckinghamshire. At the helm was the brilliant Ian Toynton, who'd directed *Widows*. It was all in safe hands until one day Verity rang me in near-meltdown.

'What's the problem?'

'Well, Ian has an actor up a tree . . .'

I thought I'd misheard. 'A tree, did you say?'

'Yes. A tree. You need to talk to her. She is refusing to come down.'

The actor was Linda Marlowe, who was playing the part of ex-convict Esther Freeman. As part of the action the women would be using horses as the getaway vehicles in the raid. In one rather iconic scene they needed to line up and ride together on horseback over the brow of a hill. Only one actor, Anna Patrick, could ride. The rest learned on set. Linda, it transpired, wasn't so confident in the saddle as she'd made out.

'She's very dodgy on the horse,' Ian warned when I spoke to him. 'We have stunt people on standby, but now she's climbed up the tree, she's refusing to use a stunt double and she won't come down.'

'How high up the tree is she?'

'High enough! And we're filming this scene this afternoon.'

'I'll be there as soon I can.'

I climbed into my car and Betina came with me. But halfway there, amid the utter madness of Linda Marlowe stuck up a tree, I had somewhat of an epiphany. Playing on the stereo that day was a tape I'd brought back from America. I'd first heard Bruce Springsteen's wife Patti Scialfa's album *Rumble Doll* there but I'd been unable to find it in the UK. It was always playing on the stereo in our house in The Hamptons.

That year I'd brought a copy over from the States which I kept in the car. Betina had never been in my car but I noticed she was singing along.

How strange that Betina knows all the words, I thought.

'When did you hear this tape?' I asked.

'I have it,' she said.

'Oh, when did you get it? I could only find it in America.'

Something started to click. Over the last few months other strange coincidences had been happening. Fleeting thoughts but part of a larger story that perhaps subconsciously I'd been trying to shut out. Betina had bought a Harley-Davidson motorbike. Richard loved Harley-Davidsons and owned several. He was always helping her repair hers. Now Betina was singing along to a song that she could only have heard in my home in The Hamptons. I had no idea that Betina had even gone to The Hamptons.

The day I got called out to talk Linda Marlowe down from a tree is a day that has always stayed with me. It's the day the penny dropped that Richard was having an affair with my PA. A crushing realisation and one I took weeks to silently process before confronting him. Beyond belief that Elevator Face had the audacity to sit in my car and lie through her back teeth.

As for Linda Marlowe, that more pressing situation called for some high-level diplomacy. The United Nations had nothing on me.

'I don't want to be replaced by a stunt double!' Linda was crying when I trudged over the muddy field to reach her.

Ian Toynton looked worn out by the whole affair.

'It's OK. You can ride the horse, Linda. Just come down from the tree!' I shouted up.

When the shoot finally did happen, all the women cantered over the brow of the hill with some proficiency. Linda Marlowe's horse went backwards. Eventually, after some persuasion, the assistance of a stunt double was required. Ian got his shot, and I returned home to work out what the hell I was going to do. In my heart I knew my marriage was over and, if I was being honest, it had been for many years. Perhaps it was a relief. But the betrayal felt deep and very painful. Before I ever had the chance to confront Betina, she arrived at my house one afternoon.

'I'm leaving La Plante Productions. I've got a job as a photographer in New York and I'm going to take it,' she said.

I decided to say absolutely nothing.

'Fine. I'm very happy for you. Good luck with it.'

I didn't ever confront Betina over the affair. I mean, what would be the point? But I did confront Richard. He admitted to it but brushed it off as nothing serious.

'She followed me to The Hamptons. It was a stupid fling,' he said.

'You need to leave. It's over,' I told him.

What I didn't know then was just how embroiled the two were with each other. Betina was, in fact, pregnant. For me, that was a final kick in the teeth. Finding out months later she'd given birth was probably the only time I'd ever shown my distress. I'd been at a friend's for dinner and someone casually, and rather unthinkingly, announced, 'Oh, did you know Richard's had a baby boy? They've called him Ben.' Ben was the name I'd chosen if ever I'd had a boy. More than that, I'd always wanted a boy. My sister sat opposite me and watched as I blinked back tears. She understood how deeply it cut me.

'Lynda and I are going to go now,' she announced, and she ushered me from the room and took me home.

I don't think I ever grieved the loss of my relationship with Richard, but I did know that if my marriage ended it would take with it my last chance to have a child. Now, that was gone. When divorce proceedings began Richard hired one of the best lawyers in the States. He wanted the house in The Hamptons and so much more. 'He's not getting a brick,' I vowed. And in the end, he didn't.

* * *

She's Out and the first series of *The Governor* screened within two months of each other in 1995. Of course, Ann Mitchell shone brightly once again in the role of Dolly Rawlins in *She's Out*, as did the other actors. It was strong, but I'd written it out of loyalty to Verity. It was *The Governor* where I really felt that same excitement I'd had when I'd first written *Widows*.

When it got commissioned for a second series that year, I felt a mixture of relief and vindication. A hard-hitting prison drama had achieved viewing figures of eleven million. Not bad for La Plante Production's first solo project.

This time around I wanted to show more of the brutality of prison life. There were blatant attacks directed at screws, though it wasn't only overt violence that interested me but the low-level torment of working in a prison: the never-ending noise. In one prison I visited, inmates had driven one officer to near insanity by shouting his name 'John' over and over again –psychological torture that eats into an officer's brain.

Then, there was the violence between inmates. Rape, namely male rape, had never been seen before on British TV, yet as my research found time and again it was a reality of prison life. I wanted viewers to see that. Moreover, I wanted to show the different effect rape had on men than women. To do that I ran parallel storylines. First would be the rape of a female member of staff – the prison psychologist, Annette Bullock – at the hands of an inmate crazed on crack cocaine, Snoopy Oswald. Her rape happened backstage during rehearsals for the prison musical. Visually, it was rather explicit, but a few grunts and moans off-camera would not have communicated its horror. That said, much of the footage did get left on the cutting-room floor. When I watched the original cut from the edit suite it felt relentless in its violence and we worked to tone it down. In the aftermath, Annette would refuse help. Instead, she would suffer the trauma of delayed shock, culminating in a breakdown weeks later.

For the male rape, I'd chosen a model prisoner – Brian Samora, played by the wonderful Jake Abraham. Brian was due for release, the guy everyone rooted for. He'd taken his prison education seriously, but after being pinned to the bed and raped in the medical wing by a twenty-stone inmate called Burt his personality would change completely. Unable to admit what had happened, he'd carry the shame of that violation. Eventually he'd be found dead, having hanged himself. For Jake, I know it was a very harrowing scene to act and reduced him to tears on several occasions.

For me, writing those scenes was also hard. Just as I did during the writing of *Entwined*, I needed to build in lighter moments to *The Governor* to relieve the tension: not just for the viewer, but for myself.

All the ways contraband got smuggled into prisons became a constant fascination for me, so I featured it. Fire extinguishers filled with alcohol – God forbid there actually was a fire! One carpenter working in a prison was bringing in vodka in condoms tied around his belt and covered over with a lumberjack shirt. In one prison I'd visited, the explosive Semtex had been wrapped around the spools on a VHS cassette tape. I had to admire the ingenuity. The climax to the series, the prison theatre production – *The Mikado* – with its costumes, make-up and preparation, also gave me the perfect backdrop to the final break-out scene planned by former IRA terrorists in the final episode.

Of course, it was the male rape that had the media frothing before the series aired. Publicly, I made no apologies for it. Nothing of what I'd written was untrue. I hoped it would cause consternation. Prison life can be horrible. What seemed more mind-boggling to me was that throughout the whole two series of *The Governor* I'd only been allowed two 'fuck's per hour. Any more would have been bleeped out. Against a backdrop of such brutality, the fact that a four-letter word could bring the nation to its knees seemed preposterous to me.

And not long after the second series of *The Governor* aired, I received a letter. It was from an outraged headmaster of a boys' school somewhere in deepest, darkest Middle England.

'Dear Ms La Plante, I watched the second series of *The Governor* and I felt compelled to write to tell you how shocked I was. I have seen the film *Pulp Fiction* three times and nothing in that disgusted me more than the male rape you chose to put on-screen.'

Extraordinary! I thought. Was the male rape featured in the film *Pulp Fiction* not realistic enough for him? More extraordinary was that I didn't receive a single letter of complaint about the rape of Annette Bullock.

Chapter 17
Trial and Retribution

Despite viewing figures exceeding eleven million and the expectation of a third series, *The Governor* didn't get recommissioned. Just before the second series, the powers that be moved it from its weekday primetime slot to a Sunday night death knell – I couldn't help thinking that decision had an impact.

Nevertheless, La Plante Productions had cemented itself as a force in TV. Naturally, I wanted to push further. If I've learned anything about myself during the writing of this book, it's that I always wanted to throw a pebble into the water and watch the ripples. Where those ripples spread is anyone's guess. And of course, the ripples of the mid-1990s were not the same as the ripples of today.

Back then the male rape in *The Governor* had never been seen before. In *She's Out* I featured a lesbian affair between Linda Marlowe's rather twisted character, Ester Freeman, and Julia, a young doctor who'd been jailed for selling prescriptions to fund a heroin habit. Hard to imagine it was only one year previous that the first lesbian kiss had ever been screened in the soap opera *Brookside*, to much pearl-clutching outrage.

That said, being audacious was never about shock for its own sake. For me, it had to fit the scenario, fit the characters, fit the realism of the piece and also fit what I'd seen with my own eyes, through my research. I always wanted to place brutality, gruesome detail, or sexual explicitness there for good reason. If it didn't hold up, it got chucked out.

In that spirit, I also wanted to experiment with production techniques – something I'd never been able to do as a writer-for-hire. I thought back to the forensics labs where I spent so much time researching *Prime Suspect*. Wouldn't it be interesting to see more of that? Forensics had moved on apace since 1991. And wouldn't it be interesting for viewers to understand how evidence fed into a court case? Never as clear-cut as people assume, especially around DNA.

'Ah, they've got a DNA match! He or she must be guilty!' This is often an assumption made by the armchair fan, but techniques like DNA have to work alongside other evidence to secure a conviction. The permutations are multifaceted, and notions of justice are equally as ambiguous. People get wrongly convicted. Guilty criminals walk free or get convicted for lesser crimes because the weight of evidence is not strong enough. Or criminals brush up in their smart clothes in court and win over sceptical juries. Justice in its purest form is served far less than people imagine. All those thoughts were swirling around in my mind.

Again, I took the idea to ITV's Nick Elliott. In my head there were three elements to this drama: the crime; the investigation and collection of evidence; and the subsequent court case. A three-dimensional view. So, what if to show that I could also split the screen into three? Viewers could then get a sense of people working on multiple elements of a case as an ongoing process. As far as forensics were concerned it solved another problem. Showing ten minutes of a hair being unwound from a button would be exceedingly boring, but if the viewer could follow other parts of the story at the same time then it would be a unique way of telling it.

Nick – usually very gung-ho about innovative formats – had serious doubts.

'Nice idea, Lynda, but it just won't work.'

'Why not?' I asked.

'Well, think about your ordinary viewer in a high-rise with a small, ten-inch screen. How the hell are they going to follow simultaneous action on a split screen? Not everyone has big tellies, Lynda!'

I vaguely knew about the ITV litmus test: whether an idea would appeal to its perceived audience – 'Tower Block Tracey' as she has more recently become known. But I didn't buy Nick's argument. In fact, I found it rather patronising and I told him so.

'Have you ever been to a game of bingo, Nick?'

'No.' He frowned.

'Well, go. Because those ladies who watch on their ten-inch screens in their tower blocks can play eight bingo cards at the same time.'

Nick thought about that for a moment. 'You're right, Lynda. Just do it.'

The series that was to become *Trial and Retribution* turned out to be a biggie. In the end, it ran for twelve seasons from 1997 to 2009, but back in 1995 that initial commission was for a three-hour two-parter.

By then La Plante Productions had moved into larger, plusher offices in Wardour Street in Soho, at the top of Paramount House where Paramount Studios had its main offices. If we were going to kick butt we needed more than a cubbyhole in my then agent's office.

With Betina gone, I would employ a bank of script editors. Nowadays, series often have teams of writers, or what's called writers' rooms, but that was never the way I worked. Once, I did bring in two writers to work independently on *Trial and Retribution*, but it took me longer to rectify the material than it did to write it. From then on I was usually the primary writer. It had always been that way and has remained so throughout my TV career. Instead, I relied on script checkers and editors, and brought in co-writers when needs be.

Trial and Retribution posed difficulties. Because it was incredibly procedural with both police and judicial elements, experts became invaluable cogs in the production wheel. A guy called Callum Sutherland – Cass to his friends and colleagues – wrote to me asking if I needed any help. He'd not long retired from the Met Police and in the latter part of his thirty-year career he'd been a crime scene investigator: a man who is still worth his weight in gold so many years later – an absolute wealth of knowledge. Not only that, but Cass gave me access to experts whose input I would have been lost without. On that show there was a forensic expert alongside a pathology expert.

Through Liz Thorburn, I met the barrister David Martin-Sperry. I adore David – a terribly funny man. Not only did he start off by being my expert on court procedure, but he ended up writing many of the judge's directions and closing speeches. David also fires out dynamite ideas at machine-gun speed. Whatever scenario or legal rabbit-hole he suggested, I was all ears.

Watching him in court made me snort with laughter, too. Judges' eyes rolled. David has a head for excruciating detail, dripped out fact by fact.

'Is this line of questioning going anywhere?' judges often asked.

'Yes, I will be making the point shortly,' David replied. He always did deliver a killer blow but, by God, the legal cul-de-sacs he went down to get there were mind-boggling.

One day he was terribly late, unheard of for David.

'I'm so sorry.' He ran flustered into the courtroom, banging down his files. 'I've been witness to a murder!' Even the judge saw the funny side. 'Right . . . shall we get on?' he said with a wry smile.

The courtroom never did get to hear the details.

With *Trial and Retribution*, I didn't set myself an easy task. In that first episode I chose to show the harrowing case of a child murder – in truth, a decision I came to regret. Some seven years later I was to witness first-hand the trial of Soham murderer Ian Huntley, accused and convicted of killing two beautiful ten-year-old children, Holly Wells and Jessica Chapman.

To this day, I have never forgotten watching that despicable killer on the stand and Huntley's girlfriend Maxine Carr nervously twitching all the time the terrible evidence was being read. I was left aware of the never-ending anguish the young victims' parents suffered, having had to listen to what had been done to their children.

Back when I was researching for *Trial and Retribution*, not only did I sit in courtroom after courtroom observing criminal trials, but I also went out to talk to the victims of crime: among them parents of children who'd been killed. I found parents through contacts or newspaper clippings. No one ever refused to talk to me, but the work did require a deep sensitivity.

One can never imagine how parents find the strength to continue after such a tragedy. How do you see your child on a gurney? Or face their killer? Beyond belief how people do. And I've always been conscious that in novels or drama, there's a conclusion. It's one of the reasons people love to read or watch crime drama. Yet in real life, there's never such a neat ending. I can't help but think of the death of my own sister, how it haunted my parents – my mother especially – her entire life. So many bereaved parents and victims serve their own life sentence, and I developed an overwhelming realisation that there is no end. The pain of your child never falling in love, never having children, never living a life – that loss extends way beyond a death.

During those meetings I needed to remain composed throughout, but there were many occasions as I walked back to my car when I couldn't help but break down in tears. The detail was harrowing, but it was often the most innocuous of comments that stuck in my head.

One woman told me how she knew her daughter was dead simply because the officer who stepped through her front door took her hat off before she spoke. Incredible that such a simple gesture communicated so much. Showing those tiny authentic details would enrich any drama.

Another woman described how her daughter had been murdered twenty years ago but how she still lived with the pain, terrified to let go of it for fear of losing the memory of her child.

An officer told me how guilt haunted him after he rushed the father of one victim when identifying his son. He'd been so eager to move forward with the case, to catch the killer, that in that moment the compassion he needed to show the next of kin escaped him. A tough balancing act between respecting families of the dead and getting on with the job.

For the first time, I also wanted to show the toll that cases have on police. All serious criminal cases have an effect, but child murder is especially traumatic. Many officers struggle to continue following those investigations. Lifting the lid on that damage became my focus.

To cope with the technical challenges of the series, I needed a director who I trusted and who would be willing to push the limits. Over the years I used a variety of favourites, but Aisling Walsh became the obvious choice. She'd shown herself to be a superb director on *The Governor,* plus she'd displayed that magical quality with actors that I needed, given such an energy-sapping script.

Splitting the screen three ways would be demanding for both cast and crew. Scripts, individual speeches and scenes had to stretch out far longer to span the length of the action. That would mean extended filming days, which was costly, and employing actors who could sustain long lines at the same time as delivering emotionally charged performances.

By now, I was employing my sister Gill as my full-time casting agent. Gill had started out in the advertising industry sourcing clothes and props for adverts but had built up her own successful casting business. Way back when I was an actor, and ever out of work, I'd sometimes step in to answer the phones in her offices in Goodge Street. She'd also get me the odd commercial. Once, I secretly glanced at my file: 'Lynda Marchal: short; ordinary-looking; good for middle-class mums'. *Bloody cheeky cow!*

'Well, it's the truth, Lynda!' she exclaimed when I pointed it out.

She also thought me incredibly stupid when I asked her who the RIP agency were. The letters were written below so many stars' names in the *Spotlight* directory that I thought they must have frightfully good representation.

'It means Rest In Peace, Lynda. They're dead!' she howled with laughter. At least I'd learned something since then!

I had used Gill a couple of times on *The Governor*. Directors like Ridley Scott loved her, but it wasn't until she began working for me full-time that I realised why. Gill didn't waste time. She always got the perfect actor first time around and the fresh faces I wanted. Gill sourced from end-of-drama-school plays plus repertory theatre up and down the country. It was as if she read my mind. She found one star after another.

In that first series of *Trial and Retribution* a little girl, Julie Ann Harris, would go missing, found dead in a sewage pipe. All suspicion would fall on the child's stepfather, who was abusive. In fact, the real killer would be a sex offender living nearby whose guilt is only revealed through DNA evidence from fingerprints on a sherry bottle and a blood match to the child.

Immediately, Gill found our mother, stepfather and suspect. The stepfather Peter would be played by Lee Ross, a terrific up-and-coming actor. For Anita Harris, mother of Julie, we found Helen McCrory in one of her earliest roles. Dear soul, terribly sad to think she is no longer with us. Helen was an incredibly promising actor but had rather bottle-shaped legs and we spent ages trying to find her the right shoes to make them look longer.

In the role of Michael Dunn, the sex offender, we cast Rhys Ifans. Rhys had done little more than a Welsh TV play – a very fresh actor and an utterly shambolic man, always disappearing off somewhere and having to be hauled back to set – but a dynamite actor when he got going.

The young officer would be played by Jake Wood. Jake was wonderful, yet I couldn't have predicted that he would find the subject matter so disturbing. His character would find Julie's body. It was after watching him during the rushes when I vowed never to write a child murder again. Everyone on set became so badly shaken up by it.

For viewers, it can be hard to imagine what scripts like that can take out of an actor, what emotion they have to summon up to hit their mark. During a final court scene Rhys had to repeat: 'I didn't do it.' Take after take was filmed, and at one point he simply broke down.

'I can't do it. I'm sorry, I can't go on,' he announced.

Step in Aisling Walsh – absolutely incredible! I have no idea what she said to Rhys, but I watched from behind the monitor as she quietly walked over and whispered in his ear. That symbiosis between director and actor was very special and he redid the line one more time. Bingo. That final take was used in the episode.

Corin Redgrave, who played Robert Rylands QC, appeared from the start of *Trial and Retribution* and through numerous seasons. He was hilarious. When he first came into casting we all felt terribly embarrassed. He wasn't just part of the Redgrave acting dynasty alongside his sister Vanessa, but a very respected actor in his own right. Nevertheless, I treated all actors the same. I always made them read in auditions – that way I could spend time with them, get a feel for how they handled the part. By reading through scripts I could also help the actor interpret the directions between the lines, thereby giving the director all the information he or she needed to bring the script to life.

Aisling sat with me that day and took charge of proceedings.

'Corin, thank you so much for coming. We've got a script for you to read,' she said.

Immediately, Corin shot both of us a look that could turn a heart to stone. 'I beg your pardon?'

Corin was rather pompous, even in real life.

'The script, if you could just start from the top,' Aisling continued.

Corin looked incandescent. He tutted and reached into his bag and yanked out several audio tapes.

'Here is me in *Coriolanus*,' he said, slamming one down. 'And me in *Antony and Cleopatra* . . . And I think you'll find me here in *Henry IV*.'

He reeled off play after play, then half-rose from his chair as if to leave the room. All very theatrical, so before we lost him I stepped in.

'It's OK, Corin, the part is yours,' I said.

'I'm very pleased about that,' he said, lowering himself back down.

That said, Corin did write me the most lovely note during *Trial and Retribution*: 'You've given me back so much belief in myself as an actor and faith that people in this business really do care.' Those words meant so much to me. When I began La Plante Productions I wanted everyone to care about the creative process as much as Verity Lambert and Ian Toynton had done on *Widows*, my first experience in TV.

Besides, I knew I was safe with Corin. To have a few seasoned actors on the set of such a big production was a godsend. When you say, 'Camera! Action!' to an unknown they can completely fall apart. I've seen it many times, as well as being in that position myself. The pressure of that moment is intense. Actors forget where to put their feet, forget their lines. Corin was perfect for those hefty speeches too, to run across the split-screen time. He also needed to use props subtly. During all my time in court I'd watched barristers play with paper and pens and I wanted that recreated on-screen.

David Martin-Sperry had told me of one QC who built tension in the courtroom simply by screwing and unscrewing the top of his pen. Then he'd place it in his top pocket to relax the witness before bringing it out just as he was about to deliver a killer question. I became fascinated by this man. Unlike in American courtrooms where attorneys can stroll around, there's little room for movement in UK courts. Props like pens take on their own character. Corin studied that QC, too, and developed those techniques from him.

For our lead detective, David Hayman filled the role of DCS Mike Walker perfectly: a terrific, solid, dependable actor – no starry quality about him whatsoever. David always turned up on time, learned his lines, gave a consistent performance throughout and was marvellously encouraging to new talent on the show. You'd often hear him off-set asking, 'Would you like to run over the lines on that scene?' Then, he'd help the actor: 'OK, that was great, but no need to come at me so strongly. Temper the volume on that line.'

Physically, however, David was surprisingly slight. In the end we had to bulk him out using padded shirts and jackets, plus insert lifts in his shoes to give him authority in the briefing room. Amazing how after that he could dominate the screen like he did.

David also understood continuity down to a tee. If he had a cigarette on the burn in one scene and filming was cut, he'd measure exactly the length of the ash so that when the camera rolled again it was at the exact same length. Every day, he also sat in front of the mirror and meticulously recreated the scar across his eye, sustained from an arrest gone wrong, which later became a plot line. He was one of the few actors we let do their own make-up.

Whenever I watched David, I always remembered acting alongside the great Daniel Massey, which I did in a TV production in Manchester. Massey was playing Churchill. A wonderful actor and a flamboyant man, but he could never remember from scene to scene what order he was supposed to be smoking his cigar, clipping his cigar, or stubbing out his cigar. Rehearsals descended into a complete fiasco.

Kate Buffery as David's subordinate DI North was brilliantly strident, too, and I thought she was terrific at first – a very commanding actor.

And for that first episode we used triplets for the child. Working with children can be terribly difficult at the best of times, but on such a complex production there would be take after take. Children simply don't have the concentration span so we swapped them in and out. Moreover, some scenes were so chilling. For a child to lay still and pretend to be dead on a gurney is a lot to ask, but if she had a sister sat out of camera shot then it could provide some comfort and distraction.

Many episodes later I cast a very young Carey Mulligan in the role of a girl whose murder was a complex case, as both her boyfriend and a neighbour were in the frame. Carey had that extra something – a magic you can't always put your finger on – but I think it was in her smile. *Great potential*, I thought. One problem was that she was underage at the time, and her mother accompanied her on set throughout.

So many negotiations needed to take place. During one scene Carey needed to fall down a set of stairs.

'She will not be doing that fall,' her mother insisted.

'No, it's OK. We have stunt doubles. They will be doing that.'

For the next scene she'd be laid out on a gurney with a pathologist talking officers through her fatal injuries.

'Under no circumstances will she be appearing naked,' her mother said.

'Don't worry, there will be nothing revealing,' we reassured her.

In fact, we placed actors in front of her breasts and private parts to obscure the view and had a white sheet on hand in between shoots.

In the end the director, Andy Hay, rang me tearing his hair out. Carey Mulligan's mother was turning into a pain in the arse, and that was before he'd started shooting the first scene.

'Can we replace her? Get another actor in?' he pleaded with me.

'Can we try to keep going with her?' I asked.

When I saw the rushes, I knew I'd got it right. Carey Mulligan did have that X-factor, even if her mother was a nightmare.

Many years later I watched her in a film called *Shame* directed by Steve McQueen, which I found shockingly explicit. Carey seemed to call it art. *What does her mother think about that?* I wondered.

The sheer amount of horse-trading that needed to go on during *Trial and Retribution* was breathtaking. In one early episode I asked Richard E. Grant if he would play the part of a respectable, charming wine merchant called Stephen Warrington, who turned out to be a psychotic serial killer. Richard was a well-known face on TV, not the usual actor I would have opted for, but I wanted someone whom viewers initially trusted – a household name. When they realised the truth it would be so shocking.

At first Richard was very unsure about the role.

'I don't think I'll be able to play it. I can't just flip into that character,' he said.

To become that character is a feat – the energy it needs, how disturbing it can be, the horror of it. But Richard was heavily underestimating his talents in my view.

'You can play it. You'll be brilliant,' I told him.

Personally, I thought Richard did an incredible job of portraying this seemingly stable, family man who tips into a maniac. But it was off-set that he was to cause me the most problems.

Afterwards I think he felt rather embarrassed, but before he'd even arrived, Richard's agent insisted he be given a luxury Winnebago to relax in between shoots. Other actors' trucks were standard trailers.

When Liz Thorburn checked out the price, it was going to cost around £35,000. Talk about blowing the budget!

Christ, I thought. *If Richard gets a Winnebago everyone else will want one!* Not a chance we could stretch to that. Instead, I negotiated a deal with every actor on an equal footing with Richard.

'By all means, you can have a Winnebago but wouldn't you rather five thousand extra in pay?' All of them took the money. Naturally, it's the kind of deal-making I never dreamed I'd be doing when La Plante Productions began.

In a later episode, I'd wanted a very young Michael Fassbender to play a rather colourful barrister, but the director had not been convinced. As the director had wanted his real-life girlfriend to play a leading role, I traded actors: 'If I can have Michael, you can have her,' I said. The deal was struck – and just look at Michael Fassbender now! But I'd overlooked one crucial point. Until I saw the rushes I'd not noticed how cross-eyed the girlfriend was. Hours were spent in the edit suite cutting any face-on shots.

Yet on *Trial and Retribution* those negotiations were small fry compared to the disaster that befell the production in the run-up to its eighth series. While Kate Buffery and David Hayman initially worked well together, the cracks in their off-screen relationship were beginning to show.

As I had been churning out script after script, the editors and experts had been checking and changing before we got to the final edit. Yet when each script got handed to Kate, she wasn't just reading her lines, but she'd started to count up the number of words David had compared to her.

What? This is utter madness, I thought. Whether it was fuelled by some kind of stand on women's rights, I had no idea.

The situation had started to become exceedingly difficult, not least because the pair were to begin an on-screen relationship and move in together. DI North even had a miscarriage – a deeply intimate storyline that required both Kate and David to bring out the emotion of that scenario. God knows, I knew the emotion they needed to get to. I'd suffered enough myself and those were tough scenes for me to write.

Soon, though, I had David knocking on my door.

'I'm sorry, I just don't think Kate and I can work together,' he said. David was such a fair-minded man that I knew the situation must be serious.

Kate was also bending my ear. 'David has far more lines than me in this episode. It has to be changed.'

'He is your DCI,' I reminded her. 'Naturally, he will speak more. He's in charge of the bloody investigation!'

As their off-screen relationship broke down further, I found myself in the midst of a script-writing shit-storm – trying to rewrite storylines to build in more scenes where the two never crossed paths. Yet they lived in the same flat, for Christ's sake! *Almost impossible to pull that one off*, I thought.

Everything came to a head. Rather bizarrely, Kate had started turning up to work looking like a bit of a bag lady, if I'm honest. And the line counting had reached epic proportions.

It had got to the point where working with her was impossible. After some consideration I didn't think I could have her back on set. David was an actor who I desperately wanted to remain on the show.

'I'm sorry, she's off the series,' I told her agent.

Regrettably, there was no option but to sack her. And it was regrettable because Kate had been such a strong female lead. Nevertheless, I paid her for her full contract.

While that decision did calm the waters with cast and crew, it left me with an almighty headache. I'd already started writing the scripts for the next series and now the part of DI North was effectively dead in the water. Plus, I had no female actor to play her part.

Instead, I wrote her out completely. The relationship between DCI Mike Walker and DI North would end and another detective would be brought in: DCI Roisin Connor, who would prove more than a match for Walker. *Who the hell could play her?* I had some idea. I didn't have time to risk a complete unknown, I needed an actor who could hit the ground running. I'd seen the Irish actor Victoria Smurfit on the BBC series *Ballykissangel* and thought she had the looks and dominance to take on the role.

Thankfully, very soon after Kate Buffery departed *Trial and Retribution* Victoria agreed to come on board, and remained in the series until it finally ended in 2009. What an absolute sweetie she turned out to be. Everyone loved working with her and she really grew into the part. Kudos to her – she needed to step in quickly and I'm sure David encouraged her every step of the way. My only problem was that Victoria kept getting pregnant. She must have popped three children out during those six years – firing them out like Smarties! Lovely, of course, but for a production company it became an absolute nightmare for scheduling.

Trial and Retribution reached its end in 2009, eleven years after I'd first conceived it. I am still so thrilled at the innovation and expert detail that went into making that series. David Hayman continued as DCI Mike Walker right up until the final episode. I cannot thank him enough for everything he brought to it. When ITV eventually cancelled it, there was no explanation given, no note sent to David or any of the stalwart cast thanking them for their wonderful talent and longstanding commitment. Disgusting, really, when I think about it now. But I do hope it's a production that made everyone who worked on it incredibly proud.

Chapter 18

Star Turns

My divorce from Richard was protracted and rather bitter. Not what I would have chosen. I'd also had to decide whether to keep my surname La Plante. I hadn't much liked Marchal when it had been my stage name, and I didn't want to revert to Titchmarsh. La Plante had been my professional name throughout my TV series and my books. It stayed, and now I often joke that it's the best thing my ex-husband gave me.

Not long after Richard and I split, I started dating a man I'd met in The Hamptons. The relationship didn't last long, although I did have one last shot at having a baby. I was approaching my early fifties by then and most people, including the fertility clinic I rocked up at in the US, thought I'd lost my mind when I embarked on a round of IVF treatment.

'Well, you're knocking on a bit!' became the consensus. Yet, I didn't feel so. I was incredibly fit, always playing tennis and horse-riding. *If I can carry babies to full term, I will. If I can't, I'll soon find out*, I figured. Why not try? Some people might think that's insanity, but fear has never stopped me doing anything.

Whenever I stayed in The Hamptons, I always kept British time. That meant starting work at 4.30 a.m. in the stillness of the early morning, perfect to write and watch the sun rise. By mid-afternoon I'd clock off and kayak on the bay, play tennis or relax. Every summer, friends from England and elsewhere would come and stay for weeks, too.

The IVF treatment was initially successful. I carried triplets until around a month, but one day as I was pushing my kayak out from the jetty I doubled over in cramps and severe pain. By now I knew the signs, but this felt particularly cruel. Although early miscarriages are traumatic, they are physically no more than a heavy period. Perhaps it was my age but it felt more harrowing and I knew I couldn't put myself through that anguish again.

For good reason, I hadn't told anyone about the IVF treatment, not even my family. If it failed I couldn't bear people calling me to say, 'I'm so sorry.' For all the uncovering of souls I do in my professional life I'm a very private person when it comes to my own emotions. What I had done, however, is keep my name on the adoption lists in the States, despite the fact that in the last two years of our marriage Richard had refused to continue with any adoption plans.

It's also fair to say that period of my life prompted some other moments of complete madness. Animals have always been incredibly important to me – from my childhood in Crosby right up to when I began keeping pets myself. These days there's not an animal in peril I don't try to save with donations: polar bears; abandoned dogs; horses. I'm a blubbering wreck whenever I see bedraggled donkeys on those gut-wrenching TV adverts.

In Queen's Gate I'd kept a wolfhound called Bates, named after my lovely butler, and later, I had another called Tallulah – wonderful companions. I also brought home a giant poodle crossed with a Great Dane – a Danoodle called Harold. Harold was a natural comic. A happy, loyal beast with silky brown ringlet curls. I used to dress him in sunglasses and a hat and he'd perch on the rear seat of my sports convertible. Once I got pulled over by a concerned police officer: 'Do you know there's a Rastafarian in the back of your car?' From behind, Harold's coat looked like dreadlocks.

'It's my dog!' I smiled.

Harold eventually needed a chain around his neck with my address stamped onto it. He'd often escape and climb into random taxis if ever a passenger was stood with the door open, paying the driver. Croydon was the farthest he got before I received a distressed call from a baffled cabbie.

But from the mid-1990s right into the early 2000s it was horses that became my passion. My grandmother Gertrude had loved racing and I spent afternoons with her at Aintree as a child. I rode regularly, too. And my then-agent Duncan Heath's mother had owned champion horses, so he and my accountant launched us into the equine world. We became the owning conglomerate Action Bloodstock – Action Bloodbath more like! Rank amateurs with more hope than we ever had success. But racing did become a fantastic form of escapism from loss.

Over those years we probably owned a total of twelve horses with a couple of real winners. Supply and Demand was named after a series I made with Miriam Margolyes – a lead investigator in charge of a specialist undercover squad. He was one of our first horses and also our best – a champion's heart who crossed the winning line several times under the trainer John Gosden. Bound for Pleasure was another beautiful horse. I even had a builder in an episode of *Trial and Retribution* say he was having a flutter on him.

But we had far more losses than wins and I soon realised that owning horses sunk more money than it ever made. Once, left to my own devices, I bought a handsome horse called Bandit Queen – surprisingly cheap, too. It didn't take us long to work out why. The horse weaved – meaning it swayed its head and neck from side to side. A stress response, apparently, but lethal as other horses in the stable copy it. Bandit Queen turned out to be a liability.

Another I named Freedom – after Freedom Stubbs, the boxer in my novel *The Legacy* – but he never ran a day his entire career. Not only did he try to hump everything in sight, but when he was eventually gelded it went wrong and he got sick. Poor thing had to be put down. I learned never to become too attached to a horse. They can easily break your heart. In the end, travelling to race meets at Epsom, Newmarket or further afield became too onerous for me and Action Bloodstock limped into inaction.

By the early 2000s La Plante Productions had several long-running series airing. *Trial and Retribution* and *Supply and Demand* were ongoing. The comedy duo *French & Saunders* had even written a spoof sketch called *The Job*, parodying all my work from *Prime Suspect* to *The Governor* to *She's Out*, and starring many of my leading ladies, including Janet McTeer, Ann Mitchell and Helen Mirren. I played the cigar-smoking boss – a real hoot to film. By then I'd also made the mini-series *Killer Net* for Channel 4. It didn't prompt much fanfare at the time, but when I look back now I think how prophetic it was. The seed had been planted when I'd been in LA and having dinner with the playwright and screenwriter Neil Simon.

'It's my daughter,' he'd said worriedly.

'What's happened?'

Apparently Neil's daughter had been on the internet – the World Wide Web, as it was known back then – on something called a chatroom and she'd been encouraged to leave home.

'What do you mean?' I asked.

I had no clue! Most people were still grappling with email, let alone chatrooms or computer games. Certainly, it was an alien world to me. But it did get me thinking – what if there was a computer game where someone could learn how to commit the perfect murder?

From that thought, *Killer Net* was born. Then the realisation hit me. *Christ, I only know computer basics!* Fortunately, I did have a young woman working for me as a script editor who I asked to help – she was a real whizz online, but sadly that arrangement ended rather abruptly.

'I'm not starting work until I get a contract,' she told me.

She had been working for me for some time, so her sudden professional mistrust hit a raw nerve.

When her contract arrived, I called her. 'Your contract is done.'

'OK, but I won't consider starting until you've signed it,' she said.

'Oh really?'

Admittedly it was not my finest moment, but her attitude enraged me.

'You won't consider starting? You mistrust me to such an extent that you won't start? Hear this . . .' I said stubbornly.

At that I took her contract and ripped it in two.

'This is your contract. I'm tearing it up. You're fired,' I said before slamming the phone down. Even now, I feel rather ashamed.

I'd also placed myself in a far worse position. *What the fuck do I do now?* I thought. Thank God for my cousin, the actor and writer Fidelis Morgan. She was very computer-literate and ended up rescuing *Killer Net*. I'd known Fidelis for years, but the funny thing is she and I would never have met had she not arrived at the stage door way back when I was acting with the Royal Shakespeare Company.

'I'm your cousin,' she announced.

'You are?'

Apparently so, although I'm still not sure from what side of our family! Fidelis has memories of aunties I have no recollection of whatsoever, but it's lovely that it's a friendship that has lasted many, many years.

Killer Net was set in Brighton and revolved around a group of students, one of whom has become obsessed by a video game. When he commits the perfect virtual murder it coincides with the real-life death of his ex-girlfriend.

Before the screening, I held a press conference. 'It's about interactive computer gaming,' I told the assembled journalists.

Talk about blank faces in the room. Mouths catching flies. 'What?'

The idea that people could be groomed online or crime could proliferate there was such a new concept. Fast forward to today and just look at social media and the chatrooms and porn sites and the explosion in cyber crime. Even if I do say so myself, *Killer Net* was way ahead of the curve.

In the main lead I cast Paul Bettany, who has gone on to achieve superstardom. Again, my brilliant sister Gill found him, alongside the series' other young lead: the wonderful Tam Williams. Neither had done much TV beforehand and I clearly remember Paul arriving for the audition. Despite being tall, he was rather scrawny and unbelievably twitchy.

'Would you read for us?' I asked.

Paul shuffled awkwardly in his seat. 'I'm sorry, I can't. I'm dyslexic,' he said, embarrassed.

I knew exactly how he felt. And I knew exactly how to help him.

'Don't worry about that. Go into the other room and I'll read alongside you so you can memorise the lines,' I instructed him.

Like me, he had tremendous recall once he got past the difficult words.

Killer Net's director Geoffrey Sax was a sweetheart but he wasn't convinced Paul was right for the part, yet he went along with my hunch. In fact, I rewrote the script especially for Paul. Originally, the lead had been an oversized rugby-player, which Paul's wiry frame did not suit.

When it came to watching the first rushes, he was stunning. And a couple of months later when my friend, the film producer Norma Heyman, was scouting around for an actor for the film *Gangster No. 1*, I suggested Paul for the title role of Young Gangster. She went on to use him in the end. The film was a hit and it launched his Hollywood career.

Wishful thinking, perhaps, but I had thought someone might have remembered my recommendation when I heard Paul make a speech at an awards ceremony some years later.

'There's one person I must thank,' he told the audience.

I smiled heartily across the auditorium.

'This person launched my career and for that I pay tribute to . . .'

By now I was half-raised out of my seat ready to receive the applause.

'. . . Norma Heyman.'

Norma? I plonked myself back down, feeling rather pissed off.

I know I shouldn't feel hurt by that all these years later, but oversights like that do get to me sometimes. Perhaps Paul didn't know I had passed Norma his name, but she should have given me the credit. After that, I always noticed she was a little nervous when mentioning him.

Actors can be a strange bunch. Some can be appreciative. Years before, when I was in Australia, I remember someone showing me the script for the upcoming drag-queen road comedy *The Adventures of Pricilla, Queen of the Desert*. A lovely actor called Nickolas Grace had been mooted for a starring role but no finances could be raised against him. When I suggested Terence Stamp there was some doubt he'd agree to drag. 'Believe me, once you get him in a frock, you'll never get him out of it!' I told the producers. Weeks later when I arrived home, Terence, who was a regular visitor, told me of an outlandish script that had been sent to him.

'You must do it. It will change your life,' I told him. And I was right. That film revived Terence's career at a time when it was in the doldrums. However, in putting him forward for the role, I'd ruined Nic's chances. I felt so bad about it that many years later I cast Nic as a psychiatric patient who thought himself to be a bat.

That said, other actors can be some of the most thankless people I have ever met, and I do believe I can say that with some confidence, having been one myself. The amount of times I've lined up talented people for roles or championed them, even coached them before auditions, only to hear they didn't bother turning up is quite remarkable. And then there are those you simply have to sit back and laugh about.

Once I asked the legendary Norman Wisdom if he would play the part of an elderly lech in *Trial and Retribution*. He was in his early eighties at the time, and insisted on coming to my house to inform me of his decision.

'I wanted to come to congratulate you on your series,' he said.

'What did you think to the part?' I asked.

'Well, my dear, I really don't want to play a dirty old man. I do have my reputation to protect, but thank you for thinking of me.'

Norman was so charming. And what good manners he had to see me in person to tell me the part was truly horrible.

In *Supply and Demand* I wanted to cast the comedian Freddie Starr as a drug dealer. I'd always been an admirer of his – a superb physical comic, albeit with a reputation of being quite crazy. He was bulky in size, and I could picture him with his thick-set jaw and bleach-blond hair in a big overcoat. When he came to discuss the part he was raring to go.

'A bad guy? I've hankered after playing a rough guy!' he said.

Freddie was adorable, but when it came to the first read-through, it was quite bizarre. When we got to Freddie's part he made no sense whatsoever.

'Up, err, ah, oh, um.' Instead of words, he made a succession of noises.

He'd brought his partner with him, a young woman, who then began to point to each word in the script. It was then I realised he was illiterate. He couldn't read a word of the script.

'Would you work on these lines with him privately?' I asked her.

When it came to filming, I was called onto set. Freddie had one initial line. He needed to bang through a set of double doors and shout, 'Put that bag down now!'

'Pu, eh, oh, da . . .' Freddie delivered his line very confidently, but he seemed to have no clue that he was talking gibberish.

'It's "Put that bag down now!"' I shouted to him.

'Put that bag down now!' he said, mimicking me effortlessly. Incredible! And that was how we got through it in the end. I called his line and he called it back.

Another series La Plante Productions made, *The Commander*, ran from 2003 to 2008 and stared Amanda Burton. Unlike Jane Tennison in *Prime Suspect* who Granada transformed into a wreck, its lead character Commander Claire Blake had fought her way to the top. I guess it was my way of revisiting that story and the outcome I had wanted for Tennison.

Filming *The Commander* turned into quite a mission. One actor kept disappearing. Throughout, we had cars out looking for him at all hours to bring him back to filming. Another lead actor demanded time off for an apparent neck injury sustained on set. I was faced with yet another tricky negotiation, the kind I had now become well-versed in.

Halting filming, especially on location, is hugely expensive and I needed to see for myself how bad this injury was. I travelled to the actor's home.

'How are you?' I asked before handing over a bouquet of flowers.

'Not so good,' they answered.

Apparently they needed at least a week off.

'I'm sorry to hear that.'

We chatted for a while and then I noticed something peculiar. The actor's rather small dog bounded into the living room and they bent over with considerable ease, picked it up and cuddled it.

'A week? It must be a relief your neck's better,' I said.

'Yes,' they hesitated guiltily, knowing they'd been caught out.

Suddenly the week got reduced to a twenty-four-hour rest on the advice of a doctor.

'Oh, that's terrific. You'll be back in work tomorrow, then?' I said.

'I'm not sure about that . . .'

What I'd also perfected was a sotto voce voice when persuading actors to do things they didn't want to do.

'It would be a great relief to me if you did return,' I said quietly and very, very sweetly.

They resumed filming with no hint of paralysis.

Other actors were simply hilarious. At the end of any series I inevitably ended up doing deals over which of their costumes they could buy at a discounted price. Some used it as a bargaining chip, especially if they felt short-changed on their fee.

'I really think my character would wear a long black cashmere coat.'
If I had a pound for every time I'd heard that one . . .

'Yes, but your character has two lines. You won't be getting one!'

Comedienne Dawn French even told me once of one actor who complained she wasn't getting paid as much as her male co-star. A deal was agreed whereby she could keep the Dior dress and selected designer clothes she'd worn during filming. The morning after production wrapped up she turned up with a removal van to the costume department and filled it with her complete wardrobe!

And just when you think you're doing someone an almighty favour, they completely flabbergast you. It's exactly what happened to me with the actor Joan Turner. How Joan got my number I'm not entirely sure, but one day she called me during the filming of *The Commander*.

'Joan Turner here, Lynda. Might you have some work for me, dahling? I'm rather in need.'

Joan was quite elderly by then. She'd been a terrifically talented comedienne in the 1960s, notable on the West End stage, but her life had been turbulent. She'd developed a gambling addiction and become a rollicking alcoholic and a bag lady in the 1990s, roaming the streets of Los Angeles and Las Vegas looking for work. That was following a stint in the soap opera *Brookside* where she'd played the part of Aunty Lou.

As it happened I did need a woman, though it wasn't a meaty role.

'I do need a lady in a hospital bed. She's dying . . .' I told her.

'Are there any lines, dahling?'

'No, no lines . . .'

'Well, does she thrash about a bit?'

'Yes . . . quite a lot of thrashing . . .'

'Hmm, thrashing about, you say?'

'Yes, thrashing, and rather a lot of groaning . . .'

'Thrashing and groaning . . . I think that would be fine, dahling.'

As Joan was in her seventies, I instructed the team to make sure she was picked up and taken directly to set. I had had to fly to New York the previous day for a meeting but I left knowing she was in safe hands.

'Treat her very well,' I told the crew.

However, on the day Joan's scene was to be filmed the schedule overran. When I checked in later that day, there was a problem.

'We won't get to Joan until tomorrow morning,' the producer told me.

'Ah, so where is Joan?'

'Don't worry, we've found her a lovely bed and breakfast near to the studios and had flowers delivered. We've taken great care of her and we'll film her scene first thing tomorrow.'

'OK, make a big fuss of her,' I said.

The next day, I rang to see how Joan had performed, given that she'd had to hang around overnight.

'Do you want the good news or the bad?' the producer said.

'What's the good?'

'She was brilliant. Absolutely brilliant. Lots of thrashing around, a lot of movement. Excellent acting.'

'And the bad?'

'The bed and breakfast phoned.'

'And?'

'She's removed every single item.'

'I beg your pardon?'

No word of a lie, Joan had removed the bath mat, the hand towel, the pillow slips, the eiderdown duvet. Every single thing that wasn't nailed down.

'How the hell did she get it all out?' I asked.

'We have no idea!'

After that, I never heard from Joan again and I considered it far easier to pay off the bed and breakfast than pursue her for a bath robe, bed linen and everything else she'd stripped the room of.

A few years later her family contacted me. They asked if I might say a few words at her funeral. *How could I?* I thought. *It's the only story about Joan I know!*

Chapter 19

Lorcan

Around 1999 over in the US, productions were going great guns, and no one could have known that behind the scenes I was in embroiled in a nightmare. I was attempting to keep La Plante Productions firing on all cylinders, after I had a gut-churning meeting at my offices in Wardour Street. I was asked by my lawyer, agent and accountant to be present, and I believed it was to be a kind of congratulatory meeting as the company was doing so well. Not in my wildest nightmares could I have anticipated what was about to unravel. As I sat there, I was informed that I and my company were bankrupt. At first I thought it was a joke, but when it was explained in heartbreaking detail, I was devastated. Not only was I under threat of losing my production company, but also my home. Worse still, I would not be able to pay any of my staff. Obviously, if I was declared bankrupt any hope of carrying on would have been futile: I simply would not have been able to secure any financial backing for any upcoming projects.

To this day, I cannot elaborate on this hideous episode. Suffice to say, it turned out that I had been targeted by a complex and well-hidden fraud that took some time to unpick. All I can report is that the situation was eventually rectified, and I was able to take a deep breath and move on.

However, it was a sober reminder that I couldn't ever take my eye off the ball when juggling so many productions both in the UK and overseas. It also hit home: I was on my own – no one was backing or protecting me. It felt as though I could trust no one, which was a sad lesson to learn. Nevertheless, the wheels of La Plante Productions kept on turning.

Stateside, in 2001, *The Governor* had been made into a TV movie called *The Warden*. The first series of *Widows* had also gone into production as a TV series. *Widows*, however, continued to be a frustration for me. In fact, several of the paper-thin contracts I signed as a writer-for-hire came back to bite me years down the line.

What so many writers don't realise is that when they sign on the dotted line for TV they may be signing away screen rights to their creations. On screen I own none of the characters in *Widows* and none in *Prime Suspect*. Not that I understood that at the time. With hindsight, I felt I was so poorly advised throughout all these negotiations, and naively never had a lawyer present to instruct me on what I did or did not own. I basically signed away my life because I thought everyone was acting in my best interests, I now do not believe that they did.

As far as my contracts are concerned, I think it's scandalous that writers can be bound by a few scraps of paper signed twenty or thirty years previously when they are starting out on their careers and grateful for a commission. More on *Widows* later, but even when I was in a position to buy my rights back for that work it didn't happen.

I don't wish to harbour endless bitterness, but only to stress how important it is for writers to be able to monitor and protect legally their product. Also to know that they are surrounded by people working in their best interests. Sadly, over the years, I realised that was my naive hope. All I can say is that it's a blessing I have such valued friends and family. Uppermost, and perhaps the most important, if you knock me down it is guaranteed that I will get up.

For *Widows*, Disney now held the rights. In fact, it had been me who had pitched *Widows* to Disney's Jeffrey Katzenberg some years before. What a palaver! On arrival, it felt like I was being beamed up to a meeting with God. Before I'd even got to Jeffrey's office, I needed to pitch the story to a gaggle of assistants in an ante-room. It took me around an hour to go through the plot step by step: I acted out the heist, I played each character while copious notes got taken. Not a single person cracked a smile.

'Jeffrey will see you now . . .' I was told, feeling rather exhausted. When I got ushered in, I barely noticed this tiny man sitting behind a gargantuan desk.

I'm not entirely sure Jeffrey Katzenberg understood *Widows*.

'Is it a comedy?' he asked.

'No, it's a drama,' I explained.

'Pitch it to me!'

Christ, I've spent the last hour doing that, I thought. I don't know what came over me, but I thought *Fuck it* and launched into another hour-long pitch delivered in a thick American accent.

'So, you got these four broads, they're plannin' a heist . . .'

Jeffrey stared blankly. He asked zero questions, and at the end of my epic performance, he nodded and said, 'Thank you very much.'

When the US version finally got made in 2002, I had no input when it came to the direction that the production company wanted to take the story. And that direction was lunacy. Apparently, four widows couldn't plan an armed robbery and carry it out – there couldn't be any violence at the hands of the fairer sex! Instead, the widows' husbands would die stealing a valuable painting and the women would finish the job. Only they couldn't kill anyone or blow anything up. *What? Seriously?*

Rather reluctantly, I spent three months in LA writing the script. The money was exceedingly good and given the financial sure-footing I needed it was work La Plante Productions couldn't turn down. And the mini-series did end up having an all-star cast of Mercedes Ruehl, Rosie Perez, Brooke Shields and N'Bushe Wright. It was also in the superb hands of director Geoffrey Sax who'd been flown over from the UK, but who did have a terrible time managing Mercedes Ruehl. Did I love working on the US version of *Widows*? Not really. Did I go along with it? Yes; I didn't feel I had much choice in the end.

At least in The Hamptons, I was able to unwind with friends. And it's a place where, once you move out from the spectacle of the super-rich like the Vanderbilts, there are some truly genuine people. But like in LA, the film set can be fickle. One thing I never got used to were guests putting in a no-show simply because a better invite came their way. In fact, when one couple did just that, I never invited them again. Perhaps I'm simply a bit too British!

And some of my social circle there strangely ended up reconnecting back to my North-West roots. In The Hamptons, Cilla Black was often a guest. I'd met her through the actor Patti Booth, a dear friend. While long lunches out with those ladies were a lot of fun – The Champagners, I called them – I dipped in and out. Actually, I've never been someone who's given a toss about who's sleeping with who, who isn't, or who wants to sleep with who – tiresome conversations for me. I suppose my working life has always been so rich that I ploughed myself into that far more than any ongoing social soap opera.

We did have some hilarious drunken escapades, though. Cilla once brought over her new CD, but my stereo in The Hamptons was a complicated affair that juggled five discs at a time. I put it on after a few too many glasses of bubbly and we sat back and listened.

'It's exceedingly good!' we all agreed. Admittedly, it was a departure from Cilla's usual style, what with its heavy blues guitar, but I loved it. Cilla waited patiently for the track to end.

'This is not my album,' she said, rather irritated. I felt so embarrassed. My stereo had shuffled up American guitarist Bonnie Raitt instead and when Cilla's track did eventually play it didn't receive quite the same enthusiastic fanfare.

Cilla also visited me once at home in London. It was after my father had died. By then my mother was living with me full-time, waited on hand-and-foot and living Barbara Cartland's best life in her own quarters. One time, Cilla popped her head round the door to say hello.

'What did you think of her?' I asked my mother later.

She looked faintly disgusted at Cilla's heavy Scouse accent.

'Very common,' she said.

Even in her old age, my mother never lost her sharp critique. In my fifties I still felt its sting.

'Are you going out looking like that?'

'Yes, Mother.'

'Well, your hair looks terrible. It doesn't suit you like that at all.'

'Thank you very much.'

Being a close friend of Cilla's, the late Paul O'Grady was also a regular in The Hamptons. The first time we met, he'd come for a party and had been staying in a bed and breakfast, which he hated.

'Can I come over?' he asked.

It turned out Paul and I had a lot in common. He knew the same music-hall greats as I did when I first started out as an actor. He did make me laugh.

'Don't worry about me, I don't eat breakfast!' he said when he appeared that morning at 8 a.m., just as my cook was serving up a Full English.

'I'll just have a cup of coffee,' he said. 'Oh, and a sausage . . . oh, and some bacon too . . . and perhaps an egg.' By the time Paul reached the table he was juggling a mountain of food. Not bad for a man who didn't eat breakfast.

Although I'd always been surrounded by good friends, as I neared my late fifties it did bother me more and more that I'd never had children to fill my life. Many years before, when I was still an actress and doing part-time work in a cafe in London, I remember seeing a woman park up in a blue Rolls-Royce Corniche car. A little blond-haired boy sat on the back seat. *One day, I'm going to have both*, I remember thinking to myself. Yet perhaps it was never meant to be? Occasionally, I walked around my UK home wondering who I would pass it all on to. I felt the same if I was ever in The Hamptons. Although I have always been proud of what I've built myself, through my own hard work, I sometimes questioned whether it had all been worth it.

Then one day, in the summer of 2003, I was at a friend's home in The Hamptons. His groomed lawn stretched all the way down to Accabonac Harbor and we'd been relaxing in the late afternoon sun. Out on the water a family drifted in on their kayaks and I followed one woman as she waded through the shallow water with a child aged around eighteen months clasped to her hip. Again, the boy had luscious blond curls. All of a sudden my heart lurched. *I'll never know what it's like to carry an infant on my hip like that*, I thought.

But life happens when you least expect it. The next day I received a phone call. A baby was due to be born in Florida, a state where I was still registered for adoption.

'You're at the top of the list. Would you like the baby?'

I couldn't catch my breath. My heart was thumping. I knew I had to make a decision quickly as so many other hopeful parents were on that waiting list.

'OK,' I said. There wasn't a muscle in my body that didn't think I wouldn't be able to cope. *I'll do it*, was my gut feel.

'Can you be here in the next twenty-four hours?'

'Of course.'

It wasn't until I got off the phone that the doubts began to creep in.

What if I'm too old?

I remembered a conversation I'd had with my friend Pat Booth not long before. I'd confided in her that I'd still like a child and that I'd kept my name on the adoption lists in certain states.

'Lynda, it's what you've always wanted,' she'd said, encouraging me to say yes should the opportunity arise. *I should at least see if I bond with this little baby*, I thought. I hadn't even asked the child's sex or its heritage. Whenever I'd visited adoption agencies there was a raft of questions like: Do you want a white baby? Are you happy with a Latino child? Do you want male or female? I honestly didn't care. All I knew was that this little baby's mother couldn't keep her child but had no preference about whether the baby went to a couple or a single parent, so long as her medical bills were paid and the baby was looked after.

My attorney was more cautious. Filming was due to start on a season of *The Commander* back in the UK, and he was very thorough in guiding me through a rather complicated process. What I hadn't appreciated is that to adopt I would need to live in the state of Florida for at least six months while the necessary paperwork was completed, in order to eventually bring the baby back home.

'Lynda, you do realise you have a TV series starting!' he reminded me.

'I'll sort something,' I said.

It all happened so quickly that in between my nerves and excitement, I barely had a moment to think. But when I saw my son for the first time I knew it was the right decision. He did look rather like a squashed potato, but he was tiny and beautiful. Later, I was to find a small raspberry birth mark on the back of his neck in the exact same spot I have one. For me, it was a sign. Did I fall in love with Lorcan the first time I held him? No. In truth, I felt so frightened with all these people watching on. The thought that I wouldn't be a great mother flooded me. That changed, however, when I brought him home. I called him Lorcan – an Irish name meaning fierce. As a baby he lived up to his name.

In Florida, I relied on the kindness of so many people. If ever I feel jaded, I only need to think back on that time and know that there are truly kind-hearted people in the world. Not long after I arrived, reality set in. For the first few weeks I stayed in the penthouse suite of a hotel in Boca Raton before Lorcan and I moved into a six-month let in Del Ray, on Florida's south-east coast. But I *did* have a TV series starting and I *would* have to commute back-and-forth to the UK. I needed help, and fast.

'Call this woman. She's wonderful and she has six children,' my attorney told me before slipping me the number of a woman called Jane McDonald.

She was right. Jane was unbelievably generous when I called her.

'What do you need?' she asked.

'A nanny, I think.'

'OK, well, I have one fantastic nanny called Rosemary. She's in Cape Cod at the moment but I'll call her and ask if she can come to you.'

Jane had three nannies looking after her children so if Rosemary wanted to she could come to me. Jane also sent cots and blankets, toys and clothes.

As soon as I heard Rosemary's voice, a wave of calm washed over me.

'Having some trouble here, need some help,' I told her when we spoke.

'That's fine, ma'am. I'll come right over,' she replied in her soft Louisiana drawl.

Rosemary Scidmore appeared like an angel and the wonderful thing is she's still with me twenty years later. Wherever I've travelled, she's travelled – and when I sold my house in The Hamptons she moved permanently with me to the UK. What a remarkable woman she is. To have the safety of someone who'd helped rear Jane's six children was the best gift I could have hoped for.

In the first few months of Lorcan's life I had fully expected to juggle work and a baby, but the formal adoption process itself was gruelling. So many tests to see if I was physically fit: medical check-ups to test my heart, lungs and stress levels; blood tests for this, that and the other. Across my left shoulder I have a large rose tattoo and that also caused alarm. I'd had it done years before but I needed to be cleared of hepatitis.

What I hadn't expected was a battle with the press, hot on the story of a fifty-seven-year-old adopting a child. Someone had leaked my temporary address in Del Ray to the UK tabloids and within weeks I was being hounded, reporters rummaging through my bins both in the US and at home. If I ever went out with Lorcan in his pram I had to shield it with a cloth to stop photographers stealing a picture. A complete nightmare! What's more, I couldn't understand what all the fuss was about. So what if I'd adopted a baby? Every report I read smacked of: 'How dare she? How dare she become at single mother at her age?' It felt unbearable. As if I hadn't considered all of those things, and worried about them. *Leave me alone,* I thought.

One journalist, *Daily Mail* columnist Lynda Lee-Potter, did corner me.

'If I can interview you for an exclusive, it'll take the heat off the story,' she persuaded me. I agreed, but regretted it soon after. The feature-length article felt horrendous. Even the headline: *Who says I'm too old to be a mother?* echoed that same sentiment. Lorcan was seven months old at the time – an exquisite bundle of happiness who had changed my life, yet the article kept banging on about my age. Mick Jagger had his last child aged seventy-three! Did that attract the same headlines? Absolutely not! And what about Charlie Chaplin? Still fathering children into his seventies. I hate such double standards.

One of the worst offenders was the columnist Anne Robinson. To this day, I do not know what that woman's problem was. I didn't know Anne, although she claimed to know me from childhood in Blundellsands. She also accused me of lying about my age – claiming that I was five years older than I really was. I didn't thank her for that one bit, as it could have derailed the adoption process. Of course, the authorities on both sides of the Atlantic had my passport and birth certificate. *What kind of woman does that?* I thought. She hammered me to the extent that it became a joke in my office in London that if she and I ever crossed paths the outcome wouldn't be pretty.

'I'll chuck a bowl of pasta over her,' I promised.

Then one night I was in the Ivy Restaurant dining with the businessman Ivan Massow. Who should I spot on another table but Anne Robinson? I told Ivan the story.

'I've vowed to throw pasta over her,' I laughed.

Thankfully, Ivan persuaded me that that would be very undignified.

'Why don't you just tell her how you feel?' he suggested.

'OK, I will.'

When I walked over and tapped Anne Robinson on the shoulder she became very flustered. I spoke calmly and clearly.

'You don't know me, but I'm Lynda La Plante. I don't why you have been unrelentingly nasty but you have destroyed my life for a year. One day someone is going to do that to you.'

'This isn't the time or the place,' Anne brushed me off.

'Neither is a newspaper column with two million readers,' I snapped back before returning to my seat.

Throughout Lorcan's life, I've felt so incredibly protective of him, especially in the face of any criticism levelled at me. I have never wanted him to suffer as a result of my public profile and have always done my utmost to shield him from the worst of it. He will always be my beautiful son.

Incidentally, I did buy that blue Rolls-Royce Corniche and Lorcan sat with his blond curls on the back seat just as I'd dreamed of so many years before.

Chapter 20

Catching a Killer

Lorcan changed my life forever. Often you don't know how you feel until you're faced with loss, and I'll never forget bumping into an actor friend at a formal dinner in London. Like me, she'd had difficulty conceiving but had given birth to a son through IVF many years before.

'Come and meet my son,' I said, beaming.

I felt so proud to show Lorcan off, but I could sense her hesitation.

'How's your son?' I asked. I pictured him as the gorgeous little boy I'd seen walking beside her when he was a toddler.

'He passed away,' she told me.

I was dumbstruck. On the way back to my seat, the tears started flowing.

I felt a great sadness for her, but also what rose up in me was an intense feeling of love for Lorcan. He'd become a fixture in my life. Simple things made me cry – like hearing him whistle for the first time. Silly when I think about it now.

As soon as I was able to bring Lorcan back to the UK we established a routine that would define us for years to come – the majority of the year based in England and long summers spent in The Hamptons.

My mother enjoyed Lorcan for the last two years of her life, even though she was in her early nineties by then and didn't step outside of the house much. In fact, I didn't tell her about Lorcan for some time, not until just before I brought him home.

'Mother, I have something to tell you. I have a son, and here he is,' I said, thrusting a picture of Lorcan under her nose.

'Well, he doesn't look like anyone from my side of the family,' she said.

Having Lorcan gradually shifted my perspective on work, too. Running La Plante Productions was a 24-7 undertaking. As well as our numerous TV series I'd also brought in producer Sophie Balhetchet in 2001 to head up a film arm we named Cougar Films. We had several feature films in development and in 2003 secured vital investment to develop further projects.

Novel-writing, however, remained my passion, even though I wasn't in a position to write full-time. But I longed for those summers in The Hamptons when I could switch off from the day-to-day, wake up early to write and then spend late afternoons with Lorcan splashing around in the pool or taking him to his various playgroups. Singing 'The Wheels on the Bus Go Round and Round' became a sheer delight.

Creatively, I was also very productive. I'd had it in my mind for a while to explore a young female detective, way before I ever considered resurrecting Jane Tennison. Instead, Anna Travis was born.

As a character, I didn't want Anna to be weighed down by quite the same discrimination Jane had endured. She'd be young, naive but also a graduate on a detective fast-track. So many women I'd started meeting in police forces up and down the country were joining via that route rather than working their way up from a 'bobby on the beat'. Her education and intelligence in the 2000s would prove more beneficial in solving serious crime than the experience of rising from the entry route of police constable.

Anna was also rather attractive, and she knew it. Plus, she'd have her father's legacy to draw on – the now deceased but highly respected Detective Chief Superintendent Jack Travis. Her superior would be Detective Inspector Langton, a long-in-the-tooth officer who'd seen it all and whom she greatly admired.

Just like all the crime novels or dramas I've produced, I wanted each investigation to remain the focus. It's what I love about writing crime the most – the jigsaw. How do I piece together the motive, the evidence, the clues? I always start each novel by asking the question: how are they going to catch this killer?

More often these days, writers want to get into the minds of killers. They want to spend time with them, see the world through their eyes. Or writers want to delve into the minutiae of the private lives of every single character – a kind of soapification of the story. That's never interested me as much as what criminals do to their victims, or to the officers working on those cases. Or how experts painstakingly piece together evidence, or how cases get solved.

Do I ever feel sympathy for criminals? Rationally, I can equate their horrific behaviour as being the result of something terrible that has happened in their lives. I do feel sorry for people who have been born into violence and abuse, but in my heart, I have no sympathy. And these days, I despair of stories of elderly people being conned out of their life savings, or killers preying on the vulnerable. Criminals strip decent people of their trust and dignity. *What kind of world are we living in?* I think. Plus, when I see the lack of resources going into the institutions supposed to protect people or rehabilitate people, it makes me weep.

Not long ago, I read about a female prison officer who had been working in a sandwich shop before she answered a job advert for the prison service. One week she was spreading fillings between slices of bread and the next she was cutting down bodies of men who had taken their own lives in their prison cells. She had next to no training. Without the right support, who can mentally prepare for that?

As a writer, I'm also continually looking at whatever is coming down the line. What's going to be the next big thing to hit law enforcement? I recently learned that criminals are now wearing the same protective suits as forensics teams. All of it can be bought online – the perfect marketplace for criminals. The lengths they will go to cover their tracks never ceases to amaze me. But the wonderful thing about Anna Travis is that she gave me licence to once more step ahead of the curve.

Having great contacts here and in the States gave me terrific access to people, many of whom I'm still in touch with today. Through my ongoing relationship with Tom Fontana, I was able to tap into any number of experts. Drug squad? Ring this guy, he'll help you. Facial recognition? Ring this woman – she'll tell you everything you need to know. And just like everyone I've called on over the years, experts do want to help – they really do want you to get it right.

Admittedly, it's also catapulted me into some nail-biting situations. Through one contact in the UK, I was in the privileged position of witnessing a major drugs bust while embedded in a police force. The respect given to me was remarkable. For days beforehand I sat in briefing rooms while the raid's final execution was planned. Five big-time operators had been dealing quantities of heroin and hash from properties in a seemingly well-to-do crescent-shaped street in London.

One morning when I walked into the briefing room I mistakenly thought a group of junkies had been rounded up.

'Hello.' I nodded.

Some had long hair, covered over with Beanie hats. Their jeans and jackets had seen better days.

'These are our undercover officers,' my chaperone told me.

Then the dogs and their handlers arrived. One beagle didn't just run towards the smell of drugs, he got so excited he skidded in, tail wagging furiously – an adorable little creature.

Before the raid itself, I was stationed in an upstairs dental practice alongside surveillance officers. From that vantage point we could view the entire street. What shocked me most was the conveyor belt of pick-ups by young boys on bikes. County lines operations, as they are now known.

Hours went by before a main suspect appeared.

'Target one is out.'

Sure enough, when I looked down a guy was standing in the street.

'Target two is now joining target one.'

The tension in the room ramped up as officers below got ready to swoop. However, when I looked again both men were gazing up in our direction.

'Shit, I think they've got us,' one officer announced.

Months of planning could have fallen apart in that split-second.

'Target three is now joining target one and target two.'

Three suspects were now on the pavement, staring up and pointing animatedly. Panic charged through everyone like an electric current.

Another message got relayed. Panic over. Two white doves had been dancing across the guttering overhead. The targets hadn't spotted us at all – they'd been momentarily captivated by the birds.

In the end, officers rounded up all five targets, properties crawled with police and trucks stood by as men were led out handcuffed.

Over in New York, I'd been given the same privileged access. One high-ranking officer in the NYPD, Camille, had been a fan of *Prime Suspect* and got in touch to ask if I needed any help. It was through her that I got introduced to top guys in the drug squad.

Camille is also an amazing woman. She's short and squat and drives around in a beat-up car. Once when she was an undercover cop on a drugs bust she disguised herself as an elderly lady on a mobility scooter. The baguette sticking out of her shopping trolley was a camouflaged police radio.

Another wonderful story she told me was when her unit were hot on the trail of a Puerto Rican gangster. Other officers were insistent on breaking down the door of the apartment where they suspected he was hiding. Camille had a better plan. She rapped on the door.

'You've got my daughter pregnant!' she screamed in Spanish.

Within minutes he was leaning out of the top window, eager to find out who it was.

Imprinted in my mind is also the time she led me into one department buzzing with a sea of mostly young men. Piled up on desks were mobile phones.

'This is our elite mobile team,' she told me.

Projected onto the walls were interactive maps where other officers were tracking movements: the paradox being that as technology has advanced it's become far easier for crimes to be committed, especially fraud, but thankfully it is also easier for criminals to be caught – one reason why many use burner phones that are discarded after just one call. How technology has rapidly changed policing since I first started writing is mind-blowing. Digital forensics are an entirely new and expanding area of expertise.

All these experiences fed into the Anna Travis series, but information can also lodge in my brain for years before I use it. Snippets of paper get pinned around my office while a story simmers. As a writer you become a magpie, drawing in ideas from here, there and everywhere. And the best part about writing novels is that there's no budgetary constraints. If I want fifty officers on a drug bust with a helicopter circling above, no one is telling me it's too expensive. The freedom is thrilling.

Writing the Anna Travis series led me to some absorbing storylines. As an avid watcher and reader of True Crime, it's hard to know why some subjects fascinate me more than others. Yet, when I get the bit between my teeth I find it hard to let go. Often, it's the horror that draws me in.

Fentanyl, for example, is a drug I've become utterly obsessed with. Its scourge is only now coming to light in the UK, but I was looking at its effects in the US in the mid-2000s. Addicts frozen like zombies in the street – unable to move a muscle. The high is more intense than crack cocaine. I first heard of it through a high-ranking officer in the NYPD.

'There's nothing we can do to stop it,' she admitted.

The synthetic opioid drug is now responsible for two-thirds of drug deaths in the US. Cities are awash with fentanyl and now it's here, on our streets and in our prisons. One prison doctor I spoke to recently described how men are found paralysed in their cells. Another woman told me about the undead propped up outside London's Victoria Station – truly dreadful.

Back then, my research on fentanyl eventually formed the backbone to the novel *Deadly Intent*. Anna gets called to a shooting of an ex-police officer in a squat, exposing an unexpected link to the drug-smuggling business.

For *Deadly Intent*, I also used the expertise of a surgeon friend of mine. My villain, Alexander Fitzpatrick, would have had his face and body completely rebuilt. Stage-by-stage he took me through every single procedure, from liposuction to facial reconstruction, to inform the book's opening sequence. He also reviewed the chapter. If ever an expert tells me something can't happen or I've got it wrong, it gets discarded.

'Lynda, there's no way we could pull that body out from that well in under an hour! It would take two at least!'

'OK, thank you. Rewrite on its way.'

The bottom line is that experts' input is too crucial for me to ever ignore it.

Some years later in 2009 when I adapted the Anna Travis novels for TV it was the fentanyl storyline in *Deadly Intent* that caused me to tear my hair out. Forensic pathologist Dr Ian Hill had been my blood spatter expert for years and a person I have the highest regard for. Over many hours, he's helped me understand the patterns blood makes depending on the crime. I've even sat in his lab with beetroot juice spurting out of my mouth to trace how it might land in a certain scenario.

On that particular shoot, the spatter against the wall in the opening scenes became crucial to understanding who the real killer was. The pattern would reveal that a man over six feet tall was in the room when the trigger got pulled. When I arrived on set I couldn't believe it. Someone in the scenery department had gone crazy with a pot of paint.

'Who's painted this wall red?' I shouted.

'We wanted the squat to look dark!' announced the director.

'How the hell is blood going to be visible against a red wall?'

It's situations like that where some directors can miss so much.

Horror also led me to seek out another storyline for Anna Travis: that of the gruesome discovery of Elizabeth Short in 1947 in Leimert Park, Los Angeles, in what became known as the Black Dahlia case. I became consumed by it – a crime that felt beyond murder. The body of Short, a twenty-two-year-old waitress, was discovered by a passer-by. She'd been severed in two and propped up in plain sight, leading the passer-by to confuse her for a mannequin. Despite her extensive injuries, no blood was found at the scene, suggesting she was killed elsewhere and positioned for show.

To this day, no one has been charged with Short's murder yet several suspects' names have emerged. I still find it hard to comprehend that justice has never been served. Could I recreate a copycat killing? It was a daring plot line for Anna Travis but one that I pulled off in *The Red Dahlia*. Through telling that story I also wanted to expose the vulnerability of young girls. A warning sign perhaps to those walking alone at night. Not long after I wrote it, I delivered a lecture at a university.

'It's your responsibility to protect yourselves,' I told the young women in the audience. 'Walk in pairs. Get a taxi home. Text someone when you reach your front door. Do not believe you're protected out there: you're not.'

One girl raised her hand.

'I feel uncomfortable being forced to protect myself. I know what I'm doing,' she said.

I understood the sentiment, but having spent my life analysing crime I also arrive with a heavy dose of realism.

'How tall are you?' I asked her.

'Five foot eight,' she replied.

'Well, you're far more difficult to attack than if you were five foot two. Until there's the manpower to deal with perpetrators, stay safe.'

Awful things to have to say to teenagers, especially in light of the despicable murder of Sarah Everard in 2021 by Wayne Couzens, a serving police officer, but a message I've always hammered home to women out alone.

The Anna Travis novels also provided me with an opportunity to revisit DNA forensics and look at its advances. In the novel *Bloodline,* Anna goes on the search of a missing person but dark secrets are revealed about his past and his own parentage.

Again, the help of experts helped me track every new development. That DNA is now used to unlock many investigations, particularly decades-old cold cases, is quite astonishing. As I revisited that research, I discovered how it is now possible to trace killers through familial DNA – samples taken from a sibling or a cousin. It became a riveting plot to pursue – the slow-moving story of Travis, Langton and the team, piecing together each fragment of the blood forensics to solve the case. And its pace became a lovely counterpoint to those big smash-and-grab stories like *Deadly Intent* and *The Red Dahlia* that can leave me drained whenever I've finished.

Now, whether it's a body found in a burned-out building or in woodland, or a spot of blood that's seeped into a floorboard under a newly fitted carpet, there's an expert on hand for all of my queries. Sometimes, I'll spend fifteen minutes with one checking a fact. Others I'll talk to for hours to fully digest the significance of a discovery. For example, the UK still doesn't have a full-time expert to analyse pet hair, unlike in the US. So many crimes these days can now be solved through tracing animals to owners.

And these days I find myself shouting at the TV if scriptwriters or directors take dramatic licence with forensics. I hear things like, 'We'll have that toxicology report back in two hours.' Nonsense! It would take around two weeks.

'He's been stabbed with a six-inch blade.' Rubbish! If you haven't recovered the weapon it would be impossible to know until a post-mortem takes place.

'She died at 7.30 p.m.' Bullshit! Pathologists can never pinpoint time-of-death with that accuracy. Instead, they'll deliver a timeframe in which a death has occurred.

And while other novelists or dramatists may see the wait for forensic results as slowing down the action, I've always used it as a way to focus on a different part of the investigation – officers opening new leads as they wait for results and reports. 'We're understaffed at the lab! There's a huge backlog for swab tests,' always has a place in one of my stories.

What I've also become deeply moved by is that while forensic scientists are often quiet, hardworking and objective people, they too feel the emotion and weight of the work they carry out, often similar to that of investigating officers. After all, it's the veracity of their evidence that's on the line and can make or break a conviction.

Some experts I am completely drawn to, like Professor Patricia Wiltshire, whose work starts when the pathologist's investigation ends: such a quiet and unassuming woman, who looks as sweet as someone's granny. Yet as a forensic ecologist she can uncover secrets not obvious to the human eye. Pollen can identify whether a body has been moved. Disturbed nettles hold another set of clues. It was her evidence that fed into the Soham investigation and helped catch the killer Ian Huntley. You have to take your hat off to that.

And it's many years of painstaking work with experts that led me to one of the greatest honours of my life. Fast forward to 2013 and I was awarded an honorary fellowship by the Chartered Society of Forensic Sciences – the only lay person ever to have been admitted – a tremendous privilege and recognition of the lengths I go to to get the facts right. It's also opened up a whole world of forensic conferences for me to attend. There, I can sit in lectures covering all kinds of topics, and visit the stands of companies at the forefront of forensic discovery – truly mind-boggling!

However, it was the relationship between Anna Travis and her superior DCI Langton that I also found myself picking over in the Anna Travis series. Bringing the characters of Travis and Langton together as a storyline bubbling under was never conceived from the outset to be a continuing theme, yet the more I wrote, the more I enjoyed exploring these two complex people and the tension between them. Langton does fancy Anna rotten, but as a high-ranking officer he also knows that any relationship with her would be the kiss of death for his career.

Anna knows how to flirt with Langton to manoeuvre her way up, but equally knows he's far too old for her. In exploring all my characters, I've become my own expert in the minutiae of human interaction. And in the series both those roles were played magnificently: Kelly Reilly played Anna, and has now gone on to great success in the US series *Yellowstone*; Ciaran Hines was absolute perfection in the part of DCI Langton. Funny to think I first met Ciaran when he appeared as a chilling villain in *Prime Suspect* series three – such a versatile actor.

Yet of all the characters I have written this pairing seemed to attract the most attention. I cannot tell you the amount of people who had a view on whether Travis and Langton should or should not be drawn to one another. 'He's far too old for her! Even the mere hint of attraction isn't right!' Would you believe I had employees arriving at my office to tell me that?

But that's also the terrific thing about being a novelist. These characters are my characters. I can do whatever I like with them. I know them, I understand them, and I can move them in any way I want to help them solve the case – that complex jigsaw that has always kept me going.

Chapter 21
A New Chapter

TV had changed so much since I started, and this hit home as La Plante Productions headed towards two decades of programme-making.

On demand channels were in their infancy around 2010. Reality TV was dominating the airwaves – a genre of programmes I've never been able to fathom. Botox, bonking and bikinis. No thank you. And it would be no great loss to me if *Love Island* became submerged! Dreadful.

Those years saw a shift in me. In 2005 some of my worst fears almost came true. Lorcan must have been around three when I collapsed suddenly in the handbag department of Harrods. Very frightening, and nobody could work out what the matter was. That Christmas the same thing happened when I was walking my dog in Richmond Park. One minute I was upright, the next a passer-by was scooping me up from the pathway.

My visit to A&E was memorable. A chap in the bed opposite had a companion glued to him, way past visiting hours.

How lovely, especially at this time of year, I thought.

I soon realised they were chained together with handcuffs. Even prisoners have to use the NHS at Christmas!

Naturally, every anxiety I'd ever had about being too old to adopt consumed me. More than anything, I needed to make sure Lorcan was taken care of, should anything happen. I put my house in order, making the necessary practical and financial arrangements. Thankfully, after extensive tests and a wonderful surgeon who saved me from open heart surgery, it was discovered that I had a heart murmur – a condition that was easily solved.

One doctor seemed rather shocked when I was admitted for one procedure. I asked if three TV screens could be installed in my hospital room so I could carry on working. The Anna Travis series was ongoing at the time and when he walked in I was sat up in bed, editing furiously to meet a deadline. He looked at me agape, as if I'd grown two heads.

And it was while I was in hospital that my mother collapsed at home. I could only be discharged a couple of days later to see her in her own hospital bed. The guilt of not being there for her felt dreadful, but I also had to smile. My mother's last words to me were Flossie at her very best.

'Well, you've put on some weight!' she said as I hurried in.

'Thank you, Mother.'

After that she slipped into unconsciousness and died a few days later. We buried her in her beloved Liverpool football strip alongside the items of Dail's that she had requested. My home felt emptier without her.

Another health scare a couple of years later required a little more intervention. After a biopsy I was diagnosed with cancer of the uterus. I would need a hysterectomy. I suppose I could have felt utterly devastated by that news, and it did shake me, but my womb had never been much of a friend to me over the years. Besides, I was still very fit and my recovery time from surgery was minimal.

Friends who came to see me the next day fully expected to find me laid out in my hospital bed and groaning.

'She's in the garden!' the nurses directed them outside. I'd leapt up that morning. I couldn't laze around. In my mind there's nothing worse than feeling sorry for oneself for too long!

Besides, I wanted to get home to Lorcan – having his young energy around the house gave me so much fight. Unfortunately, there was always someone to remind me I was no spring chicken. On one occasion I was in a restaurant with Lorcan. A lady approached us misty-eyed over his lovely blond curls and wide smile.

'I've been watching you both. It's so lovely how deep in conversation you are,' she commented. She leaned in to speak to Lorcan. 'Do you see your granny often?'

'I'm his mother, and I'm expecting another shortly!' I snapped.

She scuttled off rather quickly.

Faced for the first time with my own mortality, I felt even more protective over Lorcan. That only intensified when police officers called me one day. By the time of my operation Lorcan was happily in primary school but police had got wind of a kidnap plot to snatch him.

I couldn't quite believe what I was hearing.

'Is this serious?' I asked.

It was deadly serious. The gang in question apparently knew everything about Lorcan's school: who picked him up, what time he was picked up. Terrifying! And for months afterwards I had to pay a security guard to accompany him wherever he went. Try explaining that to other worried parents! It was just another way my profile could be used to punish him, and I wasn't going to let it happen. Mercifully, the threat receded after some months.

As far as work was concerned, there were some real highlights. Lorcan and my brother Michael accompanied me to Buckingham Palace in 2008 to receive my CBE – a very long day for Lorcan of waiting in line, but an exceedingly proud moment. It also allowed me to continue with various charities I've worked with over the years, including The Prince's Trust. Recently, to help raise funds I auctioned off a Damien Hirst skull print that used to hang in my office.

Ronnie Wood of the Rolling Stones was at the event, and told me that when he was on tour he used to watch boxsets of *Trial and Retribution* and the Anna Travis series *Above Suspicion*. Lovely to have him as a fan!

As well as the prison charities I've supported over the years, I've also continued work as an ambassador for Variety, the children's charity. I still love that when I'm in Liverpool I host a lunch or dinner for youngsters. Everyone gets a book and I often give as an auction prize the opportunity for one lucky person to have their name used for a character.

In 2009, I was inducted into the Crime Thriller Awards Hall of Fame – another huge honour.

Several La Plante Production series such as *Trial and Retribution* and *The Commander* started to wrap up towards the end of the decade, and I turned increasingly to novels and various film projects. One story I had stumbled upon a couple of years beforehand had captivated me: that of Jean Lee.

In 1951, Lee became the last woman to hang in Australia alongside her lover and an accomplice, for the murder of a seventy-three-year-old bookmaker, William 'Pop' Kent.

I'd never researched in depth a female killer before, mainly because most of them, like Ruth Ellis, had been done to death. But there was something about Jean Lee's largely untold story that grabbed me. I became a bit of an obsessive and read as much about it as I could.

Australia is also a destination where I've held many book events. The schedule is gruelling – sometimes I don't know what city I've arrived in – but readers there are always so engaged and inundate me with interesting questions, often lifting me from my jet-lagged state. To pursue a film project there would be incredibly exciting.

The research on the project took months and the more I uncovered about Jean Lee the more fascinated I became. Lee had become an alcoholic who picked up men at racecourses in a scam with her lover, Robert Clayton. He would appear claiming to be her husband and extract bribes from anyone she was caught with in a compromising situation. They would rob strangers along the way.

Lee's trial was a spectacle. She admitted to the entrapment and killing of Kent but fooled around the entire duration, even trying to get her lover to kiss her as the evidence was being heard. The groundwork for a film script became an exploration of who Jean Lee was before the alcohol, the crime and the prostitution gripped her – a tragic story.

Even up to the point of her execution, she believed the state would never hang a woman. Dressed in little ballet shoes and pedal-pushers, she sat drawing wedding dresses in her cell, convinced she would be married rather than sentenced. Rumour had it she died of shock before the noose was even placed around her neck.

When complete, the script was one project I had confidence in. Nicole Kidman had been visiting London and I'd been able to get a copy of it to her manager.

'I love it, Lynda!' she told me when she rang to discuss it. Her manager also thought it was a perfect vehicle for Nicole and one of the most compelling scripts he'd read. That feeling when a project is up and rolling and about to take off is very special.

The Australian film director Gillian Armstrong also came on board and we had a terrific production team lined up. All that was needed for its go-ahead was a last tranche of funding from Screen Australia – the government's film funding body.

In Sydney I sat in front of a panel of three, pitching the film. One young girl was captivated by it.

'I'm blown away by the story. Is it true?'

'Yes, it all happened,' I said, going on to explain some of my research.

Another woman on the panel similarly felt it was a strong script.

'Nicole Kidman's on board,' I told them.

Surprising to me that that received less of an enthusiastic response than I had anticipated – rather lukewarm, in fact.

Then, one man in the room piped up. 'You know what the problem is, don't you?'

'No, do go on . . .'

'Well, everyone knows the ending, don't they?'

'And the problem is?'

'Well, the ending's not a surprise,' he continued.

What? Had I just heard him correctly?

'How many films have been made about *Titanic*?' I asked.

He shuffled around rather nervously.

'It fucking sinks! Everybody knows that!' I shouted.

What discussion had gone on behind the scenes at Screen Australia I do not know, but I have my suspicions. I'd been warned that the subject matter may be too much of a hot potato for the Australian government. Knowing the finer details of the story as I did, Jean Lee probably should never have been hanged.

The last straw for me was when the same chap concluded, 'I can't see the point of this. It's not even as though she's a particularly nice person.'

She's a killer! I wanted to scream.

At that point, I knew funding wasn't going to be forthcoming, and Screen Australia and I parted company. Most disappointingly, my completed script on Jean Lee is still sitting on a shelf in my office, waiting to be made. Someday I hope it will be.

Of course, those fans I mentioned still keep me going. I was back in Australia in 2019 on a book tour when an elderly man approached me.

'I was in the cinema in Melbourne on the day they hanged Jean Lee. The film was stopped for the news,' he told me.

What a powerful memory, I thought. On that trip I was also given a private tour of Old Melbourne Gaol where Lee was held, and where there are wonderful documents of her time there.

Back home, it wasn't long before I was battling similar limited ambitions. One project that had excited me from the outset was a commission from the BBC to research the Brontë family for a two-hour special. Again, I dived in. The Brontës had fascinated me since childhood. I used to scare my little sister Gill at night by telling her ghost stories. One night, after an epic tale, I crept along the corridor to the loo when I heard a voice calling, 'Let me in – let me in!' There was a dreadful tapping noise on the window.

When I burst into my grandmother Gertrude's room, crying that there was a real ghost, she looked very confused.

'Don't be silly! I'm listening to a story on the radio called *Wuthering Heights*,' she laughed.

When I think about it now, it's probably the first time I understood that stories in books could be adapted to other mediums and brought to life.

Yet tackling such a well-trodden subject is fraught with decision-making – there's already an established narrative about the Brontës. Charlotte, Emily and Anne are always portrayed as young, adolescent women writing. Yet the more I uncovered, the more I found aspects to their lives that hadn't been explored on-screen.

I became preoccupied by one of the Brontë sisters, Elizabeth, who very little is known about. She had died at the age of ten of starvation, three years after the children's mother, Maria, had lost her life to cancer. And the only son in the Brontë family, Branwell, descended into alcoholism in early adulthood. Leafing through diaries and letters and papers, I discovered that one of his first memories was standing on tip toe and looking into the coffin of his dead sister, laid out in the long drawing room in the family home, the parsonage in Haworth. Incredible! Wouldn't that define a person, a family?

That expansive Yorkshire landscape often depicted in the Brontë story is also at odds with the reality of their lives. At the time the family lived there, the parsonage was tiny, with no running water and an outside privy. Claustrophobic beyond belief. Their father, Patrick, lived, worked and ate in one room. Imagine those young girls with an alcoholic brother, vomiting and passing out, and no indoor toilet? And Charlotte, it turned out, was stunted in growth. I believe she may have suffered dwarfism. She also had rotting teeth and was balding. By the time she was visiting publishers in London she had fake hair pieces covering her head.

While I wanted to celebrate the remarkable talent and achievements of the Brontë sisters, and highlight the impossibility at that time of them attracting a publishing deal under their own female names, I also felt compelled to move viewers beyond the sanitisation of the Brontë saga. I wanted to take people back to the tragedies that befell their childhoods. My God, the secrets inside that house. *I have to present this story differently,* I thought.

At the BBC, I submitted a first draft. A producer called me.

'We've read it, Lynda.'

'And?'

'It's not going to fly.'

'Right. And the problem is?'

'Well, could you sex it up a bit?'

'Sex it up?'

Immediately, I understood what commissioners wanted. They wanted the Brontës as teenagers. Mostly, they wanted what had already been seen before. They didn't want a back story. They didn't want the reality.

'But the back story makes them who they are as adults. It's important to understand it, to see how these girls wrote,' I argued.

'We don't want it.'

I received the message loud and clear. Would I sex it up? Absolutely not. Why commission a writer to research and then disregard their vision of what they've discovered? Perhaps if I'd been starting out I may have felt differently, but I don't think so. *I'm done fighting this*, I thought.

I was finding it increasingly difficult to face people who had no notion of what I wanted to bring to the screen. At La Plante Productions, too, it was becoming harder for me to hold my enthusiasm. I found myself going into the office less and less. Novel-writing simply became a better outlet for my creativity.

Yet one can never predict what's around the corner. Just as I was winding down the La Plante Productions offices in 2014, I was invited to an evening at Buckingham Palace – a celebration of RADA, of which the Queen had been a patron. A pleasant enough jolly for a cold February night, and I stood in line beside Angela Lansbury and shook hands with Her Majesty. That did seem to put Joan Collins' nose rather out of joint. She swept past wondering how I'd bagged a spot. 'I stood where I'd been asked to!' I replied.

John Hurt was also there. I don't think I'd seen John since our RADA days. 'We're so old. There's hardly anyone here our age!' we confessed to each other. I'd not long turned seventy and John was a few years my senior. Everyone did look rather young and glamorous.

Halfway through, we spotted the actor Ian Holm in a corner. He was in his eighties, and when we tapped him on the shoulder he couldn't remember either of us! I'd last seen him during his disastrous and short-lived appearance in *The Iceman Cometh* when I was with the Royal Shakespeare Company in my thirties.

Towards the end of the night, a loud, energetic man bounded towards me. 'Are you Lynda La Plante?'

'Yes...'

'Steve McQueen,' he said, beaming. 'I want to make a film of *Widows*.'

'Right. OK.'

I'd not met Steve before, but he was a larger-than-life character. He'd not long released *12 Years a Slave,* a very impressive movie. Apparently he'd been obsessed by the series *Widows* since childhood, in particular Eva Mottley in the part of Bella O'Reilly. I'd not thought about *Widows* for some time and it was lovely to hear his enthusiasm.

'Do you own the rights?' he asked.

'I don't own them, but I'll get them,' I promised.

Disney still owned the rights to *Widows* but with the TV series already done and dusted in the States it had been sitting with them for more than a decade. Plus, I'd not long sold half of my TV back catalogue and I was in a financial position to buy *Widows* back.

The next day, I called my agent Duncan Heath.

'I want the rights to *Widows* back. Can you please start the ball rolling with Disney?'

In the States, my agent was Peter Benedek of United Talent Artists. For years he'd dealt with any TV and film work on that side of the Atlantic. I also called Peter and asked him to make some calls and approach Disney with an offer.

Weeks went by, and still no news.

'What's happening?' I checked in with Duncan Heath.

'Don't panic, we're sorting something,' he reassured me.

The next time I spoke to Peter, he hadn't made headway either. Peter is one of the best-known and most influential agents in

Hollywood yet he claimed to have called Disney but couldn't find anyone there who knew about *Widows*. *Very strange*, I thought.

'Can you keep going on it, please?' I urged him.

I even called Steve McQueen myself through his agent to let him know I was waiting to hear back about the rights and to ask if he was still interested. It was then that I sensed that something odd was afoot. Apparently Steve was filming and unable to take the call.

By now it was nearing winter 2014 and there was still no contact made to Disney. Emails had been flying back and forth between myself and Duncan Heath, but no one seemed to know anything. I was due to fly to LA that November, so I arranged to meet with Peter.

We sat eating dinner in the restaurant Spago in Beverly Hills.

'What the hell is going on with *Widows*?' I complained.

Peter looked at me blankly.

It seemed ridiculous to me that after six months no one had been able to locate someone at Disney to see what offer could be made.

'It's crazy!' I continued. 'I have Steve McQueen wanting to make a movie. He's just released *12 Years a Slave*. The project is virtually green-lit.'

Then, Peter frowned and adjusted his glasses as if something had just sprung to mind.

'Oh, wait a minute. I think that project's in development,' he said rather casually.

'In development?'

'Yeah, I heard so.'

'What? How? That doesn't make sense. With who?'

'With Steve McQueen and 20th Century Fox.'

'What?'

Suddenly, the penny dropped. There'd been a wholesale buy-out behind the scenes. No one had bothered to tell me. Not only that, but Steve hadn't contacted me about a script either. My own characters, and he was too busy to take the call. Instead, *Gone Girl* writer Gillian Flynn had been drafted onto the project. I was cut out completely – not even a courtesy call.

The announcement that *Widows* was in development graced the pages of *Variety* magazine that same month. Should it have bothered me? After all, I'd had my struggles with *Widows* in the thirty years since I wrote it. But yes, it should bother me, and it still does. In that moment, I realised something – all the people whom I had trusted, all the people I had employed to represent my interests over many, many years had done a big fat nothing. I'd been cut out of the deal.

The following month, in December 2014, I sacked Duncan Heath and I sacked Peter Benedek. The funny thing is not one person from Duncan Heath's office rang me to ask why. Some of them had enjoyed my hospitality for weeks every single summer in The Hamptons. Unbelievable. *Good riddance to old rubbish*, I thought. Steve McQueen would later contact me as his film progressed, some two years down the line. Before then I would have a few more battles to fight.

Chapter 22

Tennison

Many years ago, when I was still married, a Hollywood producer came to my home for dinner. Josef Shaftel was in his late seventies, a small Jewish-American man with a greyish beard. I have no clue where my ex-husband Richard found him, but when he invited him over, Josef had not long been declared bankrupt. At first I wasn't too enamoured by this unexpected guest, but Josef turned out to be very interesting.

'I was a major television producer,' he told me.

'Doing what?'

'I worked on one of the most successful TV dramas in America.'

'What was that?'

'*The Untouchables.*'

What? The Untouchables? My jaw dropped. I'd been a massive fan of special agent Eliot Ness battling organised crime in 1930s Chicago. And that night, Josef regaled us with stories about the 1950s series, but also about his relationship with the notorious crime boss Lucky Luciano.

'He wanted to star in the show, but he was cross-eyed. I persuaded him not to, said he risked being recognised.' Josef laughed.

One day, Josef got a call. It was a major Hollywood studio asking him if he wanted a movie deal on the back of *The Untouchables*' success.

'Bring something to us. We need a fresh idea, a blockbuster.'

A few nights later Josef was at a dinner attended by none other than Orson Welles. An idea struck him and he approached the director, cap in hand.

'Mr Welles, have you ever thought about making *Citizen Kane II*?'

Apparently Welles stared wistfully into the distance. '*Citizen Kane II*? Why yes. What an idea!' he said.

When Josef went back to the studio, he negotiated enough money so that Welles could research and write the film from Paris, where he was living. Months went by. He rang but got no answer. In the end, he flew over to see what was going on.

'How's the writing going?' he asked. 'The studio would love to see a couple of pages.'

'It's going great. I'm halfway through,' said Welles. 'But I'm running out of money. If you can secure another payment, I'll be able to deliver.'

Josef secured the cash – rather a lot of money – but weeks ticked by and the studio executives were tearing their hair out.

'We need to see some pages. A script. Anything!'

Josef hot-footed it back to Paris to talk to Welles.

'The studio's going apeshit,' he pleaded. 'Can you give me a couple of pages? A synopsis of the story? Anything?'

After a moment, Orson Welles leaned in. 'I've written nothing. Nothing at all,' he said. 'I lied.'

Josef couldn't believe it. '*You lied*? Why in God's name would you *lie*?'

'*Nobody* could write *Citizen Kane II*,' Orson Welles thundered.

In that split-second, Josef Shaftel's career died.

I adore that story. Orson Welles shoving two fingers up to anyone who thought that he could simply replicate the genius of *Citizen Kane*. Of course, today writers or teams of writers would be drafted in. A studio would likely be onto *Citizen Kane IV*, probably with little regard to the original and probably not even to Welles himself.

Rarely does anyone have the brilliance or power of Orson Welles, but that quest for integrity is something that inhabits every writer I know who truly values what they do. And it's something that I became acutely aware of when I started to look back at the character of Jane Tennison in 2013.

What prompted me? Well, again it was my wonderful fans. I'd been due to speak at a book event in Sheffield. When I walked into the auditorium, the front row was mysteriously empty.

'Is it reserved for the Lord Mayor or someone?' I asked.

'No,' my host explained. 'There's a group of sight-impaired readers coming in with their guide dogs.'

How brilliant, I thought, even though I did end up being distracted by a row of dogs farting, snoring and rolling over while my talk got underway.

At the closing Q&A session, one woman put her hand up. Had I ever thought of creating a sight-impaired detective? I never had but it was definitely something to think about – my readers do have fascinating ideas! Then, she asked what I knew of Jane Tennison before she became DCI in *Prime Suspect*? Where did she get her coolness from? What did she do when she was younger?

That got me thinking, too. What *had* given Jane the hunger to demand she step into the dead man's shoes of DCI Shefford and take over the Marlow investigation? After all, she'd been overlooked for promotion many, many times. How did she develop that toughness to deal with discrimination through the ranks?

When I'd written the original *Prime Suspect,* I was armed with stories from Jackie Malton and the other women I'd met in the force. I'd also imagined something of Jane's past, but only scant details. I knew that she came from a nice family, had parents who were still alive, plus a sister. I knew she'd been at police training college, started out on the beat and worked her way up. That was really the extent of it.

The more I thought about it, the more that fleshing out of Jane's pre-1992 story became engrossing to me. But I could also see the danger signs. Revisiting such an iconic character twenty-five years later needed to be handled very carefully. If I was to meet Jane Tennison as a twenty-two-year-old, the research would have to be flawless. And the development of her character to become the feisty, resilient DCI we knew from the TV series had to be gradual. I needed Jane to feel fresh, not clutching at the past glories of an original script or Dame Helen Mirren.

Initially, my then-publisher Simon & Schuster commissioned a two-book deal. I was incredibly buoyed by their enthusiasm. *Tennison* did feel like a risk to me, but an exhilarating one. And the more I dived into the research, the more I couldn't wait to get started.

As ever, I was exceedingly lucky. Cass Sutherland had been around in the Metropolitan Police in 1973 when Jane's story would start. Even better, Cass's wife, Ann, had begun her career as a WPC constable in Hackney in East London. Both were able to unlock that world for me first-hand. Even walking into the actual station, up its stone steps and through its double-fronted doors was so evocative of that period. The stone-flagged corridors and winding staircases. Retracing the physical remnants of that history was critical to me building who Jane Tennison was.

Other details about the era were an absolute joy – the music for starters: Janis Joplin; Led Zeppelin; Cat Stevens. Wonderful. Then there were the shops lining the high street – Woolworths, and Saxone shoe shop. And, my God, the clothes! In 1973 I was still a jobbing actress, bopping around in my Biba dresses and performing cabaret at the Country Cousin. Reimagining that was nostalgic. I became utterly lost in the process.

Through Cass, I was also invited to a lunch of more than three hundred retired former police officers, some of whom had worked around London in the early 1970s. Now I attend every year. The women there are amazing! Even in their eighties they are boisterous and energised and very, very funny. My admiration for them is infinite.

'I brought the Krays in,' one of them whispered to me. Others had stories of turning up to work in the 1970s and there being no women's toilets. One WPC told me that the capes they wore as part of their uniform could conceal their fish suppers wrapped in newspaper. Secretly, they could have a bite to eat while out on the beat: invaluable snippets of information.

Then there was the technology – or lack of technology – the officers had to work with. For me, that was the most difficult aspect to get my head around. It felt so strange to force myself to unlearn all the knowledge I'd amassed over many years of crime writing.

I'm rather ashamed to admit it, but in a later Tennison novel, *Dark Rooms*, I wrote an entire storyline that included the use of computers, assuming communication between officers had advanced by then. Cass took one look at it and shook his head. 'Lynda, I'm sorry. The computers have to go.'

'What do you mean?'

'We wouldn't have used them until later!'

'Argh! You're kidding?'

That was one very tough spell in front of my computer as I stripped out all mention of officers sending emails.

Even the computerisation of criminal records didn't happen until the late 1970s. Crimes were recorded on cards or officers needed to look them up on microfiche. CCTV was in existence but not relied on in investigations in the way it is today. As for the luxury of mobile phones – forget it. Welcome to the world of landlines and teleprinters – absolutely no tracking of a suspect's movements through mast signals whatsoever.

Forensics, too, were basic by comparison. Certainly no DNA. And scenes of crimes were managed very differently. Crime scene officers would have worn white coats and gloves but they didn't cover their hair or go through half of the rigmarole they do now. Cross-contamination of evidence was considered, but in nowhere near the same detail.

In one later Tennison novel, when Jane arrives to a crime scene to find a bloodbath on a carpet, I'd placed duckboards – the wooden boards officers step across – at the scene. Cass put me straight on that too.

'I've had a look, and duckboards didn't come in until the mid-1990s. We would have thrown some cardboard down.'

'Right-o. Thanks, Cass.'

Delete. Delete. Delete.

In that first novel, I was keen to reflect the attitudes of women as well as the attitudes towards women. The naivety of Jane Tennison was incredible, just like the naivety of many of us – myself included. Constructing her going back to that hellish place became exciting. Who was Jane? Well, she was a bit of an outsider, even to her own family. Her parents were appalled she'd opted to join the police force. But she was also conscientious. She didn't drink. She didn't smoke. Rather straight-laced, actually. She did everything right to be taken seriously within that viciously sexist establishment.

The only big mistake Jane would make early on was to fall in love with her superior, Detective Chief Inspector Bradfield. An affair with a married man was wrong and she knew it. And Bradfield's subsequent death marks her for the rest of her career – it's how she learned to put her emotions in a box, and shut it tight. One reason why, when we meet her in 1992, she'd never been able to get her private life together.

For the plot of that first Tennison novel, I also wanted to show the interplay between victim and perpetrator. The first ever murder case Jane would investigate was that of a drug addict and prostitute called Julie Ann Collins, strangled with her own strapless bra. For that story arc I'd been to a prison to interview a young man – a seventeen-year-old – serving a life sentence for strangling his girlfriend.

Of course, when you meet someone like that in real life they will often downplay their culpability – reduce their crime to an unfortunate accident: 'I didn't mean to kill her.' Throughout our meeting he repeated that several times, and explained to me that he'd been desperately in love with his girlfriend but that she'd been an addict. He described how she tormented and abused him if he didn't arrive at her home with drugs.

Unbeknown to him I'd also read through the police files. It had been a savage attack – no accident. Besides, no victim ever deserves to die, and certainly not like that. Nevertheless, there was a realism to that toxic, drug-fuelled relationship that I wanted to explore. I also wanted to show what drugs can do to a beautiful teenage girl: how a person can become a stranger to the people closest to them, how they can steal from their loved ones, become dangerous to know.

In my second Tennison novel, *Hidden Killers,* I wanted to show how Jane's naivety becomes further eroded when she goes undercover with CID to catch a sexual predator. She is attacked by him, but hits against a dilemma. She believes her assailant is being fitted up for a more severe crime by her superiors and questions whether to challenge them. Imagine battling that as a low-ranking female officer in 1974!

Every book I wrote in the Tennison series, I shaped Jane further. I loved watching her grow. I loved that she made mistakes. I loved that there was a softness and vulnerability to her and that, at times, her confidence got shattered. Her evolution became so interesting to me because every time she took a professional hard knock I had to find ways to build her back up to the point where eventually, in her forties, she would walk into that office and demand to be put on the Marlow case.

From the outset, *Tennison* had the clear potential for TV. Yet, I wasn't convinced that I ever wanted to go down that route again. Jean Lee and the Brontës felt like wounds I was still licking. And if I ever did, it would need to be spot-on. Besides, *Tennison* could never be a pale imitation of *Prime Suspect*. It had to stand on its own two feet. It's one of the reasons that I called that first book *Tennison*. No one could repeat *Prime Suspect*: not me, not Dame Helen Mirren, not anyone. It was a unique moment in time. Why try?

Funnily, it was ITV who ended up contacting me. Neither *Tennison* nor *Hidden Killers* had been written, but the deal with Simon & Schuster had been signed. I promised to send them a manuscript when it was ready, which I did. And, in 2014, ITV were in need of a hit. A major series called *The Great Fire* had flopped and *Tennison* became a project the network was keen to land. Initially, I discussed it with Peter Fincham, then ITV's director of television. It can be tricky when you've established relationships with TV networks, as I had done with Nick Elliott and his successors. A new broom always wants to shape the channel their way.

Much to my relief, however, Peter jumped at the idea. Over the moon, in fact. Immediately he could imagine the Janis Joplin soundtrack; he saw the Vauxhall Viva police cars; how powerful that period could appear on-screen. He also understood that

Tennison needed an actress of some calibre to handle the contours of Jane's character even at that young age. However, Peter had suggested it as a series for ITV's Encore, the channel's newly launched paid-for platform on Sky (now no longer running).

'Why would you broadcast it on there?' I asked. I put it to him that the brand could bring in millions of older and younger viewers to ITV.

'I can't argue with that,' Peter conceded.

Tennison was eventually commissioned in 2015 by Kevin Lygo, then head of ITV Studios. He'd read the manuscript that had been discussed with Peter the previous year. He loved it, too. *Wonderful,* I thought. In particular, he'd loved the detail of life in the 1970s and felt that the part women played would make a refreshing backdrop to a crime story. After all, as we are still seeing, the gender politics of the recent past are as real today as they were then.

From the outset, however, I'd made clear to Peter, Kevin and ITV that if it were to go ahead I did not want to produce the show myself. With hindsight, I wished I had. As far as timing went, the scripts needed to be turned around quickly and I wanted to put my energy into getting it right. Plus, producing takes a lot out of you. I also felt I'd been given enough reassurances that the project would be in excellent hands. Kevin was *very* enthusiastic. Before we finalised the commission he'd come to my home for a meeting. He stood in my music room and made a lot of promises he couldn't keep. Yet at the time, Kevin persuaded me.

'It's a wonderful project. I have every confidence in it. Most of all, it's your project. You own it. It'll be your show and we'll do everything to help with that,' he said. More importantly, the casting of Jane and others would be my call. *Good,* I thought, because it did need experienced hands.

In the weeks that followed the production company NoHo, part-owned by ITV Studios, were assigned to work on the series. At first that also filled me with confidence – a partner in a true sense of the word. I had experience with ITV Studios and, I naively believed, any collaborator would recognise my experience in writing, casting, police procedure and attention to detail.

I didn't know much about NoHo, only that it was headed by ex-Channel 4 commissioners Camilla Campbell and Robert Wulff-Cochrane. But its experience, or lack of experience, quickly became clear. NoHo may have been familiar with the commissioning process, but not with the nuts and bolts of production. I felt they were simply out of their depth.

The producer who had been assigned to the project from ITV didn't fill me with much enthusiasm either. I'd first met Steve November as a script editor when I'd made *Above Suspicion*, based on the Anna Travis novels. Funny how people stick in your mind, and I never forgot him. Bizarrely, his name was Steve Frost at the time.

In one of the read-throughs he'd stopped proceedings. 'What does POV mean?'

'I beg your pardon?' I asked.

The forty-something Steve Frost did not have the excuse of being a novice script editor. POV is standard lingo.

'It says "POV wallet". What does that mean?' he repeated.

'Point. Of. View,' I said slowly and with some disbelief.

'So who's point of view would it be?' he continued.

Beyond belief that this man had been sent to check my script. When it came to *Tennison*, what was also obvious was that he'd not bothered to read the book. In fact, he seemed to rather pride himself on not having engaged with any of the source material.

Anathema to the way I or my own production company worked. Steve November did depart ITV before the filming of *Tennison* started, not that that made much difference in the end.

Red lights started flashing after my initial meetings with NoHo. From the off, they appeared to have little clue about who would direct the series. My preferences were made clear but one director was dismissed immediately. The other wasn't available, I was told. Already, I was starting to feel like an unwanted amateur. David Caffrey was drafted in. I knew David. I'd used him on *The Commander*. He was fine, but not my first choice.

Then, because of their lack of day-to-day production know-how NoHo drafted in a line producer – a Scottish woman named Rhonda Smith.

Meanwhile, Peter Fincham departed the channel. Very regrettable in the development of the *Tennison* series, I felt. I do believe Peter would have handled the whole unfolding car-crash rather differently. And he would have honoured both his and Kevin's promise of it being my show. When Kevin Lygo was promoted as Peter's replacement all the enthusiasm he'd shown me at the outset of the project began to mean very little to me.

Yet Kevin said the most flattering things. As soon as he understood there were some teething troubles he reaffirmed that Jane Tennison was my invention. Nobody would be working on the series had I not created such a wonderful character – a character that keeps on giving – he told me in March 2016. Yet by that time David Caffrey had rewritten much of my script, changing even the killer of Julie Ann Collins from her boyfriend to her father. With a golf club for Christ's sake! I wasn't altogether surprised. NoHo's Camilla Campbell hadn't been able to fathom how someone could be strangled with their own bra. One meeting felt like pulling teeth.

'Look, the killer grabs at her top, her strapless bra comes loose. He has it in his hand. She says something abusive and he strangles her with it.'

'Well, I don't really see how that could happen.'

'Oh really?'

I explained again, this time with hand gestures.

'No, I just don't see it,' she said.

'Oh, for fuck's sake. I'll go upstairs, get a strapless bra and pretend to strangle you with it so you can see,' I said, completely exasperated.

'Oh no, no. That's just being silly now,' she tittered.

What do I have to do to show you that this was a real, horrific crime? I thought.

At first, I tried to shut out the tsunami hurtling towards me but I was starting to feel humiliated and demoralised. What I found so odd was the belief at ITV that this new version remained true to my work. It was entirely unrecognisable from my work. All of the warmth and humour had been stripped from Jane. And the detail of the period had also been disregarded.

At their disposal would have been a beautiful old station in Hackney just begging to be filmed in. No one went to look at it. Instead, a set was built that looked prefabricated and utterly sterile – no atmosphere whatsoever.

As for casting, that was tragic. The choices made no sense. David Caffrey hadn't even bothered to turn up to a pre-casting meeting with me, which perhaps says it all. There were a couple of very fresh and promising actresses I had in mind for Jane Tennison, including the actress Callie Cooke. For the role of Jane's sister I wanted Florence Pugh. Neither of them got the part. According to NoHo, Florence, who did come in to read for the part, hadn't much to offer.

'She really must be cast,' I stressed to the room.

I was overruled. Yet as I write, her films to date have grossed two billion dollars. I knew she'd be a star. Not bad for an actress with 'so little to offer'. And so much for Kevin Lygo's promises of final casting decisions being my call.

In the end NoHo, supported wholeheartedly by ITV, chose the actress Stefani Martini as Jane Tennison. I have no intention of disparaging a young actor, but she simply wasn't right for Jane. Pretty, yes, but with none of the range needed. I was told she was chosen for her authority as well as her girlish enthusiasm and charm. Simplistic at best. I needed someone young, naive but with an inner steel that could be developed over time. I just didn't feel Stefani had that. During the read-through she seemed to twitter around the role rather than confidently inhabit Jane's complex character.

As for the part of DCI Bradfield, that was an even sorrier saga. Of course, I came out of left field with my first suggestion but I really did think it would work. I'd been glued to the sports game show *A League of Their Own* hosted by James Corden. The ex-cricketer Freddie Flintoff captained one team and I found myself drawn in by him. *What an interesting Bradfield he might make*, I thought.

After I contacted Freddie's manager and met with Freddie I put it to him:

'Have you ever thought of acting?'

'I'd love to,' he answered, although he admitted that a lead part scared him.

'You have something,' I reassured him.

And he did – a quiet charisma.

Freddie was due to travel to Australia shortly afterwards but while he was there he agreed to put together a short tape of him acting out a scene, which I enthusiastically showed NoHo.

To me, it would have been such a coup to give him his first major acting role.

'He's not good enough.' That was the immediate response. It felt as though he'd hardly been considered.

Back to the drawing board, I thought. Next I wanted the actor Steven Waddington to play the role. He'd come to my home to read for it, and he was brilliant – Bradfield exactly as I'd imagined him. Bradfield needed to be older, not necessarily drop-dead gorgeous but charismatic – a superior that Jane looked up to. Why else would she go against all of her principles and have an affair?

I'll never forget sitting with producer Rhonda Smith.

'What do you think?' I asked after he'd left the audition.

'Well, he does absolutely nothing for me,' Rhonda chirped.

'Oh really? He does nothing for you?' I said through gritted teeth.

Another actor arrived to read for the part.

'Well, he's absolutely terrific. He's been in *The Borrowers*,' she said.

I didn't give a hoot whether he'd been in The Askers, The Takers or The Givers, he couldn't bloody act.

'Well, I find him very attractive,' Rhonda concluded.

In the end Australian actor Sam Reid was picked, a decision I was not consulted on. A dreadful choice. Again, Sam has, and will, shine brightly in other roles, but he simply wasn't right for Bradfield. Chiselled? Absolutely. Good-looking? Sure. The right age or demeanour? Not even close.

'Well, we all think he's really sexy,' came the missive from ITV Studio's then Controller of Drama, Victoria Fea.

'OK, but can he act the part of Bradfield?'

It was one vital question that no one seemed to be asking. And Bradfield had a lot of lines. In the end his delivery was so static that instead of finding a replacement, NoHo brought in a voice coach for Sam. I also thought he needed an acting coach and I suggested as such.

And it was the same Victoria Fea who, when concerns were raised about how little this version of *Tennison* resembled my book, said, 'If you watch *Wuthering Heights* it's only half the book.' It was a comment that I found incredibly condescending.

By this stage, I had serious doubts over whether or not I wanted to continue. Not only had it registered with me that Kevin Lygo had not kept his promises, but I could see the headline reviews already. I may not have legally owned the rights to Jane Tennison on TV but she was mine. My professional pride couldn't bear the disaster of getting it wrong. What I realised is that nobody working on the series had ever wanted my vision of *Tennison*. Instead, a sensationalised version supplanted it – a version that they thought would sell better.

Filming ended up being delayed by a month so that further rewrites to the script could be made by an uncredited writer who had also been drafted in without my say-so. And when May 2016 eventually rolled around and filming started, it was obvious to me that everything was so badly wrong.

Physically, Stefani Martini as Jane was equal in height to Sam Field as Bradfield, even taller with a bun on her head. Helen Mirren in the original series had been five foot four. It was absurd! Plus, they featured Jane smoking in Julie Ann's autopsy. *Smoking? What? In an autopsy?* And *drinking* with Bradfield in a bar! A policewoman in the 1970s? Turning over in my head were all those wonderful women I'd met from the force, how I'd listened to their first-hand accounts. How could I sit back and watch this happen?

Of course, by the time we met Jane in 1992 she did smoke. In fact, she was failing miserably to give up. But in *Tennison* Jane starts smoking much later – not until book three. Why feature it so early? Where was the space for Jane's character to develop as the pressures of the job took hold? What were they going to do – have her in therapy by 1976? Ridiculous!

Another aspect I felt very strongly about was the scene when Julie Ann's body was found. All that I wanted visible was her ankle and a high-heeled platform shoe under the tarpaulin. I didn't want anything gratuitous. It was a period piece, for Christ's sake. In any case, I wanted the horror focused on her addiction. What did NoHo do? Had a poor extra laid out in the rain with no tarpaulin whatsoever.

In the autopsy, I also wanted parts of Julie Ann covered. What did NoHo do? Stretched her out completely naked for the duration of the scene. It was too much. Besides, I've become more conscious than ever of what that entails. As far as I've had the power I've tried to protect actors: one nude woman on a gurney while twenty-or-so mainly male camera men, sound technicians and crew gawp is not on. I have done it, but I rarely want to put a girl, or anyone, in that position for more time than is necessary. These young actors are not paid enough to do that.

For those reasons and more I wanted to be on set every day. Despite everything I was seeing, in my heart I still wanted *Tennison* to be a success.

Yet ITV seemed hell-bent on producing something abysmal. Two weeks in and Kevin Lygo and Victoria Fea had had a meeting. On reflection, Victoria told me, they had decided that it wasn't desirable that I came onto set. *Wasn't desirable?* Apparently, given how negatively I felt about the production, there was a danger I could become a destabilising force. More insultingly, I was told to keep my powder dry until I'd seen a final cut.

In my very long career, I can honestly say that that was one of the most upsetting things I've ever had to endure. A pariah on the set of my own story – a story I'd been promised command over. It would have been a farce if it wasn't my reputation I was fighting for. Sadly, it did prompt me to ask the question: would Ian Rankin have been treated in that way if a production team had tried to meddle with his beloved Rebus? I don't know the answer, but I think I can make a decent stab at it.

And I can't forget the final twist of the knife – *Tennison,* the title, was changed to *Prime Suspect 1973*. Later, I found out this was at the hands of Kevin Lygo himself. He thought it crazy not to use it to bring in audiences in their millions to the series. Another way of treating audiences like they're dumb, in my view – another Tower Block Tracey moment. *You're missing a crucial part of the jigsaw,* I thought. The way that you bring audiences in their millions is to create brilliant, fresh, compelling TV that people want to watch. I have always endeavoured to respect the viewers of my series, their ability to follow the plot and even solve the case.

It was exceedingly hard to keep my powder dry as they had requested, but it simply got worse. Eventually, I could not accept the humiliation and total disrespect of everything I had created and although I did not want any negative press it was too late to solve anything. I withdrew my name as the script writer, and was no longer attached to the production. The reviews were as I expected: 'Fails to step out of the shadow of it's original' was the consensus. 'None of the heft needed', 'Clunky' and 'Why should we invest time in these characters?' Honestly, I couldn't disagree with the critics. After the final episode, when Bradfield is killed in an explosion, one review even described Sam Reid's performance as being so wooden that he would have burned and died very quickly! Ouch.

Up until that point, I'd been in talks with ITV about the sale of my remaining TV back catalogue. With regret, I withdrew that offer and sold it elsewhere. As for *Tennison*, I was asked if I would consider continuing to a second series and beyond with the same production company, NoHo. Had they handled the production correctly it could have been a solid commercial opportunity for the broadcaster: nine books and a returnable TV series. But I refused to endorse any further series. What had begun as an exciting, hopeful project had become one of the most damaging episodes of my recent professional life. A warning to fellow writers that when it comes to TV adaptations of our work, we are often the lowest common denominator. I wasn't myself for months afterwards. And while I retain a tremendous respect for ITV as a broadcaster, it did make me question so much about its current production values. Over the years I've worked with outstanding people at ITV. Perhaps I'm getting sentimental in my old age, but the whole *Tennison* debacle made me so very, very sad.

Towards the end of 2016 another long-standing relationship was beginning to draw to a close. I'd been with the publisher Simon & Schuster since the early 1990s – a wonderful publisher – but I was now out of contract. It's not uncommon for authors to be approached by other publishing houses enquiring as to whether they would consider moving. That had begun happening to me, and it was pause for thought. With Steve McQueen's film of *Widows* now confirmed for release in 2018, wasn't it the perfect time to reissue the books? I owned rights to the first two and Simon & Schuster held *She's Out*. Yet there seemed to be little enthusiasm. Disappointing for me that no one could see the potential. Then, a publishing plan got sent to me outlining a new vision for the trilogy. It became one I couldn't ignore. Sometimes, no matter how painful it is – and it was painful, like a divorce – you have to say goodbye. Again, I'd worked with some incredible people at Simon & Schuster and I thank every single one of them, but that November I made the move to my current publisher, Bonnier.

To have a new team behind me, and a renewed faith in my work, meant so much. More than that, a subsequent four-book deal meant I could keep writing Jane Tennison – what a privilege. It allowed me to breathe again. I didn't have to wrestle with networks or production crews or juggle scripts that would be abandoned anyway. I didn't want to fight like that. Now it was just me, my imagination, my computer and my brilliant research experts. Sheer joy.

And, I have loved every moment of completing now eight in the young Tennison series. It's seen Jane cut her teeth as a detective in the Dip Squad – the surveillance squad of the Met Police. It's seen her caught up in an IRA bombing at a London Tube station. So much of that tense political period became a compelling backdrop to Jane's day job. I also wanted to shed light on what it's like to be surrounded by that panic and devastation.

Murder Mile was set during the 1978–1979 Winter of Discontent – where the severe economic downturn prompted waves of public sector strikes. In Peckham, Jane was promoted to a detective sergeant in CID where her treatment further forced her to become the maverick officer she develops into. I also wanted to introduce two male gay characters to the story – one a suspect, the other an officer – to explore how biases against homosexuality at that time would have affected an investigation.

Jane kept me glued to my desk during the Covid-19 pandemic, investigating the death of a nun in *Unholy Murder*. And the minute I could travel again, I began research for what would become the penultimate book in the series, *Taste of Blood,* where Jane finds herself plodding along in a rather boring Bromley station, investigating a domestic murder, before her nose leads her in a different direction to catch a killer. Typically, Jane feels compelled to uncover the truth and quickly becomes embroiled in the world of psychics and mediums.

That storyline drew on my own fascination with the world of mediums. As well as the dukkerin I met researching *The Legacy*, I also used to attend medium sessions at the College of Psychic Studies in Earl's Court. One very famous psychic, the late Doris Stokes, used to tour and I went to see her on several occasions – one of the first spiritualist superstars in the UK. Doris had a wonderful interaction with her audience. Of course, some mediums are utter cranks but I don't believe that she was.

In the States, too, I found very reputable mediums through dear friends of mine in The Hamptons. I got so intrigued by the way they operate, how they hook into links, use images and smells. In one session I watched a girl in the audience who was distraught. The medium had contact with a man with the initial S. It was the girl's brother – an addict who'd been in rehab and whom she'd promised to look after.

'He wants to tell you not to blame yourself,' she said. 'He couldn't have lived without drugs and he didn't want you to find him dead. It's why he went away.'

If I was a sceptic, the rest of that interaction left me in no doubt of these people's powers.

'Did he have a record collection? Not vinyl, but CDs?' she asked.

'Yes,' the young girl replied.

'He's left them for you. He's asked that you play them in the order he has left them. They have a message.'

Before he died the girl's brother had stacked up his entire CD collection on his bedside table.

At another private session I was witness to, one middle-aged couple believed their son had killed himself by driving into a tree. They received a message to say he'd died of a heart attack. To see the comfort that brought them and the closure was truly something. Now, when people ask if I'm a believer, I have to say yes. I believe it, because I've seen it.

However, the funniest medium I met while researching *Taste of Blood* still makes me howl with laughter.

'You'd think I'd have known that my husband was leaving me, but I had no idea!' she told me. I do love a medium who can see the funny side.

Of course, it is my many readers who have also kept me going throughout the Tennison series. As I write, I am nearing its end. In the final novel Jane will try to join the AMIP Squad – the elite major incident squad, now disbanded within the Met. No woman had ever been a part of it and, as she discovers, she's not welcome. It's where we meet DCI Shefford, Sergeant Otley and all the protagonists I wrote about more than thirty years ago.

I was asked recently if I would ever revisit Jane after she'd left the force in 1996, whether I'd ever bring her back for one final investigation. And whether I'd ever kill her off. The answer is no to all three. I could never kill off Jane Tennison. She's a part of me and she always will be. And I'll miss her terribly when I type the final word of my final Tennison novel.

Chapter 23

In My Prime

On the night before the final episode of the calamitous *Prime Suspect: 1973* screened on ITV, I went to a party. Norma Heyman's son David was throwing it for Norma's birthday. He and his wife Rose were wonderful hosts. David had made his name as producer of the Harry Potter films and so it was a star-studded evening at their home in Central London.

All good parties gravitate to the dining room and it was there that I sat with Norma's ex-husband, John.

'I hear you've been having a terrible time, Lynda,' he said.

My list was long, from feeling humiliated and undermined to having been forced to read the Tennison series' abysmal reviews.

'Don't let it kill you,' he advised me.

'How can I not? It's dreadful.'

'The best revenge is success. Forget it. Move on. Be successful.'

Sadly, John died four months later, but I've never forgotten those parting words – a gift, in fact. And the best part of it: he was absolutely right.

Before I'd moved to my new publisher Bonnier they'd presented me with a plan of how they might republish *Widows*, and I'd been impressed. It's still hard to believe I wasn't going to make a single penny from the film, but the books were in my ownership.

The same week as Norma's birthday party, I got a call to say republication would go ahead. Terrific! Not only that but I was asked if I would update parts of the text on the *Widows, Widows' Revenge* and *She's Out* trilogy. It was collaboration as I understood it to be – the kind of collaboration I'd enjoyed way back in 1983 with Verity Lambert.

Suddenly, the world started to feel hopeful again, although it did take some time for the pain of *Tennison* to fade. As far as Steve McQueen's film was concerned, that became a slightly different story. Gillian Flynn had completed the script, but now Steve was banging on my door, asking if I would look over it.

That did feel rather cheeky, but in my heart I wanted the film to be a success so I agreed. I sat for hours and wrote note upon note upon note. The script was appalling. There was no humour to it. It fell flat for what was supposed to be a blockbuster. To me, it didn't have any of the essence of the original – odd, given that Steve had been such a fan.

I returned the script with my notes and not long after Steve contacted me again. Would I read and make notes on a second draft? By now, I was starting to feel a little like a used dishrag. More than that, I did ask myself whether it was salvageable. It lacked so much. *Why am I doing this?* I thought. Perhaps I needed to wash my hands of it in the way I had done with so much of *Widows* over the years. Steve hadn't had the courtesy to include me from the outset. 'I'm sorry, I'm not available,' I told him. Besides, I wanted to plough my energy into my own work.

Widows the film was due for release in November 2018, and in the August of that year I was in LA. *Cold Shoulder,* the series for which I'd created that terrific pilot with Kelly McGillis way back in 2000, was still on my mind and Tom Fontana set out to pitch it once more. While I was there, I was invited to see a first cut of *Widows* in a private viewing room in the 20th Century Fox studio lot. Credit to Steve, the cast he had lined up was fantastic: Viola Davis in the lead of Dolly Rawlins (renamed Veronica Rawlins), Elizabeth Debicki and Michelle Rodriguez in the parts of Shirley (renamed Alice) and Linda respectively, and the wonderful Cynthia Erivo as Bella (renamed Belle). Lovely, too, that Ann Mitchell had been given a small part in a nod to the original.

However, that's where my enthusiasm ended. *Why bring in this star cast and give them so little to work with?* I thought. I suspect 20th Century Fox had wanted an action movie with a rip-roaring heist at the centre but what they got had the feel of an art-house movie. Where was the warmth? The fun? Viola Davis didn't smile once.

I understood that Steve also wanted his film to communicate a larger message about race. Fair enough, but I'm not sure it worked. As for the heist, that was ridiculous. The women hauled Tupperware boxes on their backs. Preposterous! Then there was a rather bizarre subplot about Veronica Rawlins' son having died. And the ending? Christ almighty! That was Viola Davis in a diner, drinking coffee, staring blankly out of a window. She catches the eye of Elizabeth Debicki, and the screen goes blank. *What?*

'It's a *big* film.' That was really all I could say about it.

Final edits were underway on *Widows* as I returned to London, and I received another message from Steve. Would I watch the film again and meet him at The Ivy Club for a coffee afterwards? Sure, I agreed, although it was hard to see how it could be improved without a rewrite.

Steve and his producer Iain Canning were waiting for me, but Steve seemed in a terrible rush.

'I'm doing edits in Soho. I don't have long,' he said.

Honestly, I found Steve McQueen quite rude.

'Do you have anything to say?' he asked.

'Yes, I do. There's no humour.'

Steve looked rather taken aback. 'Pardon?'

'Well, it's lacking in humour.'

'Give me an example,' he barked.

'Well, you've got all these women who have never fired a gun in their lives and when they practise they hit their targets. At the very least you could inject some fun into that. How about they miss a few?'

I ran through some more sequences with Steve.

'Hmm, yeah, hmm. Right, well, I don't have much time,' he repeated.

'But the biggest note I have is the problem with your ending,' I continued.

'What?'

Surely I can't have been the only person to have been given notes on it? I thought.

Steve looked incandescent and turned to Iain Canning. 'Have you been talking to her?' he snapped. Iain and I had only just met.

'No,' he replied.

'What's wrong with the ending?' Steve barked again.

'Well, it's depressing. I've spent two hours watching four fabulous women pull off a heist, then it cuts to Viola Davis sitting in a diner looking miserable. It drops like a stone.'

Steve seemed very irritated. 'So, so?'

'Bring someone in, have them sit opposite her. Have her say, "Underneath the table is one million. I want a library built in the name of my dead son." Finish on a high – they've bloody done it!'

Steve got up to use the bathroom, then headed back to the Soho editing suite with my notes. And when I was invited to the premiere in London that November I did notice that Viola had been given more on-screen smiles. Not only that, but he had used the ending I suggested. Of the seven notes I'd given Steve, six were used in the final cut.

Sadly, Ann Mitchell's part had been cut to a single shot. Ann looked wonderful on the red carpet, but it did feel to me like a rather poor way to treat her, given she owned the role of Dolly Rawlins from the start.

'So, you used my ending?' I said to Iain Canning as we shuffled out of the auditorium. He didn't say a word. And it would have been churlish of me to reveal any of that to the waiting press. Or my feelings about the film, which by all accounts had been improved. Instead, I stuck to my script: 'It's a *big* film,' I repeated over and over. Beforehand I'd even sent Steve a good luck gift of a leather notebook. In it I'd written a tongue-in-cheek message: *To write down the notes for your next movie. Love, Lynda x*

Privately, however, it is still incredible to me that the sum total of thanks I received from Steve was a bouquet of flowers sent to my home in The Hamptons. And when I reflected on the turbulence in my professional life over those past four years I had to draw some very difficult conclusions. *What a dirty business we are in. It really can be horrible,* I thought.

What did lift me were my books. They looked absolutely terrific and went on to sell great guns – way beyond my imagination. Even so, I hadn't even been allowed to use any of the stills from the film's promotional artwork to boost them. A copyright issue, apparently, but I later heard that it may have been Steve who put his foot down. Instead, I worked with my publisher to redesign the covers. They looked stunning.

Terrific, too, that Ann Mitchell agreed to read for the audio version. She was superb and I dedicated the *Widows* book to her. That winter, thirty-five years after the original, *Widows* went straight into the *Sunday Times* bestseller list – an incredibly special moment for me, and perhaps a little bit of closure on a story that has seen so many highs and lows over the years.

* * *

Where did all those years go? In 2018 Lorcan turned fifteen – the terrible teens. But he was also maturing into a surprising young man. He's absolutely brilliant with computers and anything mechanical – where he's got that from I have no idea. But Lorcan is also a lovely, kind and generous boy who's rather private, too. He hates the limelight – unlike his mother!

In the last few years, I don't know what I would have done without him. That same year *Widows* smashed the book charts, I had another hurdle to overcome. I'd never thought of myself as seventy-five – age really does creep up on you – but there's nothing like a knock to your health to remind you. A routine operation to remove cataracts was going to make my life easier. My sight had become a problem, though only when it came to reading very small print. Added to that was the onset of the crippling pain I now have in my neck – I've had so many MRI scans I'm practically radioactive!

The cataract operation didn't go as planned. Apparently I was too old for laser treatment. *Too old?* That was a shock – I've never considered myself to be too old for anything. Instead, I could have my cloudy lenses removed and replaced with artificial lenses. My vision would be as good as new. What a monstrous lie that turned out to be.

I had both eyes operated on at the same time, which was probably a big mistake. And the operation didn't go well. Fast forward a few weeks and I was a walking danger zone. Initially, I'd been given round glasses with a little hole in each lens to wear while my eyes got used to the light. Yet as the days passed, nothing improved. At home I was bumping into doors and falling down stairs. In the park, I was tripping over kerbs and paving stones. Passers-by must have thought I was utterly paralytic.

And meetings became a nightmare. I'd never noticed before how everybody's offices are painted white. I couldn't see a bloody thing.

Bright sunlight also gave me an almighty headache, and still does. In all seriousness, it was terrifying. *How the hell am I going to write anything?* I worried. I couldn't even see my computer screen. The titles I'd been working on for Bonnier started to look like a faint hope. *Me? Not work? Not write? Shoot me now,* I thought.

One saving grace was my business partner Nigel Stoneman. Nigel had helped me set up my most recent venture, La Plante Global, in 2014 after I parted company with Duncan Heath. He had worked across the publishing industry for many years and I'd known him for ten of those. After the fiasco of the *Widows* film rights buy-back, it was so important to me to find a team who understood and appreciated my body of work and whom I trusted.

La Plante Global is now my own company that looks after my books, my TV and my film work in the UK. Through it, I feel reborn. In the States, I moved to the William Morris Endeavor Entertainment agency – WME – for representation after I gave Peter Benedek the heave-ho. With my eyesight shot to pieces, poor Nigel became my carer at work for a while. Whenever I was in New York especially, he guided me through the airport and to all my meetings. And at home, dear Rosemary was juggling both Lorcan and myself.

As far as my books were concerned, I needed a new strategy and fast. Until my eyesight improved I would have to dictate them. Yet to develop a story to that level, I would have to plot in my head for hours, work out all its twists and turns and paint the faces of the characters in my mind. For the dialogue, I needed to have rehearsed every line. Wonderful Tory – my PA – spent hours sitting in my office listening to me bang on while she typed away on the computer. She really was incredible. And alongside Tory, I also had a secretary called Veronica who spent hours with me as I paced the office, gradually talking through the plot. In The Hamptons I found a brilliant court stenographer who picked up where Tory and Veronica left off. She was wonderfully fast, but on one occasion she stopped me in my tracks.

'Wait!' she shouted, holding up her hand, which she did often if I was talking too fast. 'I'm sorry. I'm tired and I need a break,' she continued rather tearfully.

'Of course.' I apologised. I did have a habit of forgetting how long I had been pacing around the small room. But it wasn't until we parted company that she opened up.

'Working with you has sometimes given me sleepless nights,' she confessed.

'Really. Why?'

'It's the voices, Lynda. The way you talk through each character in a different voice is chilling. It's as if you've been possessed,' she said.

When I think about it now, probably she was right. Without me being able to focus on a computer screen to write or edit, every character had to come alive in my head. Only gradually, through that process, did the new novel *Dark Rooms* take shape. But I simply couldn't have done it alone. Without all those people *Dark Rooms* would never have seen the light of day!

* * *

With the young Tennison series of books ongoing, I wanted to challenge myself once more. Again, I have to thank my readers. One woman at an event came up to the table afterwards to get her book signed.

'Whatever happened to Harry Rawlins' son?' she asked.

What did? I thought. I had no clue. The last time I'd left him was in 1985 when he was being brought up by Harry's mistress and Harry was dead.

My imagination began to work overtime.

Funnily, I had been considering a male protagonist for a while. For years in the police force I'd been meeting some really great guys. Down-to-earth, dedicated coppers who endure a lot during the course of their work.

Yet male crime leads are often portrayed as alcoholic, rather bitter, and can't keep their flies zipped up for more than two minutes. Why can't I write a guy who has a wonderful marriage? One that has had a happy childhood? One that is a genuinely good bloke, albeit a bit of a maverick when it comes to solving crime. Enter Jack Warr, my newest creation.

Honestly, I'd quite like Jack as a friend. I love spending time with him. He's not so well read and he's not hugely ambitious, so he might irritate me a little too! But the Harry Rawlins' idea opened up many angles for me to work with. Jack would be Harry's son who had been adopted after Harry died. His adoptive parents would have been lovely people, and his childhood idyllic. My first book, *Buried*, would focus on Jack solving a crime but in the process also discovering who his real parents are. A fire at a cottage and a charred body would take him back to near where Dolly Rawlins and her accomplices planned the heist in *She's Out*.

I was very excited about *Buried* and developing my new character Jack Warr. Also, I was eager to discuss the numerous offers of it transferring to the screen. Yet again, though, I hit against a massive legal problem. Jack Warr discovers who he is only by tracing the women involved in the series *She's Out* – namely Dolly Rawlins. However, as I don't own any of the characters from *Widows*, I would be prevented from taking it further. Heartbreaking once more to be haunted by signing the rights away more than thirty years ago.

Just as I had not predicted the situation over *Buried* when I embarked on the Jack Warr series, I also had no idea of the extent of the disaster that was about to befall everyone. I'd just celebrated my seventy-seventh birthday in 2020 when the Covid-19 pandemic hit – two weeks before publication of my first Jack Warr novel. Suddenly, we were in lockdown.

Normally, I'm happy at home – and over the next couple of years I embraced being a recluse. However, it did mean that all my promotional work suddenly got shelved.

Book tours can feel relentless, but I also love them. And I'm constantly reminded of some classic moments by Nigel, who accompanies me. One of my bugbears is being placed in a no-smoking room in whichever hotel. Despite several attempts, I've never been able to kick the habit. On one occasion Nigel found me in my bathroom on my hands and knees having a sneaky puff and blowing smoke into the flushing toilet.

'What the hell are you doing, Lynda?' he cried.

'It's an old trick I've learned!' I winked.

It would have been so embarrassing if I'd set off the fire alarm.

As for the bad lighting, bad light switches and the fancy bathrooms: don't get me started! Beautiful to look at, but what a nightmare. In Dubai I must have spent a good half hour trying to locate the bath taps – it filled from a hole in the ceiling! Who the hell looks upwards? Then there's the technological enigma of scanning QR codes to watch TV or working the air-conditioning remote control. All I ever want is a good bed, a nice pillow and a decent Caesar salad.

And to attend some events, I've risked life and limb. I hate turning invites down and so on one occasion I found myself having to charter a private helicopter. I was scheduled to be interviewed by the actor and broadcaster Judi Spiers in Devon a couple of years ago, but then realised I was also booked for a charity function at Epsom Racecourse the next day. By air became the only way to make both. Where Nigel got the pilot from I have no clue. He didn't appear to know the way to Appledore and at one point I'm sure we were veering towards France. Every storm possible hit us and when he announced he couldn't find the field to land in, I almost had heart failure. In the end I had to ring Judi and ask a group of guests to stand outside with their umbrellas open just so the pilot could see.

'I'm still on my L-plates,' he merrily announced on the return leg. It's rare for me not to see the funny side, but I had been utterly terrified.

But at any event it's always the fans who keep me going. Without fail someone will ask me if my hair is naturally red. Yes, it is. And I've had readers in fits over some of my storylines. One woman was incandescent that I'd killed off Lorraine Page.

'I'm so sorry, I had to!' I found myself apologising.

Others get very emotional when asking about *The Legacy* or *Entwined*. It means so much that people are touched by books that have meant a great deal to me over the years. And I can also guarantee that someone will also raise their hand: 'Weren't you in the series *Rentaghost*?' they'll ask. Yes, I was, although I still find it frightfully embarrassing. It was way back in 1980 when I was still an actress. My good friend Christopher Biggins asked if I'd do a quick stint on the UK children's programme. I played the tiny part of the hay-fever suffering ghost Tamara Novek. I would never have agreed if I'd known it would come back to haunt me all these years later!

Yet the energy I gain from being in a room with viewers or readers is boundless. For a crime event, I think many people are surprised at how much laughter there is!

After all these years, I also still enjoy the rounds of press interviews I do along the way, although these too can be fraught with mishaps. On one tour of Australia in 2014 I was booked on a late-night arts show. I lost my way to the dressing room and almost ended up on the Australian equivalent of *Question Time*. That said, the sandwiches and wine in the green room were delicious!

'Who are you?' I asked the other guests as I took my seat.

Bit serious! I thought.

It turned out I was surrounded by politicians.

Thankfully, I was rescued by a woman from hair and make-up before I made an utter fool of myself. She proceeded to sculpt my hair with so much lacquer it resembled the nose of an aircraft. Truly, I could write another epic about my hair on tour. By the time I'd reached Brisbane the humidity had made it so big and frizzy that I needed to buy some heavy-duty conditioner to tame it.

Lockdown would deprive me of all of that fun. And I also became acutely aware that I had a garden to stroll around – wonderful koi carp to look at in my pond, and I could swim every day. So many of my readers were imprisoned indoors. Thank God for Lorcan who catapulted me into the twenty-first century. That same year I began my regular Facebook Live sessions. Admittedly, I can't always get to grips with how the live feed works but Lorcan is on hand to sort out any technical hitches while his mother, the dinosaur, panics.

Thankfully, even after those lockdowns lifted, I've kept them going. I adore logging on every month and chatting away. Granted, it isn't the same as face-to-face. I can't see anybody, for starters. But I do continue to receive fascinating questions from all around the globe.

I've also launched myself into the world of podcasts – who knew what one of those was fifteen years ago? Yet I've loved every minute of teaming up with my long-time colleague Cass

Sutherland and creating the podcast *Listening to the Dead*. We began recording the first season before the Covid-19 pandemic but through the power of Zoom we were able to keep going throughout.

Listening to the Dead has not only been a terrific learning experience for me, but a chance to reconnect and discuss forensics with all the fantastic experts I've used over so many years. Listeners might even be able to hear the cogs in my brain whirring as I pick up new ideas for my novels.

In 2020, we began by taking listeners through each strand of forensics from forensic ecology to fire investigations, DNA, digital forensics and fibre analysis, to name a few. Amazing to think we have now finished our third season, which focuses on the forensics of solving famous criminal cases. The use of a handwriting expert in uncovering the identity of Wearside Jack – the man who falsely purported to be the Yorkshire Ripper – I found particularly interesting. And, how fingerprint evidence was used in solving the Great Train Robbery. Cass and I have many ideas about what we would like to uncover next.

As for Jack Warr, I am halfway through my fourth novel as I write. Although an appalling period to live through, I used the pandemic to get stuck into more of his story. What else to do but watch True Crime on my big-screen TV and research and write? Jack is turning out to be quite a character, and through him I'm exploring the effect crime has on the mental health of officers – men in particular who may not put themselves forward for counselling, despite it being offered.

Cass and his wife Ann have been a wealth of knowledge about the mental strain policing can put on a person. And I've also spoken extensively to psychologists. But there are moments of real fun too. When Jack does end up in therapy he spends more time trying to make the therapist giggle than he ever does confronting his own problems.

Readers' reactions to Jack have been humbling too. *Pure Evil*, the third in the Jack Warr series, shot straight into the *Sunday Times* bestseller list. Almost forty years since I penned my first novel, I sometimes have to remind myself how lucky I am to be able to spend my life doing what I enjoy the most and making readers happy. Added to that I'm working away on a new TV script – a rather dark and twisted tale. Watch this space.

At home, Lorcan is twenty-one – unbelievable! And I turned eighty-one in 2024. Rosemary has switched from being Lorcan's carer to looking after me. And I've another child to take care of these days: Hugo, my magnificent Russian Borzoi wolfhound. He gallops like a racehorse, but he's been the most worrisome animal I've ever owned – and the most costly. He's needed open-chest surgery twice after choking on pampas grass. And the chemical cosh he's under makes him the most needy and temperamental dog I've ever lived with. But I love him dearly, especially when he howls at the TV in unison with any music that's playing. He's my first operatic pet – it must be his classically trained Russian ear.

During the writing of this book, dear friends have been remembered and dear friends have passed. I'm appalling at funerals – I can never stop the tears. Thankfully I won't be around for my own (I've always said I want to die on a bed of roses and that fantasy still stands!) and only occasionally do I look at something I've treasured and wonder who I would leave it to. I mean, who the hell would want a massive carved eagle on a plinth, outstretched with full wing span? Still, writing a will is very depressing. It's all about looking to a time when you won't be here. When my will was complete I felt so relieved, and hopefully in a fit of temper I won't start changing my mind about who gets what.

Truthfully, though, money has never been an incentive in my life. Granted, I've made enough to enjoy a very secure life. But I've also worked hard throughout, and taken some hard knocks. It's sometimes difficult for me to digest those moments, such as *Widows* being made into a multi-million-pound epic in 2018 with my name on the billboard yet only receiving a bouquet of flowers as payment. But satisfaction did come in the success of the original novels – I suppose I've always learned the hard way how to make my own success and I think there's a lesson in there for everyone. You may be down, but you're not out. Keep at it and keep going.

And novel writing still excites me after all these years. I feel as energised as I always did – just like the day I wrote the first word of *The Legacy*. To be honest, that I'm often described as 'prolific' can feel a bit demeaning. The dedication and research I commit to every single book or script comes as standard. I may be prolific, but I'm also a driven perfectionist. And I do believe that hard graft pays off.

I was recently asked at a book signing if I'd ever thought of retiring. I thought about it for a nano-second.

'Why would I give up doing something I enjoy so much and that continues to be a constant fascination?' I replied.

Another reason is that I still get commissioned, and supported, by my publishers. But really, I wouldn't be anywhere without my army of loyal fans. They are the reason I keep going. And while the body creaks a little more these days, in my mind I feel like I'm only just beginning. I have no intention of stopping until I drop off the face of the earth.

I've led a terrific life, and I continue to live a terrific life, and I hope you've enjoyed reading about it. Eight decades on the planet and counting. At heart, I'm still Lynda Titchmarsh from Crosby. And there's a saying: you can take the girl out of Liverpool, but you can never take Liverpool out of the girl. Perhaps that's why I'm such a fighter. I love that city and I'm proud to have been born there. It's that part of me that stares furiously at the rejected files on my shelves with the thick black felt-tip titles. That inner rage never leaves me. *Bastards*, I think.

But I know that my life isn't about failures. I also look out and see floor-to-ceiling shelves that contain all of my published novels, alongside my BAFTAs and other awards. It never ceases to give me such a feeling of pride, and to acknowledge how many wonderful people have been part of making my career a success. For them all, I give thanks from the bottom of my heart.